SPEAKING THE TOOTH IN LOVE

A Dentist Reflects
on His Mission to the Middle East

ADAM ALGAM, DDS

**Christian
Medical & Dental
Associations®**
Changing Hearts in Healthcare

The Christian Medical & Dental Associations was founded in 1931 and currently serves more than 19,000 members; coordinates a network of Christian healthcare professionals for personal and professional growth; sponsors student ministries in medical and dental schools; conducts overseas healthcare projects for underserved populations; addresses policies on healthcare, medical ethics and bioethical and human rights issues; distributes educational and inspirational resources; provides missionary healthcare professionals with continuing education resources; and conducts international academic exchange programs.

For more information:
Christian Medical & Dental Associations
P.O. Box 7500
Bristol, TN 37621-7500
888-230-2637
www.cmda.org • main@cmda.org

ISBN 13: 978-1-7344968-9-5
Library of Congress Control Number: 2020934751

Printed in the United States
First Printing April 2020

To Grace, Amy, David and Rae.

Your love made this journey possible.

Rather, speaking the truth in love,
we are to grow up in every way
into him who is the head, into Christ

Ephesians 4:15, ESV

ACKNOWLEDGMENTS

This account is certainly just one man's interpretation of culture and events in the Middle East. Anything of value is not original as I learned from some many others who took me under their wings to let me learn from their wisdom and experience. I'm indebted forever to my dear brothers and sisters on the field who loved my family well, rejoicing with us and crying with us through our exciting years of work in that desert soil. May God bless you and strengthen your hands for the work ahead.

I'm also very blessed to have a cohort of caring and amazing friends in the US who have helped me in this effort to turn a mix of journal and stories into a manuscript.

Kelby M., you motivated me early on by finding some helpful information in my journals and asking me to share more. I hope you can use this account to make a few less mistakes than I have while learning to love these desert people.

I appreciate the encouragement and professional editing I received from Jackson and Kelly K. Thank you for the sacrifice of so much time and for your awesome organizational skills. Your friendship and support throughout the years has be invaluable.

I also certainly appreciate John F. who aimed to make me a better writer and saved readers from many headaches in the process. Your timeliness was superb and your grasp of the English language is profound. You should consider getting a job in this area!

Bob S. was a huge encouragement and proofreader already having some personal history in the Middle East. Thank you for your insights and clarifications to make this a more adept account.

Spoonee M., you came to my rescue without hesitation, and I appreciate you having been a pillar of friendship and wisdom in my life for many years.

Gallant H. I appreciate your nimble interpretations and guidance on my manuscript

Your professionalism and skill was readily apparent, Teresa B. Thank you for getting me to the finish line with excellent formatting and design.

As for my favorite son, David—you were a great encouragement to actually help me get this done and I appreciate your critical and insightful edits throughout the process. I hope your upcoming novel is a success itself! I look forward to holding it in my own hands soon.

Last but not least I owe much thanks to Grace. Thank you for all your help in reading and rereading these stories of life that we shared together. Your details and memories were essential and it was (usually) fun to remember this special time in our lives. I know you made this a much clearer account even as you have made me a much better man, sometimes even against my will. You are much loved and I look forward to the next chapter for us.

FOREWORD

Every soul belonging to Christ will at times struggle with discovering the Lord's plan for their life, the good works which God has prepared beforehand for them (Ephesians 2:10). In *Speaking the Tooth in Love* Dr. Adam Algam shares the challenges of his journey—the blessings, the frustrations, and the ultimate confirmation that he was indeed on the path the Lord had designed for him.

One of the greatest deterrents for a Christian to venture into an unfamiliar culture is the vast number of unknowns—a new language, unusual clothing and housing and cultural peculiarities, to name a few. Dr. Algam and his family were certainly challenged by these recurrent obstacles in their efforts—sometimes in hilarious ways, and other times in ways that tested the strength of their resolve to reach their new patients and neighbors with the love of Christ. What they discovered, however, in the midst of the many newfound societal challenges, was the undeniable universals that are present in each of us. We all struggle against both physical and spiritual disease, and that struggle is ultimately and fully alleviated in the life, death and resurrection of a Middle Easterner named Jesus. As Dr. Algam succinctly states, "…we are really just the same; two groups of broken sinners who require a great rescue" (p. 256).

As I graduated from dental school almost 4 decades ago, invigorated by my newfound faith in Jesus Christ, I remember thinking, "Now that I have been entrusted with this precious Gospel, how can I spend my life just working on teeth?" It didn't take long for me to joyfully discover that the Lord can use even a dentist for His glory. Dr. Algam beautifully illustrates how dentistry can be a platform for sharing the Good News of Jesus Christ, and also for growing in our knowledge of its broad applicability to all of life. Each filling we complete, each denture we fabricate, each abscessed tooth we remove, is an opportunity to point with excellence to the One who lived, died and rose on our behalf.

So for whom has this book been written? First, anyone working with Muslims—whether domestically or internationally—can glean great insight into how to interact and minister in a culturally sensitive way. Secondly, any dentist who takes seriously our calling as "ministers of reconciliation" (2 Corinthians 5:18) will be inspired to more creatively and consistently share God's love with their patients, both domestically and internationally. But in an even broader sense, all who desire to serve Christ in their chosen profession—whatever they might be—will be challenged to recognize the eternal possibilities God creates as we travail in the temporal realm for His eternal glory. May you be blessed by Dr. Algam's story, as I was, to more fully "confirm the work of (your) hands" (Psalm 90:17).

Dr. William Griffin
Vice President for Dental Ministries
Christian Medical and Dental Associations

TABLE OF CONTENTS

بسم الله الرحمن الرحيم

PART 1
LANGUAGE & CULTURE

Chapter 1
FIRST STEPS

The surroundings were not familiar at all, and the sun was way too bright and hot to match up with my expectations for a morning awakening. There was a weird carnival-like song playing outside from a truck as it went down the road. It reminded me of the call from an ice-cream truck, but with more of a new age style.

I laid there, unmoving, trying to reconcile my environment to my memory. It sunk in then that I was in the Middle East. After planning and thinking about it for almost six years, we had finally made it there during the previous night, and the hard work of the last 24 hours hadn't just been a dream after all.

The bright sun explained itself when I looked at my watch and realized it was already afternoon. I had slept deeply like someone on sedatives after we staggered into this place in the middle of the night. As I went into the next room, I saw it wasn't just me. Grace and the kids were still zonked out and laying in strange positions around the couches and beds. I took out my phone and captured the scene; the first picture I took after arriving in the Middle East.

Our friends Benjamin and Valerie had done a yeoman's job of trying to find us an apartment before we got there, and that included following an elaborate list of requirements and preferences that we had given them. Looking back, it was totally unfair to ask them to do anything like that for us, but we didn't know better.

Maybe in the US, you can have someone find you a ground-floor, three-bedroom apartment easily, but in the Middle East, it was an effort suprême. But we didn't know that at the time, and it had seemed like the best option to have somewhere to call home immediately, with three young kids in tow.

The problem is that apartment shopping in the Middle East is accomplished mostly by visiting in person and through word of mouth. There is no handy app or website you can use. In the West, you assume a certain level of quality for every apartment you look at in a similar price range, but in our new country, the variability between living spaces was wide.

In any given ready-to-rent apartment you might look at, there might be glass windows or just open holes in the wall. There may be electric wiring already in use or just a promise that it would be ready tomorrow as you spied bare wires hanging down from the ceiling. The place might be filthy or clean, but always a pledge came for its deep cleaning before you moved in to live there. Usually, what you saw during the visit was exactly what you got on move-in day.

All that said, Benjamin and Valerie had found a promising place at the last minute, but hadn't had time to seal the deal, and so we were supposed to go there day one and sign the contract if we agreed it could work for us.

Until then, they had found a temporary place nearby, where we could crash; some friends of theirs who owned the apartment were out of town.

We hadn't even really seen the place or neighborhood until this first morning as we had gotten in during the middle of the night and had no orientation of where we were. Picked up at the airport by some other friends, Faoud and Laura, they had greeted us with open arms and delivered us to our new neighborhood, with a watermelon to boot.

Waking up in this afternoon sun, I now stumbled into the kitchen with the hope of finding some coffee to help me revive a bit. The usual Christian drug of choice in the form of ground coffee wasn't there. However, there was a promising jar of something called "Nescafe Red Mug" on the shelf.

I made myself a cup and realized I had accomplished everything on my to-do list that I had thought about and worried about for this past year. Suddenly, new needs and tasks to accomplish on this side of the pond were swiftly multiplying in my mind. I guess this is why Jesus was so adamant about telling his disciples on the mount not to worry about what will happen tomorrow, because there are enough needs for today.

I struggle with this teaching, knowing it brings freedom and reliance on God's faithfulness, but always wanting the control of being able to wrestle with the problems on my own. I'm the kind of guy who appreciates the manna but intends to stock up on it, so I'm not in need for the coming days. Being dependent on daily bread is chafing and pride-destroying.

A year ago, the prospect of moving to the Middle East had felt daunting. Like planning to hurl ourselves over an impossible canyon, we had planned our steps to the other side. God had been faithful to us in so many ways along the road, and we had actually drawn closer to Him and each other in the process. *Lord, may you help my faith again with new challenges to come on this side?*

Grace and I would often reflect over the coming years about how hard and impossible it had looked to move our lives from the US to the Middle East. Every small decision we made to get there had required some amount of dying to ourselves, our comforts, and our self-made plans. Once we had actually done it, we felt such joy.

Looking back, all those tiny struggles and deaths now seemed like nothing. In fact, we had often said to each other with a bit of guilty glee that if only people knew how unusual and exciting this kind of life and work was, everyone would be leaving the US to do the same. Of course, if that were the case, then not everyone would be able to come, so we felt ourselves the lucky few.

The effect of the Nescafe on my mind did not resemble the picture of a happy day that is depicted on the front of the jar. After a few years of Starbucks coffee jostling around in my body in the US, most other coffees simply had little effect on me anymore and especially this freeze-dried powdered stuff.

But the Arabs seemed to love the stuff, so I endeavored to get used to drinking it around them while always seeking out a place that might sell unground coffee beans that I could enjoy in private. I found a pretty good spot in the *balad* (or old city) of the capital that Faoud told me about where they roasted coffee beans from Colombia. Another time in my on-going struggle to find coffee, I heard of a new Brazilian coffee house that had opened.

Before I even got a chance to go, my colleague Benjamin "the Brain", whose love for good coffee actually probably outdoes mine, had slipped in there himself. Not knowing what to select, Benjamin had asked the new and proud owner which type of coffee bean he preferred himself. The owner admitted that he didn't like drinking coffee using a French press or filter drip system. While he had invested quite a bit of personal money into this business, which was his livelihood, he never tried any of these beans that he was selling.

Benjamin then asked him what he liked drinking, and the owner confessed that he preferred only Nescafe. Benjamin, perplexed, asked the man, "Why do you think the Arabs love Nescafe so much?"

The helpful owner answered, "Perhaps … because it is dee-licious."

To our dismay, the hope of a new coffee place was obliterated because who can with any self-respect buy coffee beans from a man who prefers Nescafe? However, the fun thing was that the man's response of "Perhaps … because it's dee-licious" became a catch-phrase for our friends and us over the years to describe any kind of seemingly unexplainable cultural preferences in the Middle East, of which there were many.

The Feast of Ramadan

The other new cultural phenomenon we experienced upon our arrival in the Middle East was the month of Ramadan. Ramadan had just started on the day before we arrived, August 1st, and our friends were quick to coach us up on behavior modifications mandatory during this festive month.

The Quran mentions this month very briefly in saying that you are supposed to fast during the lunar month of Ramadan from the time in the morning when you can distinguish two hairs until the time at night when you can no longer distinguish two hairs (essentially sunrise and sunset). This fast is not described in detail in the Quran, but traditionally it is a fast from food, drink, sex, and smoking.

There are substantial penalties associated with breaking this fast, both cosmically and locally. Some Muslims will tell you that God never forgets if you breach the fast, and it will always be a mark against you no matter how many good things and fasts you try to do to make up for it. If you do break the fast for any reason (and illness is an accepted reason not to participate), then you must make it up during a later part of the year. If you can't or don't want to make it up, you can absolve yourself by giving money to the mosque. They calculate it as a certain amount of payment needed for every day missed to satisfy God's demands.

Because of the monetary and spiritual penalties associated with breaking the fast, religious leaders have added even more rules to discourage you from making mistakes. Because of these additions, other activities are now universally banned.

For instance, everyone knows you can't swallow during Ramadan because there could be something that got into your mouth like a bug or a tiny leftover piece of food. If you consume that, then you have broken your fast. You may not even know it, but God does, so it's better just spitting all day to avoid any swallowing.

One time, I heard that they had instructed people not to receive any dental anesthesia during the fast because that could get into your digestive system and cause you to break the fast. As you can guess, this resulted in me always having very little business and work during the festive month. It's hard enough to get people to go to the dentist during an average month, but then everyone had a good reason not to see me, and no one in their right mind wanted to come to me unless they were already blatantly breaking the fast due to illness.

I often scheduled our family vacations during this time because I felt like a lumberjack on Earth Day whenever I stayed.

On the local level, our friends were quick to warn us about eating, drinking, or smoking in public (I guess the other part of the fast goes without saying). If the police see you doing any of those things, they will give you a ticket at best and haul you down to the police station for a little stay at the worst. Little tolerance is offered to foreigners and non-Muslims who are not following the fast in public.

This fast meant that for us, it becomes a month of hiding when you eat or drink and a lot of home-cooked meals because you are not going to find many restaurants open at least during the day. They start to open up around 4 pm, and then you can go and buy food for takeaway, under the pretense of course that you are buying it for the *iftar* meal coming up after sunset and certainly not to eat right now. Of course, we weren't the only ones buying it under pretense as we came to find out the majority of people hiding out when they were eating during the day were not Christians and foreigners.

As easy as these rules seem to follow, only a few hours later, when we decided to head over and look at our possible apartment to move into, I made my first slip-up.

Walking down the street, I lazily took a big swig from a water bottle I was carrying, then caught myself. It was August in the Middle East, and I was flat-out thirsty, but I realized you couldn't do that and quickly looked around to be sure no one saw me.

I then gave the water bottle to one of my kids. Kids are great in general, but especially awesome during times like this because they are allowed to eat and drink during Ramadan. I quickly realized they could also act as my proxy in public for carrying my illegal beverages around, and that is what they did.

The *iftar* meal is a lot of fun to participate in, whether at a restaurant or in the home of a friend. I remember the first time we experienced it we went to a restaurant in the capital a week after we arrived to get a little taste of home. They took everyone's order around 5:45 pm, and we knew it wasn't time to eat until at least seven.

As we drew near to the time to break the fast, everyone's attention focused on a TV screen they had brought in where you could see a very official-looking group of Muslim scholars gathered and waiting to proclaim the end of the day's fast. The waiters brought out all the food and put it in front of everyone at all the tables, and then we waited.

It looked delicious and was steaming hot in front of us, but we couldn't eat it just yet. We waited for five minutes, then 10 minutes, then 15 minutes. We were all intently watching the TV, trying to figure out what the signal would be. I was kind of hoping for something obvious like the firing of a pistol.

Honestly, that first time, I never saw the people on TV do anything unique— I just suddenly noticed all the people around us throwing back a plump date and then attacking their plates of food. Relieved, we then eagerly joined them and started devouring.

The fast of Ramadan is an indispensable occasion of pride for Muslims, and I can't tell you how many times my neighbors and friends have pointed to this fast as a sign of their sincere devotion to God and sacrifice for Him. They love to talk about it and share about how hard it is to carry out.

I think the cycle of years when the lunar month of Ramadan falls in the summer are truly tough seasons to abstain from drink, especially throughout those long, hot summer days. I can't imagine being a day laborer during those times, and thankfully for that reason, the workdays are cut short during Ramadan.

However, all that said, from an outsider's perspective, I have to say I was rarely impressed because most of my Muslim friends softened the blow of Ramadan by changing their daily routine. We saw this change sometimes in the capital and almost with everyone living outside the big urban centers that during the fast month, they completely flip their schedules. All the streets go quiet during the days of Ramadan, and it's a lot like living in a ghost town where you know people must be there, but you see no one as you carry on life for yourself.

The typical solution to the challenge of Ramadan for our friends was to stay up all night eating and drinking, and then right before sunrise, they gorged themselves with a big meal and went to sleep. Waking up around 4 pm or so, they fasted the required three hours approximately until they could eat again, and then they ate with relish another massive meal after the sun had set.

The kind of smile, wink, wink joke during Ramadan is that everyone actually gains weight during this month of fasting. It's truly considered the only religious fast where people knowingly stuff themselves with food before and after fasting (or sleeping), and it causes critical health problems among the people.

Every year diabetics get entirely out of control, and other medical issues increase, especially obesity. When my friends would bring up their "fast" and remind me of how hard it was, I thought to myself that I carry out a fast like that every night. I never eat when I'm sleeping either.

Jesus in trying to release people from many man-made laws that the Pharisees had burdened people with said in Mark 2:27, "the Sabbath was made for man, not man for the Sabbath."

I don't know exactly what he would think of the Ramadan fast, but with all of the additional rules and burdens laid on people, over time, this became a kind of fast that was made for men and by men. Who wouldn't want to participate in something like this when you flip the schedule and end up having a party every night?

Guess who is cooking all day long to get ready for these big meals every day? It certainly wasn't any of my friends. Grace would often tell me how exhausted her women friends were during this month trying to cook all day long for the men and keep up the children.

To be fair, it's true that we mainly saw legalism around us which made us cynical, but I should mention that there is a group of Muslims who follow the fasting in its proper light and keep their sleep at a standard time.

I met several people who were diligently seeking God in a meaningful way during this month.

One woman I worked with told me that she often felt closer to God during this time and tried to listen to Him. We often prayed that people like her would truly succeed and find Him during this month of fasting, the way that many others had found Him before.

If you ever try to carry out the fast yourself while living in the desert, to experience how it feels, it doesn't take long to discover that it is difficult. Those devoted people who observe it by the actual terms of the tradition are tough folks who I respected. I just wanted more spiritual returns for their efforts.

When the fasting month is drawing to an end, everyone starts looking to the sky. The moon wanes more and more until it disappears, and everyone waits for just the tiniest sliver of moon to reappear and denote the next lunar month has come.

The official call comes from some religious higher-ups in Saudi Arabia who probably have the biggest telescope or something. But finally, the day comes when the moon is sighted, and everyone knows this is the last day of fasting; the real feasting is coming.

This party at the end of Ramadan is called *Eid* (feast) *al Fitr* (of fast-breaking) and lasts about three days as everyone now enjoys feasting and spending time visiting their relatives and friends. Kids usually receive gifts during an *eid*—it seemed like toy guns were always popular because our car undoubtedly got shot at for the next few days.

Everyone also got a new outfit to wear on that special occasion. Over time, I heard that a common consideration for the new clothes after the month of fasting was that you usually needed to buy them at least one size larger then you wore at the beginning of the month. This *eid* at the end was usually a fantastic time for visiting neighbors and people that we had been building relationships with throughout the year.

We often would go on the third day of visiting, which they reserve for non-relatives. It's nice because with so many people coming and going, you can actually get a quick 30-minute visit in and then go and do another. Typically, any visit to a house will require one to two hours, even to simply check-in and say hello.

* * *

Eid's a Wonderful Life

The most memorable Eid al Fitr visit that I made happened much later after we had left the capital and moved on to our clinic work in Manara, but it's one of my favorite Ramadan memories, so I'll mention it here.

It was a visit to one of my neighbors in that town. He was the nephew of my landlord and the grandson of my next-door neighbor, so as you can tell, everyone was related on my street except for us.

He and I had started an English-Arabic discussion several months before, where I would teach him English for a while, and then he would teach me Arabic. I was using a discussion book for this exchange, which I had brought from my language school, and it covered broad-ranging topics from ordinary life. As the book went along, it grew in helping one learn Arabic vocabulary to share Christianity through the gospels and biblical stories.

While I frequently was teaching him English medical vocabulary because he was a nurse and had an interest in getting better with his work language, he increasingly began teaching me biblical and Christian terminology. The result was we were reading together through parts of the Bible—to help my Arabic, of course.

After meeting with him for a while, I had gone over to his house and hung out with him and his brother. He asked me in front of his brother if I could give him an *Injil* (a New Testament), and while I was very excited, I held my feelings in and calmly asked him if he had permission from his father to study the Bible.

I had been warned that it could cause a lot of problems if you go around parents in a situation like this or try to be secretive. In the end, you might end up with a lone believer who is ostracized from his family once they find out about his faith, instead of having the opportunity to bring light to the entire family. Plus, the *mukhabarat* (secret police) may find out about the proselytism, which is illegal, and arrest you and kick you out of the country when they hear from a disgruntled family member.

So, I had reckoned it was just better to be upfront, honest and be sure his dad knew about it so that no matter what, there wouldn't be any repercussions for him or me later. And who knows, maybe that would leave the door open for his whole family to come to the Lord in the end.

Nevertheless, to my surprise, he exclaimed, "I don't need my dad's permission!"

I looked at his brother for help, but he supported him, saying, "He's old enough—he doesn't have to ask our dad."

So, I said, "Great!" and told him I would look around and try to round an *Injil* up for him from somewhere. I wanted to act as if the thought had never crossed my mind. I took a little over a week before I presented it to him, grateful to have come across a copy.

So, months into our study, I wanted to visit him and his family, and I had never met his dad although I had seen him walking to the mosque for prayer often enough. After yelling the normal, "*Salaam alaikum!*" (Peace be upon y'all) greeting outside the gate, I got a welcoming, "*tfuddul,*" response from someone on the porch.

I walked up the steps and entered through the left door into the men's salon. I was surprised to see the room already full, and almost every gentleman in the room looked the same. I mean, that is usually what we all say stereotypically about foreigners, but these men truly were all cut out of the same cloth. They were all medium-build and thin; wearing black suits, white shirts, and black ties, these men all had a cigarette in hand, and the place was full of smoke.

My friend greeted me. Rescuing me, he pulled me aside to a corner chair and sat with me as I received the welcoming cup of coffee. We communicated with our usual mixed *Arabisi* (mixed Arabic and English) back and forth with some general greetings, and I asked how the *eid* was going and that kind of thing.

Soon after, the men who had been heavily engaged with my friend's dad all got up and headed out almost as a group, their *eid* visit completed. His dad came over to us, and I made some cordial greetings and told him I was enjoying meeting with his son every week. I couldn't help it, so I decided to ask him who all the men in the black suits were who had just left because it had seemed a bit curious.

He replied that they were all his subordinates from the office, where he was the director in a neighboring town. I told him I had no idea he was a *rajul kabiir* (big man) to have all those men working for him.

I asked, "What are you the director of in the other town?"

He responded with what I'm sure was a tiny grin and said, "I'm the director of the *mukhabarat* for that district. You know, we watch people like you."

At that moment, time froze, and my mind was exploding. I surely felt that he was implying he knew exactly what kind of foreigner I was. I mean, I did work at a place that says "Jesus is the light of the world" on the front gate, but the whole time I thought I had been kind of on the down-low after moving into the neighborhood.

I don't really know where it came from if not from above, but I was able to say without missing a beat, "Well, we really appreciate you guys keeping us foreigners all safe here."

After that, I pretty much realized that everyone there knows why you are there, especially if you were working where we were working.

Chapter 2
LIVING THE DREAM

After shaking off the jet lag of our first day in the capital with our new appreciation for Nescafe, we knew from Benjamin that we already had an appointment time set up in the afternoon to go check out a potential apartment.

We arrived at the beautifully named Muizz Kreishen Street, looking for number 5. It turned out to be a three-story stone apartment building set on the slope of a hill with a small but straightforward garden and BBQ set up to the right side; a grand entrance stair headed up from the street to a large double door.

These doors were framed by two large stained-glass windows that were bright red and green, and that had seen better days back in the 1950s when they built this place. We later discovered that at night, you could turn on the backlights to these windows that would give off a Christmas-like feel with the glowing shards of green and red glass mixing romantically on the stones.

As we greeted the landlord and walked in, we met a formal looking apartment complete with what was likely all original furniture from the days of Fairuz and Frank Sinatra. No less than four large chandeliers were glowing incandescently as you walked in, arriving at a mirrored ceiling overlooking a large wooden dining-room table. There were two salons to the right full of ornate draperies and fancy but now dated couches.

We wanted a furnished apartment here in the capital because we would be moving to Manara after 12 months and could buy all of our stuff cheaper from someone up there, maybe a fellow foreigner moving out. As we moved deeper into the apartment, we realized that it didn't go too much deeper. There were two small bedrooms, one bath, and one small office with a kitchen off to the right. We would find out later that Arabs generally will spend all their money on their entry rooms at the expense of their actual living quarters because hosting and impressing guests is so important in their culture.

A guest would never actually penetrate someone's house beyond the salon at the front, and they would certainly never go into someone's kitchen or bathroom, so why spend any money back there? We knew of some Arab friends who had spent thousands of dinars entirely building out their front entrance and salon room while they lived in a small bare room that was just cinder-block shells while they waited to earn enough money to complete the bedrooms, bathroom, and kitchen.

This apartment had the same kind of priority, and we noticed the carpet was worn out in the bedrooms, and the furniture was pretty tired. In the kitchen stood a loud and very olive-green Westinghouse refrigerator that was probably more appropriate for a post-WWII museum.

Buddhas and Burgers

Maybe more fascinating to us were the decorations everywhere. There was a relatively large ceramic Buddha sitting in the main living area. Next to it was a large framed picture of the *Kaaba*, which is a small black cube, the central shrine for Muslim worship in Mecca. Grace's favorite painting in the main room was a large stag that was in the process of being eaten alive by a ferocious dog during what was possibly a hunt.

We couldn't understand what kind of philosophy or personality could connect all of these ideas, and we were unquestionably surprised a Muslim would allow a giant idol of the Buddha in their home. Were they trying to show us how Western they were to appeal to us as renters? We didn't know.

* * *

We needed a ground floor apartment because Grace had had untreatable severe leg pain now for more than two years. She had been to every doctor she could find starting from her internist and moving on to the neurologist and every other specialty as she sought a cure or at least a diagnosis for this strange phenomenon. She, in many ways, was like the woman described in Mark 5:26 who had spent so much of her money on doctors but still was no better off than before.

Like that woman, she had faith that Jesus could heal her even if she could reach out and touch the edge of his garment, but to this point, there had been no miracle. We had many dear friends praying for her around the US as we made all the preparations for our move to the Middle East. She no longer could stand or walk for normal amounts of time, and she often had to brace herself against a wall. I had gotten in the habit of scouting out chairs when we entered a new room because she would often sit down as soon as she could find a chair available.

Although it would give us many more options and be much cheaper, the idea of Grace climbing stairs every day up to a second- or third-floor apartment (in the Middle East they call this the first- and second-floor) seemed impossible, so we knew we needed the ground level.

The problem is that usually, the ground level apartment is where the older couple of the family live, and their sons build and live on the floors above. The result is the whole family is living together in the same building that keeps going up and up. In our situation, the grandparents had passed away, and the son did not want to move downstairs, which left this apartment opening.

We sat down at the table with the owner and asked questions and negotiated out a price for the apartment. We had seen the asking price for a total of one apartment at this point, but we knew that ground floor apartments were very hard to come by, and this was the only livable one that Benjamin had found.

The truth is that when you realize you are now officially homeless and dragging around three kids with you and ten full pieces of luggage around with you with no place to unpack them, you are highly motivated to sign a deal and find a place to call home.

We were thinking it's only for 12 months anyway and people with our calling are supposed to live in less suitable places then they came from, right? That's just part of the deal. So, we thought it was not the best place in the world. But, the location was right, the gaudy chandeliers and mirrors in the front were hilarious, and we figured we could do some fixing up and replace the nasty carpet and some other things pretty quickly. There's probably a Home Depot somewhere close.

Grace was concerned about the cleanliness of the place and the fact that all of the shelves and cabinets and drawers and closets were still full of the deceased grandparents' belongings. The landlord quickly assured us that he would clean all the apartment very thoroughly and get rid of all the books, papers, and items before we moved in.

I asked about the radiator, which I knew would be valuable in the winter, and he told us the apartment had radiators and a boiler and everything. He told us that one year's rent was to be paid six months upfront, and then the other six months in January. We shook on it, paid him some money, and he told us we could move in after two days so that they would have time to get everything ready for us.

We were about to make our departure when the landlord's younger son busted in the front door, his hands full of two heavily laden bags steaming hot and fresh from Burger King. He was clearly surprised and embarrassed to see us sitting there, catching him red-handed with the forbidden Ramadan spoils for the family.

He gathered himself, and hastily greeted us and escaped with the food up the stairs to the upper level. The wafting aroma of grilled meat lingered on this full day of fasting. So much for a Ramadan facade for this family—they had been outed, and we knew they must be thoroughly secular at this point between Buddhas and burgers. It wouldn't be the last time that what looked good on the outside would be shown to be just whitewashed with this family.

Looking back at it, we should have never signed a deal on this apartment, but we were in too much of a hurry, and we put general faith in what the landlord was telling us because we came from a country with a Judeo-Christian heritage. We generally assumed that lying was considered wrong everywhere—certainly, bald-faced lying in response to direct questions. We wrongly assumed that would never be an issue with this well-mannered elder statesman of a landlord.

Also, as we would find a couple of weeks later, we had no need for a ground floor apartment after all. One day, I noticed that Grace was standing more than normal and not gravitating towards the nearest chair like she usually did.

I asked her, "Do your legs not hurt you standing like that?"

She thought about it a second and said, "You know, I totally forgot about my leg pain, they're not hurting at all now that you mention it."

In fact, the leg pain that had afflicted her for two years had fully departed and was not to return again. It would be easy for the skeptic to say two weeks of a different diet or two weeks of an alien climate had made the change, but to us, it was Jesus.

It was as if Jesus had told her like the woman in Mark 5:34: "Daughter, your faith has healed you. Go in peace and be freed from your suffering." It was a full answer to a long season of prayers, and we knew that many faithful friends praying for her on the other side of the world had hugely contributed to this healing. May His name be praised!

Movin' On Up

Once we moved into the apartment, the reality of what we had signed on for started to hit us. The place did look much cleaner—it had been dusted and generally cleaned, but as we started opening up drawers to unload our luggage, we kept finding them all still full of junk.

We complained to the landlord, and he said he would come and get it all, but until he did that, we decided to go ahead and started emptying all the stuff into boxes so we could begin making this place home. We knew it would take him hours of work, and he wasn't anywhere to be seen.

As we started moving everything around and getting things arranged, we noticed we weren't the only inhabitants of this apartment. Roaches were coming out of every nook and cranny, and we were constantly trying to smash them as we worked. Apparently, this roach feature is one of the disadvantages of the ground floor apartment we came to find out later.

It got to be so ridiculous that we started keeping count of how many we were killing, almost like it was a competition. I'll never forget that during that first week, the record number of kills was 43 cockroaches in one day. I'm glad we've never had the opportunity to break that record again.

After three weeks of no-showing to pick up their family's items from our apartment, we finally put all of the boxes outside our door and let them know that if they wanted the stuff, it was out there, but otherwise, we weren't going to keep it for them anymore.

About that time, they brought us the first electric bill. I was surprised that is was $150, because we hadn't even been there for one month yet and it was a small apartment. That was definitely beyond our monthly budget, but the landlord told me it was likely because we were running the AC units, which were very expensive. Anyway, it was a new country and I didn't know the electric rates, so I paid for it and decided to cut down on our electricity and see what happened.

The next month after cutting back significantly, our electric bill went up. I instantly knew something was fishy because there was no way we had used more electricity now for a full month because we had been really suffering through the summer heat to meet our budget.

I asked Benjamin what his electric bill was for their apartment because ours was a similar size. I knew I was being cheated when he said it was generally around $30-40 monthly. I wasn't sure how they accomplished it, but I knew something was going on.

We were going away that weekend for a little excursion, so I decided to cut off all of my circuit breakers except on the fridge while I was away to reduce my electricity bill. I got a call the next day from the landlord asking me if I had touched any of my circuit breakers.

I was curious how he knew, but I responded that I had because I was trying to save electricity, and my bill was not accurate. He asked me to turn them all back on because they controlled an outside light in front of the house, and for safety reasons, I should never have that off.

When I got back home, it was late, and the building and entrance were mostly dark everywhere. We got inside and put some stuff down, and then I decided to flip on all the breakers and look outside. When I did, the whole building came alive, including multiple outside floodlights, stairway lights, and interior lights up on the second and third floors.

I was mad and confronted the landlord about the fact that I was paying for the electricity of the whole building, and he denied it saying that it was just that one light outside, and he would get that switched out quick.

I knew this was a simple lie from him and would never happen, just like the boxes of junk, so I called an electrician and had him come out. He confirmed that most of the building wiring had been rigged to run through my meter box, so he cut all of those auxiliary wires out and rerouted them back to the individual apartment meters.

The other problem we had already endured was electrical power blacking out on us a lot. I had already marked all of our large appliances with their amperage, and we knew we could only have a few large things on at a time, or it blew a fuse in the basement.

Literally, I would see my daughter plug in a hairdryer, forgetting to unplug something to match it, and I would yell, "Stop!" At the same moment she powered it on, the apartment went black.

These occurrences happened all the time because you always had to unplug something to plug something else in, and it was hard for the kids to remember. I asked if the electrician could give us more amps because the power went out at least once every week, and it was annoying to go replace the fuse in the basement.

He told us these apartments were only allowed 30 amps, and the government would not let him increase it (American homes usually have at least 200 amps). However, he told me that I shouldn't bother with fuses anymore because he could make it a better system in the end for us. I watched as he wound three copper wires together in a braid and completely bypassed the fuse.

I knew that Ecclesiastes tells us that "a cord of three strands is not easily broken," but I had never seen that verse applied in this way.

He said now the problem would come from the city side which was weaker and not from us and they would have to fix that themselves. Sure enough, a week later, the power went out, and I checked downstairs, but our new "handmade" fuse was still fully intact, so there was no way to get the power back on. But this time, I smelled something and saw there had been an electrical fire in a box closer to the street.

I looked into it, and it was a charred mess of plastic and wires. The next day the government utility workers came and replaced that box, upgrading it to 60 amps. We were beginning to learn the ways of this world.

Water of Life

When we hear that Jesus told the people at the feast in John 7:37, "If anyone is thirsty, let him come to Me and drink," His audacity to claim to be the source of water needed to quench our thirst and satisfy captures our attention.

But while I understand that theoretically, I never walked around too thirsty living in the West because a Seven-Eleven is on every corner along with unlimited tap water available in every home and business.

After living in one of the most water-scarce countries in the world, I have found myself thirsty living there more than any other time in my life. Knowing Jesus made His water promise in this arid part of the world has real practical application and makes it an even more dramatic statement; it must have been quite the life-giving promise to the people of that day.

After we moved in, we tried to live our lives as we would have in the US. After three days, when the first Sunday morning arrived, Grace was showering as we got ready to go to church. Suddenly, the water stopped, and she was left covered in a trickle of sediment that came out the pipe. Disgusted, she had to rinse off with cups of bottled drinking water. Before I started looking at water pumps and other things, I wanted to verify there was actually still water to pump.

I knew our water tank was on the roof, so I made my way to the top and looked into our water tank only to find it was completely dry, except for a layer of mud and sediment. I knew that the water from the government came in on Wednesday, so we had used up all our water in four days. We did survive by buying some bottled water to get us by, and it was a happy moment on Wednesday morning when the water started rushing in from the city. We could finally complete a long-overdue flush on the toilet and get a shower.

It took quite a change in our behavior to make the water last from Wednesday to Wednesday, but gradually we got the hang of it. The idea of leaving a faucet on to brush your teeth or using enough water to take a bath began to seem so wasteful to us after a while. Dishwashers were unheard of, and quick "Navy" showers became the rule for our family.

I developed a sensitivity to the sound of dripping water and would immediately rush off and address any drip because overnight, a simple drip or leak in your toilet will drain your entire water cistern and leave you out of water until the next Wednesday.

Our bodies took a little time to get used to reduced showers and cleaning, but eventually, they did. However, during the first month, I started feeling the sensation of burning on my arms and legs.

It felt like they were burning and that someone was putting push-pins into my skin. I did a little research and called one of my best friends, Mark, who is an excellent internist in the US and found out that the problem was likely something called "prickly heat."

According to him, it usually came from inadequate cleaning of sebum from the body, so I could fix it by taking more showers or making my showers more effective. Since more showers and wearing clean clothes every day were impossible (how easy the solutions are in the West!), I followed the advice not to use a towel after the shower and air dry.

I also went to the pharmacy to get a dermatological cream but found out from my internist friend that it was like nuclear-level stuff that could cause sloughing of the skin if you use it too much, so I only used that when there was extreme prickling.

After a few weeks, I got past this, and over the years, it never came back. Maybe it was a mix between my body adjusting or my changed bathing behavior, but I never experienced it again.

I was encouraged during my internet research about prickly heat to learn that bathing was done in the US only monthly until the 1930s. After that, companies like Proctor and Gamble encouraged weekly bathing to sell more products and in the '70s, started talking about daily bathing. I took pride in feeling like the Middle East was helping me get back to the roots and behaviors of my ancestors.

The day arrived for the water bill to come for the first time, and my landlord presented me with a bill for about $50. I was already cynical about receiving invoices from him by now, but if water was such a precious commodity, maybe this was a reasonable charge for how little water we were using. I quickly called up Benjamin to see what his average bill was, and he told me he never paid more than nine to eleven dollars. My blood pressure immediately started to rise, and I went outside to see what I could discover about the incoming water system.

I knew that once the water was pushed up to the roof, that it evenly went into all of the three water cisterns, so the water was equally shared at that point. So, theoretically, we should all be paying the same amount for water. At the ground level, the water came in through three different water meters: ground floor, second floor, third floor, but then as I followed the pipes, the three tubes joined into one large pipe before heading up the side of the building to the roof. The bill was based on what was shown on the meter, and surprisingly, my bill accurately matched my ground floor meter.

I asked my landlord if they all paid the same amount as I had on my bill, and he said the other two bills were for the exact same amount. So, I had investigated, and it all looked legit, but I felt like there had to be some catch or trick that I was missing. But I couldn't see how they could be deceiving me this time. Maybe because they watered the garden every day with the communal water to keep it nice and green, we just used more water than Benjamin did. All I could do was wait and see.

The next Wednesday, when the water started coming in, I decided to go outside early and reinvestigate the meters and be sure everything was copacetic. I found my pipe and meter spinning rapidly as the water came in as we tried to get as much water as possible to make it through the week. But as I looked at the other two meters, they were not spinning at all, which was curious. I traced these pipes around the house again from the city to our building and found that both of these pipes had little valves up the line, which were now closed.

The realization hit me that every Wednesday, someone was closing both valves on the other two pipes, so all the water for the building was only coming through my pipe and meter and then getting distributed on the roof evenly to everyone, but I was paying for it all. This guy was robbing and lying to me again!

At this point in my experience, I didn't know whether to be mad or just laugh at how base and ridiculous this man was in trying to deceive me. He would go to any length it seemed to steal from me and save a few dollars.

I knew from Psalm 141:10 that the wicked would eventually fail as it says, "Let the wicked fall into their own nets, while I pass by in safety," but at the moment, I wasn't feeling like a success. Knowing that he could never admit his deceit, I still wanted to let the landlord know I was on to him yet again. I told the landlord that every Wednesday morning, I would be sure all the valves were open so we could get as much water as possible since I had found his two pipes "accidentally" closed off

A few months later, when the rainy season came, we were often blessed with more water coming in compared to the average amounts. The rainy season stretches from December until February in the Middle East, although you may see a stray shower even as late as April. In fact, the Arabic word for winter, *shitta,* also means "rain" because that is the only time you usually see it or even see clouds for that matter.

Living in the capital city meant that we were pretty exposed to wind and weather without a lot of trees or natural protection. That's usually an advantage in the summer months, but in the rainy season, you can get some severe weather during the short winter months.

One day we had an example of that with a huge deluge that lasted all day long and then into the next day. We were busy studying the language at that point and getting the kids to school, so we were out of the house all day.

When we returned home, we learned about another disadvantage of living on the ground floor when we opened up the front door and water poured down the front steps out of our house. Venturing inside, already with thoroughly wet feet, we observed about 2 inches of standing water throughout the apartment.

We couldn't figure out how in the world this water was getting into the house. Was the rain pouring down the hill and running under the door into our apartment? It seemed impossible as all of the entrances were well sealed. But that's when we saw it.

Floating across our living room past the table were a couple of long, small logs. I'm not talking about wooden logs, but logs that come from the sewer. We quickly realized that we were not standing in the overflow coming from too much rainwater, but we were standing in raw sewage because the city sewers had backed up when they couldn't accommodate all of the rain. When the sewers had backed up, it had just risen until the sewage came straight up out of the drains in the floors that all Arab buildings have.

We quickly pushed the kids outside; grabbing squeegees we started pushing the sewage water out of our house. The landlord came down and to his credit, grabbed a squeegee, and we formed a line, pushing the sewage out of the front and side doors and then down a step so that it couldn't seep back in. The rain did start to ease up outside as we worked, and we gave up on trying to stay hygienic because that was an impossibility at this point.

Our efforts finally overcame the sewage even as the storm drains began to catch up and take all the rainwater to the proper place. That only began our work as we started to do damage assessment and see what we could save and what we couldn't. We bought loads of bleach and initiated the process of bleaching our whole apartment up to the level of the sewage and throwing out all the stuff that couldn't be cleaned.

Thankfully, tiles and not carpets are the norm in apartments in the Middle East, and the walls are always cement or stone, so this was an easier task than it would have been in the US where it is usually all carpets and drywall. The only carpet we had in the back bedrooms had not been affected because of a raised step at the doorway.

Once we sanitized the apartment, we finally caught our breath, but within about 12 hours, we all started getting sick. It's probably the only time I can think of where the whole family got sick at exactly the same time—and because of the situation, it was fairly obvious as to why.

Paul says in Philippians 3:8 that we should count all of our gains apart from Christ as "sewage" (the Greek word is *skubala*) so that we may gain Christ. That means we got a really close-up view of what our achievements without Christ look like and smell like if you peel back the outside and look at them from an eternal viewpoint.

It seems like even our virtues and good works can make us sick and defile us if we put our hope in them and not in Christ. We hope in Christ and hoped that our apartment woes would get better.

Baby, it's Cold Outside

As the rainy season moved into winter, it was time to look into figuring out how to run the boiler and radiators, because living in a stone building with single pane glass windows on top of a mountain was starting to get very cold. I had never personally used a radiator before, although I had memories of the radiator percolating in my old elementary school back home.

I called a plumber to come to help me get it cleaned out and started. It didn't take long after he came to figure out that the boiler was utterly wrecked and wouldn't work. I called up my landlord and told him the boiler needed repair. He informed me that it hadn't worked in three years because something inside had cracked, and he was sorry, but we couldn't use it.

I reminded him we rented the place based on the fact that it had radiators and had asked him specifically about that, and he had advertised it as an apartment heated by a radiator. He told me that in the contract, he never claimed that the radiators worked, just that it had radiators, and if I wanted it to work, he would help me buy and install a $3500 boiler, with my money of course.

I better not explain what kind of thoughts and words I may have imagined and spoken at that time about my landlord. It's best not to put that much in print, but surely what had transpired must have been ordained for my sanctification.

As winter moved in, we had a nice thermometer that reminded us of the temperature inside, although we didn't need much help figuring it out. Come to find out, in the low 50's you start to see your own breath (depending on humidity), so we could often tell about where we stood on temperature.

We bought a couple of electric heaters that did a good job of warming up whatever was about twelve inches in front of it. It became normal just to come home and get in bed because that was the only place you could get warm after we had found some Turkish electric blankets that did a great job. We'd all be lying in bed, studying Arabic, or doing homework with our toboggan hats on our heads, seeing our breath every time we spoke. Grace began to live with gloves on both inside and outside our home.

Compared to our homeland, the winter wasn't that much cooler by temperature; the issue was you could never get out of the cold. Inside our apartment, the temperature hovered between 48 and 54 degrees most of the time, and even when you would go out to the bank or to the store to do shopping, none of those places were heated, so you could never get any relief.

We found out later that our first winter there was one of the coldest on record in the capital. It became kind of a badge of honor to brag that you were living in the capital that winter because everyone froze that year. One of our friends even had to go to the hospital because of frostbite on her toes.

Still, I'll remember that winter as being one of closeness for our family. We spent a lot of time together, huddling to keep warm, sometimes bonding over our misery but generally just thanking God that we were here in the Middle East and making steps toward becoming better speakers of Arabic and better understanding the culture.

Despite all of the problems, we did enjoy a lot of good memories in that apartment. I often remember all three kids bundled up together in bed with winter caps on like peas in a pod. Probably if we had stayed in the US, our nine-year-old girl, eight-year-old boy, and five-year-old girl would not have ever shared a room although they were still at an age when that wasn't too weird.

The cold brought them together, and they had a good time bonding and playing until spring came, and our son moved into the office. We always were trying to make the most of what we had, and since there wasn't anything too exciting on Arab TV to watch, we had to get creative.

We found a small net which we erected on our dining room table and voila, ping pong was born in the apartment. Other times, the kids erected forts out of the furniture, and we always had a good time trying to find a stuffed animal lamb that would be hidden throughout the apartment.

As the weather warmed, the sun revived the earth, and the plants began to grow again; our language skills were blossoming, and we were able to engage people in more meaningful ways, which allowed us to discover a lot more about the culture around us.

Chapter 3

CLASH OF THE CULTURES

Taking out the trash on one of our first weeks living in the Middle East, I made the soon-to-be-weekly pilgrimage to the busted and bombed-out silver garbage bins at the end of the street. Once the mess of cats had quickly jumped out, which often shocked me at times until I got used to them, I was free to make my deposit of several bags.

I noted that bags of bread were visibly tied and hanging off the side of the bins, but technically not inside the containers. An innocuous-looking man leaned against a car a couple of feet away from the bins, and he watched me as I dropped my bags in. I turned around and headed back up the street only to quickly hear the sound of rummaging in the bin behind me. I turned around and looked; I saw the man grab my garbage bags in toto, put them in his trunk, and drive away.

This first garbage experience alerted me to the fact that everything we threw away was not anonymous like in the US. Each item would most likely be in the hands of someone else at a later point, so I must be aware of what we were taking out.

Most of the time, it was because the poor typically went through the trash, especially the garbage of foreigners, looking for cans or discarded items. What to us might be worthless, to someone else in a lower socioeconomic state could be of much value.

The other possibility was that the *mukhabarat* were looking through our trash to discover any receipts or communications we might have thrown away. Some colleagues of ours had recently been brought in before the secret police, and they told us the police were able to produce and present to them some letters and documents that they had discarded long ago.

Whatever had just happened that time with the man putting our garbage in his car, it changed our behavior with regards to trash. We bought a shredder for handling anything that had a name or number and deposited most of our waste from that point on at a location far from our house.

So why was the bread hanging on the trash can? Well, we had got a glimpse of that early on even when we were on the plane heading to the Middle East. My young son, David, had knocked off the bread roll from his plate of "yummy" airplane food, and it had rolled under his seat.

An Arab woman behind us had instantly started saying, "*Harum, harum, harum!*" after that, and was pointing to the roll under his seat.

I thanked her for the notice but then ignored her, not knowing why she was so perturbed. I assumed that she was alerting us to the bread, which at this point, we no longer wanted.

However, she continued shouting, "*Harum, harum, harum!*" and I realized that she must wish us to get it or do something with it.

Frustrated, I sent David after it under the seat to quiet her up, and he replaced it onto his tray. To our relief, her "*harum-ing*" finally stopped.

Come to find out, the Arabs have a strong tradition of not letting bread be on the ground or in the garbage because they feel like it is a gift from God that should be esteemed to honor this heavenly mercy from above. So, all discarded pieces of bread are set apart and never thrown away directly, theoretically for the hungry poor to pick up, but ostensibly for someone else to discard it in the end so we can remember God's gift to us.

It makes me wonder how the people here must have responded to someone like Jesus saying, "I am the bread come down from heaven" in John 6. It's much more of a statement and claim than I ever imagined before.

In Arab culture, there is a critical distinction in general between the *halal (permitted)* and the *harum (forbidden)*. The things *halal* are acceptable to God and essentially done according to His prescription, as they find in their book of traditions called the Hadith. For instance, Muslims slaughter animals differently than we do in the West. They must say a prayer over the animal, turn its head toward the *Qibla* (direction to Mecca) and slice its carotid artery with a sharp knife.

The animal generally moans or strains as the blood slowly drains out until it gives up the ghost. Then the animal can be butchered according to Islamic law, and the meat is then considered *halal* and acceptable to eat. If the animal is not slaughtered this way or, Lord forbid, the animal is a pig, the meat is considered *harum* or forbidden for them to eat.

Connected to this idea is the word *harem* that most Westerners know about: a man's wife or wives are also off-limits to other men, so they are called a *harem* because they are in the forbidden place or set-apart site of his house.

Basically, anything that they feel goes against God or the laws that respect Him are called *harum*, from a BBQ rib to a piece of bread, which is a gift from God rolling on an airplane floor.

As we began living and dealing with Arabs daily, we were often puzzled. We couldn't figure out the logic as to why they said or did the things they did. If they had only spoken a truthful and straightforward answer to us many times, we wouldn't have been disappointed, and we wouldn't have wasted our time on so many dead ends.

An Arab proverb says that "the lie is the salt of men," and we noticed that we were getting lied to daily. Without an underlying story that helped us understand the interactions, other than they all must just be evil sinners, it drove us crazy sometimes.

Thankfully, we were still in what is called the "honeymoon" phase of our time in the Middle East, which is how people describe the first months in trying to adapt to the culture. So, when people did stuff like that, we could laugh it off as being so intriguing that they did things "backwards" in this culture compared to the way we think you should do things. It wasn't until six or nine months later when one enters the "black hole" of culture shock that these things urgently made you upset, and you are ready to leave the country and go home.

Rooms to Go They Ain't

One of our first orders of business was to get some new carpets for the small back bedrooms of our apartment and to buy some new mattresses for the beds. We had rented it furnished, but we had decided those things had to be renewed because they had seen too many years of use from nameless people.

Our friend Benjamin took us to the first carpet place that we had been to at the bottom of a hill that supervises the entire city, and he showed us basically what was available in the *balad* of the capital. We didn't find anything there and later ended up in another carpet place on the main street.

We dug and dug through carpet samples and asked about prices and finally landed on a carpet style and cost that would meet our needs well. We asked the salesperson if we could go ahead and order that carpet, and he seemed a bit taken back at first.

"You want to buy this carpet…now?" he said, the question on his face.

We quickly all looked at each other and responded in the affirmative.

He informed us that only the owner of the store could sell the carpet, and he was not here. "You want to buy it today?" he asked again.

We again told him we did, so he said to wait for five minutes until the owner came back. He showed us some seats. Ten minutes passed and then fifteen minutes, and there was still no owner.

Benjamin asked the man if the owner was on the way soon. The salesman said he would call him to find out and picked up the phone and dialed a number. He talked a short bit and hung up and informed us that the owner would be here in ten more minutes.

We sighed and decided to hold out just a little bit longer because it would save us a whole trip in getting back another time. Ten minutes again passed and then fifteen and still no owner.

Growing impatient, we decided that we would be better off doing some of our other shopping and coming back a few hours later because who knew how long this man was going to take.

We told the salesperson that we would just come back later in the afternoon and try to meet with the owner then.

He seemed to be relieved and said, "Oh—so you are leaving and will come back later today?"

We responded, "Yes," and then, to our surprise, he told us, "don't come back later, because the owner is off work all day today. He'll not be back to work until tomorrow."

Going to find the mattresses was equally frustrating. We were trying not to spend too much money on American style mattresses, so we were looking at blocks of different colored foam with various levels of firmness.

We found some foam mattresses with the right softness we were looking for, and we paid for three pink foam mattresses, and they said they could deliver them to our house a bit later.

When the truck arrived, the two men lugged the mattresses up the steps to our apartment. Two were pink, and one was yellow. I immediately pointed this out to one of the men who had just sold me the pink mattresses an hour earlier.

He looked at the yellow mattress and seemed a bit surprised. He then said that these were precisely the three mattresses we had purchased from him. I then reminded him of the trouble we went to together to find and pull out three pink mattresses in his store and how we didn't like the feel of the yellow ones. He insisted that we did like the yellow mattress, and he didn't remember that happening at all.

I showed him the receipt showing that we had paid the same price for all three identical mattresses, and each color sold for different prices in his store.

He told me it didn't say the color in the receipt, so that didn't prove anything. He then suddenly abandoned that line of thinking and offered up a red herring by telling me it was a good thing that we ended up with a yellow mattress because they are so much better for your back.

The other delivery man quickly agreed, chiming in and saying that, yes, we had a lucky accident with this switch-up, but God was blessing us.

Their logic was bewildering. I stood my ground and demanded that he return the yellow mattress and bring back the pink mattress immediately.

They then said that there was a substantial return charge if we decided to swap out the one yellow mattress for the pink one we ordered. It was almost the cost of a new mattress, and that pink mattress would hurt our backs, and they didn't want to be responsible for hurting our backs.

We realized these men were not going to back down anytime soon and that they would string out this lie forever unless we had some way to prove them wrong, which we didn't.

Later, I learned to take pictures with my phone of any large item I was having delivered with me and the salesman standing in front of it, but at this point, I had not gotten to that level of mistrust.

As they quickly departed, I told them in a huff that I would never buy mattresses from them again, which probably seemed to them to be a pretty hollow threat since people don't usually re-buy mattresses yearly.

At the time, this interaction significantly bothered us because we still couldn't find the thread which ran through these events that would help us to make sense of what was going on around us in the culture.

Three Knocks

One thing that did help was that we found a little word of wisdom from our friends Benjamin and Valerie to often be true as we tried to accomplish any task in the Middle East. They had told us that to do anything here, expect that "you'll have to knock three times."

What this meant is that while in America, you can often go to a store and buy something and leave, the way of life in the Middle East takes much more time and interaction to accomplish anything. On average, they had told us you had to try three times before you were successful with any big task, and as time went on, we felt that was a very accurate estimate.

It saved us a lot of frustration in the long run because it gave us new expectations, which seemed to help our patience level. It got to the point that when, for instance, I needed to go to the internet store to request internet for our house, that I just quipped to Grace that I was going for the "first knock" to get the process started.

I certainly didn't entertain any thoughts of getting an internet installation order processed in a single day because that was unrealistic. So, when I went and waited thirty minutes to be served and then the first thing the man wanted was my passport which I didn't bring, it didn't bother me. I knew I had at least accomplished the "first knock" because I had never dreamed of bringing my passport to sign up for internet service, and now I could return for round two.

Things like this happened a lot, and you often would return for the "second knock" with the requested document in hand only to be told that they now needed something else. You would usually succeed on the "third knock" however.

I remember going to register my car one time, and they wanted a copy of my passport's first page, but I only brought the passport itself, and the man insisted he needed only a paper copy.

I returned home and made a copy and then jetted back to the DMV and gave this to the registrar. The registrar then told me it looked good, and where was the passport photo he needed to go along with the documentation?

I was incensed because he didn't inform me of that the first time around, and I let him know that in a gentle way, but he wouldn't back down.

Thankfully, I had several spare photos at the house, so I again returned home to retrieve it and again returned to the DMV.

During that time I was away, work shifts had changed and there was now a new registrar at the counter. I confidently handed her my passport, the copy of my passport, and the passport photo.

She looked at them questioningly and asked me why I brought them. I told her the last man said I had to have them all with me and she said no—those things were never required. She then looked up my information on the computer, and the car registration was quickly printed up. Knock, knock, knock.

The Silver Thread

As more and more time passed, we were picking up more clues about how to interact successfully in this culture, and the silver thread holding all the pieces together finally began to fall in place. The solution to the puzzling chain of events concerned the cultural idea of honor and shame. It was an idea we were familiar with from before we arrived, but we hadn't known how to apply it.

It is featured in almost every book that's written about the Muslim world, including the well known *Honor and Shame* by Roland Mueller. However, reading about it theoretically and seeing it work out in practical life are two different matters. What we saw was that our Arab friends and neighbors and local shopkeepers were doing everything possible in their power to please and honor us. They were the ultimate "people pleasers" because not to please or honor a person is to bring shame upon yourself, and shame was to be avoided at all costs.

One would think this should have worked out great for us, because who doesn't want to be surrounded by a bunch of people pleasers who have all your interests at the front of their minds at all times?

The problem for us and the reason it doesn't work out that way is that people can escape the penalty of shame way too easily by just *appearing* to please you.

They don't actually have to do anything that pleases you, they just have to tell you what you want to hear or make things look the way you want them to look, and then they have escaped any danger of incurring shame upon themselves.

So, when we thought back about our incident in the carpet store, we realized we had made a classic blunder. We had been so bold as to tell the salesman that we actually wanted to buy the carpet that day. How stupid of us! By telling him what we wanted, he was now required to please us, or he would be shamed.

He knew that the store owner was not going to be there that day so that we couldn't buy the carpet. But, if he told us that, we would be unhappy and he would be shamed. That's probably why he asked us the second time if we really wanted to buy it that day—he was giving us a chance to give him an out.

As good Westerners, we held our ground and told him what we wanted. So, like a good Easterner, he did what he had to do to honor us—he lied to us and told us the owner would be there soon to sell the carpet to us.

We had forced him to lie to us by telling him the only way to please us was to sell us the carpet. Once we gave up and told him we were leaving the store and would come back at another time, the salesman was then free. He could now admit to us that the owner was not coming in that day because there was no longer any shame danger to himself—we didn't want the carpet that day anymore.

If I had it to do over again, when he asked me what I wanted, I should never have openly answered him. I should have given him an out and said I wanted to buy some carpet one day and watched how he responded.

And thinking later about the mattress salesman, he had probably just made an honest mistake. Unfortunately, I had openly confronted him about the delivery mistake in front of the other man. If he had admitted this error, then it clearly would have brought shame upon him because he did not please me with what I wanted. So, he had to lie and lie again to cover up the mistake because he couldn't be shamed openly like that.

The other man was trying to help me back down by suggesting what a surreptitious mistake this had been and how good this was for my back, but I wasn't biting.

So, what should I have done? Upon seeing the yellow mattress, I probably should have pointed it out to the man privately. If he had shown signs of denial or refusal, I should have simply told him that I had changed my mind, and now I wanted all three mattresses to be pink.

This method would have pointed out the problem to him without blaming anyone for the error. Likely he could have returned it to his store and brought back the correct pink mattress and told me I made the right decision for no extra charge.

Yet, I had forced his hand and made it a public showdown between his word and my word with shame on the line. I had found out the hard way that if you don't have solid proof or evidence of your word, then you can never argue them into a corner, even if they know you are telling the truth. They will be forced to lie at all costs—to honor you, of course.

In general, as I learned more and more to conceal what I wanted, I found that I was getting lied to much less often, which made me happier. People are always more free to be honest with you when you don't want anything.

I remember a breakthrough came when I was walking by the site of a new movie theater that had been built and looked like it would possibly be opening soon. I asked one worker standing there if the theater was open yet.

He told me something like, "It is open, but not today—you can come tomorrow or any other time this week and see a movie."

I was surprised because it certainly didn't look like it was close to being already open. As I got to the end of the block, I saw another construction worker there, and I decided to ask him differently.

It was summer, so I asked him, "Do you think this theater might be open sometime in the next year?"

He responded cheerfully, "Oh yes, sooner than that—our opening date is in three months, October 1st." He was so happy to please me and even outdo my expectations.

By giving him a "next year" expectation, I had allowed him to be truthful with me and give me the actual date. The first man probably thought I wanted to see a movie right then, so he had to lie and say the theater was already in business. The silver thread had been found.

Because this thread is so important in understanding the culture and daily life of the East, that necessarily means that we must understand this idea of shame. We must follow Peter in "always being prepared to make a defense to anyone who asks you for a reason for the hope that is in you…" (I Peter 3:15).

Many of our neighbors and friends often asked us why we were there and why we were Christians and not Muslims. Talking about religion (as well as politics) is not a forbidden topic in daily conversation in the Middle East, but a welcome one. If we can't articulate the gospel in a way that resonates with their life and culture, then that probably means it will be an added barrier for them to understand the good news about which we share. So, we have to know how to present the Bible stories through the lens of honor and shame.

Does that mean we should add things or change things in the Bible so that it fits the Arab understanding of honor and shame better? Certainly not! We may never add to or change God's written Word. As Mueller fitfully points out in his book, the ideas of honor and shame are fully available in Scripture without having to make any additions or subtractions. We as Westerners never see that aspect because it's not on our radar—but it's undoubtedly on theirs.

Consider, for instance, the story of Adam and Eve. We typically get interested in the guilt and judgment that falls upon our first parents after they sin and eat the forbidden fruit. For Westerners, the penalty for sin surely has to be paid by someone like in a law court model. God will bring justice, and guilt will drive the sinners to remorse.

However, if you share this story from Genesis 3 in the Arab context, what grabs their attention is the utter shame this brings upon God as His creatures don't honor Him at all. Adam and Eve are not God pleasers. They actually do the only thing that would not please Him or honor Him by eating the fruit. Arabs intently notice that.

I remember reading this story once with a twenty-something-year-old Arab who was initially only mildly interested in the Bible. We talked and discussed all aspects of the text leading up to this point. But when we got to this point in the story where Adam sinned, his interest was piqued.

However, we had kind of run out of time together and he anxiously asked me, "But what is God now going to do about this? How does He deal with the shame? Do I have to wait until next time?"

I asked him if he knew what an Arab family would do if the father was publicly shamed by one of the children—specifically if a female did something with a man that embarrassed the whole family.

I said, "Wouldn't they have to do something to her and maybe even kill her?"

He shook his head, "Yes." The idea of the honor killing is well known in the East and often practiced still. Someone would have to die in that situation.

I told him that God had to do an honor killing as well because they had shamed Him so bad. Someone was going to have to die as a result of this sin.

It was tough, but I told him we'd talk about who that was the next time. I always tried to remember one training phrase I was taught by my good friend and future dental assistant Max, "Go slow to go fast," but it's rather hard to follow sometimes when it's so exciting to share.

By God's grace, I was able to finish that story in detail the next time, and share how Jesus took upon himself the honor-killing required. It totally made sense to him and I'll never forget how differently he grasped that story than I did.

Chapter 4
CULTURE PART DEUX

Other aspects of culture were maybe not so integral to sharing the truth with people but were very important in building strong relationships and making friends, which allowed deeper sharing to take place later.

We found out quickly that much like Latin and South America, where we had some previous work experience, the people of the Middle East were very reactionary and not proactive at all. In other words, if something was not causing a problem for them that they felt, you often never saw them do anything about preventing a future problem from happening.

For instance, it often happened that I might see a small cavity on a tooth and tell the person they needed a filling, but they would refuse and tell me it doesn't hurt yet. They would inform me they planned to wait until it started hurting extremely bad, and then they would know it was time to repair the tooth.

I might remind them that today I can fix the problem for them, it's free for them, and they have time. Maybe it will start hurting on a day when they are working, and then they'll have to go into the city losing their salary for the day and pay a dentist a lot of money to fix it. But arguments like this one would not usually persuade them. They were often concerned with the here and now and not things happening in the future.

This preoccupation with the present also means that they place high importance on the person right in front of them, which to be honest, is incredibly refreshing. In the West, when we are talking to someone, we may have an appointment, meeting, or phone call to take, and that will respectfully allow us to ignore and leave a person and do the previously planned event. The planned item takes precedence over the unplanned people in front of you.

But in the East, it's exactly the opposite. If I have a doctor's appointment in ten minutes, and as I am leaving my house a friend comes up the stairs to visit me, I will then simply forget about the appointment (not calling the doctor of course) and I will brew some coffee or tea and sit with the friend for the next hour. His presence automatically trumps my preplanned appointment, and I will not even bring it up that I have a reason to not be there with him. This circumstance is also why I generally didn't make appointments for my dental patients. I just called them or grabbed them in the moment, which seemed to work much better.

If the Phone Doesn't Ring, It's Me

There is at least one definite exception to this rule in the lives of women. One thing that Grace noticed spending a lot of time with women was that no matter what she needed to get done, the women would strongly insist she stay and continue to visit with them. It didn't matter if she had to pick up kids from school or if she had some work to return to at the clinic, they simply wouldn't budge and would act offended that she would consider leaving.

However, one time when she had been visiting for a long while, and I wanted to see what the plans were for dinner, I called her during her visit. The women asked if it was me calling, and Grace told them I was inquiring about dinner. They then almost forcefully pushed her out of the door, telling her she needed to go home and make me my supper. That was definitely an excuse that held weight in their eyes.

As we observed Muslim women, we detected that there is often a deep fear that their husband will take a second wife or divorce them if he is unpleased at all. Taking up to four wives is permitted in Islam (Muhammad took nine), and divorcing a wife is very easy—you merely say the word "divorce" three times if your wife displeases you for any reason, and you are then divorced. Because of this fact, the women know they are standing on shaky ground at all times with their husbands.

They must perform their duties well to keep the marriage, and cooking is a significant part of that. Grace and I often used this knowledge to our benefit on visits, and she would tell me that if she wasn't back by a particular time, then she was trapped in a visit, and I should call her and ask her about dinner to get her out of there.

Inevitably I would end up having to call her and say something like, "Where's my dinner, woman?" just to make it convincing and for a little fun. It seemed to work every time, and I guess I got a reputation among her female friends of being a brooding pig of a husband more than likely.

I also saw this fear of divorce very often in the dental clinic. Women might come in with abscessed molars or other big problems with their back teeth. However, they would ask me to spend their allotted time working on their front teeth, the "social six" as we lovingly call them from the upper canine to canine. At first, I refused, but I began to see that this was really their biggest felt need.

Often, they would confess to me that it was for their husbands because they had to keep up their appearances. While we in the West sometimes "let everything go" after we get married, these women are working hard to keep their husbands happy so they won't take another wife and push them out.

One time in a remote southern village located at the breathtaking edge of an escarpment, I worked on a man and then on his second wife. I talked quite a bit with the husband as I completed a dental treatment for him.

Next, as I saw the second wife, she interrogated me about her husband and whether he had said anything about her or the first wife. She was intensely interested in finding out if her husband had told me who his favorite wife was and told me I had to help her get information from him and make her teeth better or she would lose him.

It would have been comical if it hadn't been so sad to see the plight of women in these relationships so clearly.

What, Me Worry?

For men, the only thing that could break up a conversation with a guest increasingly seemed to be a cell phone call. Before cellular networks, you just drove up to visit someone, and they knew you were coming when they saw your sandals darken their tent flap. Cell phones have spread like crazy among the Arabs, and even the most remotely located Bedouin will often have two or three cheap ones for the different networks. They had never had a telephone land-line before, but cellular communications have allowed them to jump over that older technology straight to smartphones in a matter of years.

Unfortunately, in my observation, they allowed the cell phone call to take precedence over the person in front of them. This behavior was happening already in the West, of course. Still, it was surprising to me and disappointing that this lack of consistency with their culture had begun to break down and erode the old customs, which had been so refreshing at times. Increasingly, I saw the here and now taking a back seat to technology.

I often wonder if the Arab peoples are less predisposed to worry because of their culture's focus on the present. I mean, if you don't care if your tooth has a hole in it as long as it doesn't hurt, are you going to worry about your overall health and body?

Most of the time, when I question men about potential problems that I see in their lives, they only say *bi'allah* (by God) and accept whatever will happen as if they have no control over anything in their lives. When someone tells you of a terrible tragedy or an urgent problem in their life, they will often say *Hamdililah*, which means "praise be to God."

At times, I found it nice that even amid grief, they were praising God, but more and more, I was starting to see this as just hopeless fatalism. It seemed like they had a peace about it because they had resigned themselves to it, but I think it was a counterfeit peace.

An ounce of prevention is worth a pound of cure, isn't it? However, I do think that for all the positives that may come out of preplanning and being proactive, we hide a lot of worries under that banner in the West.

We can see that Jesus praised the idea of preplanning at times, especially in Luke 14, when he gives two examples that commend preplanning to live as Christians. He describes a man building a tower who must consider ahead of time if he has the resources to complete the tower. Secondly, He reminds us that the general of an army must determine if his force is big enough before he starts the attack against another army.

That said, while we must live in a discerning way, it seems very easy to let our planning run wild and turn into a bunch of worries.

Worry is said to be *the fear of being hurt*, while anger is said to be *the response to being hurt*. I can tell you that at least among the men, I didn't witness a lot of worry from Arabs I was around, although I did see quite a bit of anger. Maybe our cultural reference point predisposes us more to one category than the other.

It's interesting and helpful that Jesus taught about the problems of anger and worry at the same time to his disciples on the Sermon on the Mount in Matthew 5 and 6. In between those passages, he teaches in Matthew 6:20-21,

> *Store up for yourselves treasures in heaven, where moths and vermin do not destroy, and where thieves do not break in and steal. For where your treasure is, there your heart will be also.*

When our treasures are on earth, they can get hurt, which leads to worry and anger, but if we remember our true treasure is in heaven, we can have a heavenly perspective that counts our earthly holdings as loss for the King. We don't have to accept it fatalistically, but joyfully because Jesus reminds us we are not just animals or plants in His kingdom, but we are the very children of God. Because of that, we have family privileges.

Other Cultural Phenomena

The fascinating thing about living in another country is all of the minute and fascinating cultural differences that start to rise to the surface after you've been there a while. You really won't necessarily see those or think about them unless you make a mistake or trip over them, and then you begin to put the pieces together.

My friend Yazin and I used to meet weekly at a Canadian coffee house in the embassy district where he would help me with my Arabic homework, and I would give him equal time in English conversation. He was the classic Arab man who wanted to move to the US and get out of the Middle East as soon as possible because he was tired of all of the restrictions on his life and dreams.

He taught me many interesting and complicated things about Arab life: the convoluted laws concerning taxes and customs as they related to his business, his perspective on the Palestinian question, and the Arab passion for soccer, to name a few. But one of the things I remember most was that he had a lovely GM SUV that he had bought, and he never took the plastic off the seats.

I used to get on Yazin all of the time to just remove the plastic off the seats and enjoy his new car, but he refused. Yazin said maybe one day many years distant, he would sell the car, and he wanted the seats to be original, so he'd get a new car price.

I was reasonably convinced that a five-year-old car with five years of wear and tear would not sell like a new car just because the seats were new.

He had a proactive way of thinking it seemed, but in this case, I couldn't figure out the logic of it, and I hated sitting on his plastic in the middle of the summer.

This issue came up again when a pastor friend of mine, Kent, came to work and visit with me, and he wanted to rent a car in town.

I went to the rental place, and the owner had a brand-new car available with only a few thousand kilometers on it. Surprise, surprise, there was the original factory plastic on all the seats. I didn't think anything about it having seen it before many times with Yazin, and I knew that the rental guy was making a big deal about the car being new by leaving the plastic on the seats.

The next morning, I went out to see my friend Kent and I looked at his rental car and noticed there was no plastic anywhere on the seats. I asked him what had happened, and he said he had just ripped all of that plastic out of the car that morning, thinking they put that on for the customers.

I mean, who wants to drive around with plastic on the seats, right? However, it had truthfully been the original plastic from the factory.

I cringed, and my colleagues and I were all freaking out, thinking that the man would be so mad when we returned the car. I found a place that could put a cheaper plastic back on the seats for about $15, but thankfully when we turned the car in, the owner forgave us and didn't make us pay for any "damages."

Fruitless Anticipation

Another thing we noticed about living in the capital city and later in Manara was that many fruit trees were growing all around the area. Fig trees grow well in that climate, and it almost seems hard to kill them, which later made them an excellent tree for me to plant.

You also see mulberry trees a lot as well as peach and apricot trees in every wedge of dirt up and down the streets. Every time the season for figs or peaches would start to get close, I would see those beautiful green buds begin to grow, and I would imagine they would be so tasty in another month or so. While you couldn't pick fruit growing in someone's yard, the fruit hanging out over the street was considered fair game.

However, before we could ever get to the point where the fruit was ready to harvest, the pre-ripe fruits would all suddenly disappear off the trees. People would pick them very early and eat them well before they became ripe. I tried a fig that way to see if it was delicious, but it was horrible and a waste of potentially good fruit.

If you just wait another three weeks or so, that same fig can be a heavenly infusion of sweetness, but they never got a chance to make it that long unless they were in your yard. I still haven't totally concluded whether this has something to do with that "in the moment" inclination of the culture or not—that's what I assumed at first. How could they wait for something in the future that was not a sure thing when they could have the unripe version now, and no one could take it from them?

Nevertheless, my friend Faoud swears to me that Arabs authentically like the taste of pre-ripe fruit like green almonds, which tend to be sour or bitter. How in the world that can happen, I don't know, but I'll have to take his word for it and give up on ever seeing a ripened fruit ready for the harvest there.

Homes and Hospitality

Another substantial cultural difference has to do with how Arabs furnish and use their homes. Whenever we would visit an Arab friend's house, they would invite us through their front door by saying *tfuddulu* and into a salon reception room adjacent to the front.

If it was just a small family, they might invite us all into the same salon with them, or if there were other guests there, I would go into the men's salon, and Grace would go into the women's salon with the kids to prevent mixing between the sexes.

As I mentioned before, they typically never invite you to see the rest of the house, except on a special occasion if it is a new house or if you are a close friend. It's also known that you should probably not ask to use the restroom when you visit because the bathroom is considered a cursed place.

In Muslim culture, they have a belief in spirit creatures that are described a lot in the Quran and called the *jinn*. We typically know these creatures as genies and think of them as powerful beings living in a magic lamp because of the famous story of Aladdin or even the show *I Dream of Jeannie*.

Muslims believe that *jinn* are a unique creation of God made out of fire, and they are either good or very bad. Apparently, in *jinn* lore, the *jinn* love to inhabit the bathroom and jump down on you as you walk in or are doing your business. Because of these beliefs, Arab bathrooms do generally not contain ledges where the *jinn* could sit and wait on an unsuspecting victim and jump down on them.

Because of the fear of the *jinn* residing there, Arab bathrooms are also notoriously filthy because no one wants to spend too much time in there cleaning, or they may get attacked. Even in a charming upper-class home, you may find the bathroom there to be like something you would find outside of a US gas station. Because of this firm belief, it's really in your own best interest to use the restroom in your own home before you go on a visit.

One time Grace made an innocent mistake when entering into a bathroom. She was wearing a necklace that said *mahabat Allah* (God is Love) in Arabic. When an Arab woman saw her come out, she condemned her for wearing the name of *Allah* in the bathroom where *jinn* were. Grace tried to tell her God is stronger than the *jinn* but the woman insisted this act was simply never done.

When you make it into the salon and sit down, you'll notice the furnishings are always much the same. In a home in the capital, you will probably be sitting on a set of couches that ring the room, covered in shiny gold or silver paint and filigree. In a more impoverished home, out in a village, you will probably be sitting on the floor covered in carpets or on a very fancy looking set of mats with opulent, intricate designs.

To us, these designs of the mats and furniture were always ridiculously gaudy, but we found that our Arab friends were intensely proud of their salon furniture. They would often tell us how much money they spent on it and from where it came. In addition to the furniture, we often observed that the ceiling was molded and decorated with vibrant and garish colors. If someone was particularly blessed, they would have a multi-colored fabric ceiling, which they would tell you is from Japan.

After you admire the ceiling, you are usually guaranteed to see a picture high up on the wall, often in the corner, of an aged man. This picture is always of the deceased patriarch of that family, usually the father or grandfather who has passed away. If the dead or any other family member had ever met royalty or a president in their life, you might also see a picture on the wall of that moment in time when they saw or stood with the famous official. In the middle of the room were often several tables for serving as well as some small tables beside each chair for placing your tea or coffee.

Of the Reading of Books

After visiting several Arab homes and looking throughout some of the houses and using bathrooms because of our cultural naiveté, it finally struck me that something was completely missing that we would always have in an American home—books. The Arab home consistently and almost without exception never has any books around. There are no books on the shelves, no bookshelves for that matter, and certainly no coffee table books, bathroom literature, or cookbooks.

There is a full-fledged absence of writing in the Arab home. One time I did happen to see a book in a friend's house, and I reacted so strongly to it and pointed it out to everyone around me that the hosts probably thought I was loopy. It's a difference that is simple but also profound.

Starting with the US war in Iraq in 2003 and continuing afterward in the occupation that was going on in our neighborhood in the Middle East, Americans found that the real problem was not winning the war. The challenge was rebuilding a philosophical foundation in Iraq that would sustain democracy.

Because of that, someone had the great idea to introduce something called "My Arabic Library," which was a translation into Arabic of all of the famous books of English literature—*Great Expectations, Moby Dick*, etc. They thought that if they gave Iraqis these books, they would start reading them, and the ideas of democracy would start to sink into their hearts and minds.

Well, we all know now that they spent millions of dollars on creating these books and sending them over to Iraqi schools, only to find out later that they were never used and in one instance, were even used as landfill behind a school.

If they had asked any "fellow American" living in the Middle East, that idea of sending books would have been quashed in an instant. Anyone that knows Arabs knows that reading is not part of their makeup—except in a very few exceptions.

I recently saw in World Press that "the total number of books translated into Arabic during the 1,000 years since the age of Caliph Al-Ma'moun [a ninth-century Arab ruler] to this day is less than those translated into Spanish in one year."

We found that if we wanted to teach or tell Arabs stories, it would often have to be in an oral storytelling form because giving them a book would not meet with results that we wanted to see.

What Does Your Name Mean?

Names are another fascinating aspect of the culture in the Middle East. Back home, we are comfortable with naming our kids almost anything from a family name to something that no one has ever used before, like a piece of fruit.

If you ask an American what their name means, often they can't even tell you. That is never the case in that part of the world. Names have meanings there, and everyone knows what they are. These are the descendants of many of the people we read about in the Old Testament of the Bible, so it makes sense that names are important to them, because they were always important to those early patriarchs.

We had to interpret our names a little bit according to the culture so that people could pronounce them and remember them more naturally. Western pronunciations are very difficult for them, so you either decide to live with your name massacred continuously, or you give in and change it a little bit to make it simpler.

Once you become a parent, your name also changes. I was usually known as Abu David, which means "Father of David." Even though I had an older daughter Rebekah, and I would have been Abu Rebekah at that point in time, once a son is born, the mom and dad's name always takes the name of the eldest son. Grace was known as Umm David or "Mother of David." It's a lot of pressure on the oldest son, but they also get a lot of privileges and pampering as they are the future hope of the family. If you didn't know someone's name, you could usually call them Abu Muhammad, and most of the time, you were correct.

All in the Family

Family size is considerable in the Middle East, although studies show that it is quickly decreasing year by year, especially in educated families. We often met families with ten or more children, and many could count offspring in the twenties. The Duggar family could never get a television show here because there are families just as large on nearly every street.

Arabs want to have as many kids as possible, and I heard a few different theories on why that is. Some men told me it is just up to *Allah*, and you just keep having kids according to *Allah*'s will. If you are out of a job or don't have money to take care of your family, don't worry about it. If *Allah* wants your wife to get pregnant, it's up to Him to provide the food and money for your kids, not you.

This mindset was a fatalistic approach to childbearing, and I often saw this with dads who were not too close to their families.

The other main idea I got in talking to men was that having a large family was like an insurance policy for your life as an older person. The more kids you had, the more chance you had of being cared for when you were older. Thankfully, I saw many other dads who dearly loved their children apart from all the retirement benefits.

This emphasis on family size puts a lot of pressure on newly married couples. It is almost expected that you will get pregnant on your honeymoon and that you should try to get pregnant as soon as possible. When a couple gets married, the husband is usually in his mid-thirties, and the wife is often 15 years younger than him. Everyone is asking them when they will have kids (a son) and if the wife is pregnant yet.

The sad truth is like in the West, some couples have infertility issues there. When the first year passes and no child is born, they start to become ashamed. When the years continue like this, it becomes a huge problem, and they can become social outcasts from the community. For the women, this lack of childbearing is most terrible and ultimately leads to the husband taking another wife who can give him a son unless he is a unique and dedicated man.

Regardless, what couples typically do is change their name to a made-up name, just so they can avoid getting questioned all of the time about why they don't have kids yet.

We knew a Christian couple who went by Abu Solme and Umm Solme. Eventually, when I realized I had never actually seen their son Solme I asked them about it, and they said they had never been able to have children. But doing everyday business and daily interactions as Abu Solme had made his life better and helped him fit in where the lack of a child is not respected or understood.

Superstitions and the Evil Eye

The eye is the lamp of the body. So, if your eye is healthy, your whole body will be full of light, but if your eye is bad, your whole body will be full of darkness. If then the light in you is darkness, how great is the darkness! —Matthew 6:22:23

This mysterious passage about the health of eyeballs falls smack dab in the middle of the Sermon on the Mount. It comes between a discourse talking about money and possessions and how you should store your treasures up in heaven (vs.19-21) and another section that says, "you cannot serve God and money" (verse 24).

What bad eyes or healthy eyes have to do with money and treasures had always eluded me until we moved to the Middle East. There, I was quickly acquainted with a symbol and an idea called the "evil eye."

The evil eye symbol is usually a blue colored ceramic eyeball that people hang on their doors or in their cars or on jewelry around their neck. It is meant to ward off the curses that come from the evil eye.

What the evil eye is in itself is covetousness. Seeing something that your neighbor has and wanting it or admiring it constitutes this act. When you covet something, you are giving it the evil eye because of your greed and Arabs believe that this greed brings a curse. Inevitably, harm will then come to that coveted object because of the evil eye.

Because of this belief, we found that if we complimented someone on something they were wearing, whether it was jewelry or a jacket, they would take it off immediately and give it to us. They believed it was cursed now by our compliment, so the best thing for them was to give it to us and relieve that covetousness.

If an idea of covetousness or admiration comes by spoken language, then a special counter curse, *mashallah,* is used to ward off the potential evil from the curse. This word means "What God has willed," and I came to use it all of the time in conversations with my neighbors. I didn't personally believe it did anything, but I knew my neighbors did. I didn't want to be flinging a bunch of curses at them every time they talked to me, so I contextualized my conversations.

For example, if I saw a friend's newborn son and wanted to tell them how beautiful he was or what a blessing he was, I couldn't just say that compliment or I would be putting a curse on their son. Then, they could be sure that he would suddenly get sick or just drop dead in the coming days, and I would be the one to blame.

So instead, I would say, "Your son is so handsome! *Mashallah.* And he's wearing such cute clothing, *mashallah.*" I had to give out a *mashallah* to cover each of the compliments. We always noticed that if we forgot to say this counter-curse, someone nearby would utter a quick *mashallah* to cover our error.

This idea runs deep within the culture and apparently even subverts good old Western logic at times and crosses religious lines as well. One of my neighbors had gone to the US years before to study. After living there for 20 years, he had returned to the Middle East to have a family. Talking to him was like talking to an American because he thought like I did and spoke as I did.

I was looking at his new bright blue pickup truck one day, uttering all of the required *mashallah*s along with my compliments when he said to me, "You know, I never had any kind of car troubles until I moved back to the Middle East. In the US, my car always worked great, but here, because of the evil eye, my new car is always breaking down."

I was a bit flabbergasted. I questioned him if he truly thought that someone he drove past in town might admire his car, and because of that, his car would be cursed with engine failure. He said that certainly he believed that.

How could this educated man think that could happen—I didn't know. But he complimented me and said that we are better in the US and don't believe that evil eye stuff, so it never happens. I guess that means that the evil eye has a geographical restriction based on whether people believe in it or not.

A Christian background Arab that I also knew strongly believed in the evil eye. On the front of his house, he had a cross on one side of the door with St. George slaying a dragon, and on the other side of the door, he had a large evil eye hanging there. I guess he was covering his bases. He also had evil eyes dangling from the rear-view mirror of his Mercedes as well.

We usually tried to tell everyone struggling with these *jinn* or evil eye problems that we know Jesus, and His name is much stronger than Satan and all of his demons and all the *jinn*.

We encouraged people to call on His name when they were having issues like this one. I'm afraid they usually just hung up a couple of more evil eyes or put a *mashallah* bumper sticker on the car because it was hard to get that notion out of their mind.

Sometimes we would even see someone driving a beat-up rattletrap of a car down the highway with a big *mashallah* sticker in the back, and I'd have to wonder why they wasted their money on warding off any curses because there weren't any coming towards that car.

The hardest thing related to the evil eye for a Westerner to get used to is the stifling of compliments that these fears create in the culture. I remember during a short-term visit by a talented dentist friend of mine that he had spent a couple of hours of working on a Bedouin woman placing composite veneers on her front six teeth. Her teeth transformed in a couple of hours from some black, decayed, witch teeth to something you would see in Hollywood, and it took years off of her age. We were all excited and looking forward to the big reveal when we would show in the mirror her new look.

As she took the mirror, we all anxiously watched her only to see her look at herself in the mirror, make no visible expression at all, get out of the dental chair and walk away without a word.

My friend was a little devastated, and I would have been too. All of that effort and not even a smile on her face or a thank you from her as she left? What was the deal? She was probably in such a cultural habit of not complimenting things to avoid curses that she did us a favor and didn't say a word of thanks as she left.

I saw this attitude all of the time in daily life whether you helped someone with their teeth or whether you gave someone a gift or donated your used washing machine to someone. I couldn't help but expect a satisfying thank you or note of gratitude, but over and over, I just watched people get in a car and drive off without a word.

I guess it helps that Jesus taught us gratefulness is not a prerequisite for us serving these people in love, or even serving enemies, because it is the way God has served us, a most ungrateful people.

> *But love your enemies, do good to them, and lend to them without expecting to get anything back. Then your reward will be great, and you will be children of the Most High, because he is kind to the ungrateful and wicked. Be merciful, just as your Father is merciful. —Luke 6:35*

Sometimes I've felt like I need to see some good qualities in a person or general respectful behavior if they want me to serve them.

If you are rude to me, don't expect me to help you is the type of attitude I've had at times. But if God is good to us who are rebels and disobedient children, we must not demand any more on the front end from the people we seek to serve, even as we hope to see changed lives on the back end.

So it seems it makes total sense for Jesus to mix in this discussion about eyeball health in the middle of two passages about treasure and money becoming your gods. It was obviously an idea that was around and well known back then and still a widespread understanding of life today.

Jesus uses this context to explain his teaching that covetousness and greed are like diseases that can affect the whole body and make it dark. Yet, once freed from serving greed, our eyes are bright, and our focus is on heavenly treasures above.

Chapter 5

LANGUAGE SCHOOL BLUES

As soon as we had settled into life in the capital and gotten our apartment figured out and relatively comfortable, it was time for school. School was starting for our two older kids Rebekah and David, who were going to a small private academy in town. Our youngest daughter, Rae, was going to begin Kindergarten in a nationally run school, while Grace and I were going to attend a language school and try to firmly master the Arabic language.

Our kids were excited because they would be going to school for the first time in this new place and they had developed a sweet friendship with Benjamin and Valerie's kids who were also attending the same institutions.

The easiest of those three schools for me to manage with my cultural baggage was our older kids' school because Westerners founded it and ran it a lot like the way we do things in America. We received a school calendar and a syllabus for each grade, and we found out where the school bus route ran every day.

Ironically, the first time our two oldest kids ever got to ride a yellow school bus was not in the US, but in the Middle East. In the US, we had either homeschooled them in their early years or driven them to school every morning and picked them up in the afternoons.

Being in the Middle East, without a car for the first time in our adult lives and totally dependent on taxi services, we now had to rely on their school to come and pick them up from our apartment. The big yellow school bus would arrive every morning at about 6:50 AM, which always led to no small amount of stress. We could always hear it barreling down our street, which precipitated us yelling final instructions to the kids to get them out on the curb in time.

Our older kids' school was about 40 minutes in the opposite direction of our language school, so it was a real blessing that they could get taken there at the same time that we headed the opposite direction for our classes.

As it happened, riding the bus was an excellent experience for them to have. They had field trips at times, along with the usual after-school activities that we are used to back home. The organization of that school was a little piece of heaven.

"Baba's Here"

Rae's school was a different matter entirely. We got to meet with the principal of the school, and Rae had an interview with her and a teacher to determine her readiness for the school's kindergarten.

In the Middle East, they have two years of kindergarten KG1 and KG2 prior to 1st grade, so Rae was going straight into KG2. It seemed like a good fit as it was a school run and founded back before World War II, and it had a solid reputation for bilingual instruction.

She would have two teachers for KG2, an Arabic-speaking teacher, and an English-speaking teacher, and it appeared she would be able to learn both languages throughout the year seamlessly.

The troubles came when we began to ask those hard questions like, "When does the school year begin?" or "How much does tuition cost?" It seemed like no one, including the principal, had answers to questions like that. They just told us to keep checking back with them, and they would know closer to the time.

Finally, one day after much checking, we were surprised to find out the school started the next day. We brought Rae there, basically knowing nothing about what would happen or what she needed to bring and just hoped we would get some answers.

One thing that shocked us was that from the time we did the initial interview to the time that the school started, the principal had decided to stop the entire bilingual language learning program, which was one of her better selling points for the school.

So, Rae ended up going into a class with two Arabic speaking teachers and no English. The principal assured us that it was really fortunate this surprise change had happened because it would be much better for her Arabic learning without any chance to speak English.

We didn't buy that story (it reminded us of mattress sales) and were concerned because we didn't know how you could learn Arabic without having any teaching in a language you understood. Nevertheless, we decided to give it a shot, and it was honestly too late to find somewhere else for her to attend.

The first week was tough on her, and we picked her up each day in tears. She was so sad that she couldn't understand anything at all, and we tried to coach her to understand body language from her teachers better, but it was still challenging.

One day when I went to pick her up, I walked up to the door, and the teacher pointed at me and yelled, "Rae, baba's hone" (Rae—your papa's here).

Rae picked up her bag and ran out of the class to me, and the teacher said, "See, she is learning Arabic—she already knows 'Baba' means 'Papa' now."

I was not really impressed.

Rae's kindergarten was very close to our Arabic language school, so we would either walk with her to school, which was a little more than a mile away, or we would take a taxi all together if it rained.

Several mornings we brought Rae to school only to find out that school had been canceled for the day. The typical response from the main office was something nonchalant like, "Oh, by the way, school is closed—she's with you today." We never did receive a calendar, nor did they ever make one.

On those days, we would head to our language school with Rae in tow, and there were often many kids hanging out there as all the other parents decried the cultural failures in scheduling. We would reminisce about how well the school calendar worked in our respective countries and how everything runs so well back home.

When you are comparing the situation in another culture, I found that this idealist image of my home country always persisted in my mind—at least until you return home and realize that ideal wasn't real after all.

Anyone Can Master Arabic

Our language school started up with a set schedule with dates and times, which was very helpful together with a general idea of the courses we would be taking on our path to learning Arabic. Many of the other students were like-minded foreigners, and we all had a lot in common and a lot to commiserate about as we took the plunge into this new, diabolical language.

The students were diverse with regard to age and station in life. The majority of other students seemed much younger than us, and many students were unmarried in their early twenties and really at a different place in life than the "old codgers" who were married and taking care of children.

They called all of us newbies together and met with us in a conference room to welcome us to the school and give announcements.

I don't remember much about that meeting except for one statement made by the acting headmaster at the time. He told us that we were embarking on a very challenging journey into learning Arabic, but not to worry; statistics showed that everyone could learn a new language if they just stick with it. He then added that his assertion was true unless you have reached the age of 35, and then science tells us the brain can no longer acquire a new language at that point.

How old was I again? I asked myself. Oh yeah, 35 exactly. This meeting was not an auspicious beginning point. I hoped that I still had a few little grey cells hanging on up there, but I wasn't sure they had any spunk left.

As school got into session and we began going to our classes from 8:00 until 1:30 each day, we started getting into our routines. We generally were told to focus on three areas in particular: studying each day the Arabic we had learned, going out each day and using that Arabic with Arabs, and attending Christian meetings to practice hearing and using spiritual words.

Of the three, studying tended to be the easiest one to do because we had to go from Arabic school to pick up Rae from her kindergarten, and then we had to go home to receive our oldest two from the school bus drop off.

Once three kids were in hand, it sometimes was hard to go back out and visit people on the street or in their homes because we had to get them situated. They had homework and after-school snack needs just as we did. However, being close to a church made the Christian meetings part easier, and we often went there for the Thursday night and Sunday morning meetings.

At the end of each week, our teacher gave us a sheet to fill out and record the number of hours that we had spent on each of the three things: studying, visiting, and church meetings. This approach seemed good to me as a way to keep us all accountable to our teachers, and it spurred us on to do better because someone was going to know about it.

The surprise came the next day when they posted the hourly totals from each person on the bulletin board. By God's grace, they encoded it so that your actual name was not listed next to your reported hours because I had to read most of the way down the list until I got to the code that represented me.

This motivated Grace and me to do more, but the truth of it was that there was only so much time in a day, and we couldn't study until 12 every night like our old college days.

When the second-week results came out, there we were hugging the bottom of the sheet again. We really couldn't compete with singles and others who were putting in 30 hours of study a week in addition to the 22 hours of classes. It was yet another opportunity to be humbled in this new life we had chosen.

The Mystery of Calling

Every so often, the language school would have a guest speaker come who would present some aspect of culture or tell us about some ministry opportunity that was available in the Middle East. I would later do this same thing myself.

One day a person, Titus, working at the clinic where we were already planning to go, came and presented about all of the personnel needs and opportunities that they had at the clinic location.

Then, after telling us with excitement about all the possibilities there, he mentioned off-handedly that they also needed a new family to go to a satellite clinic, but he said no one really wanted to go there because it was desolate, lonely and cold. He said there were no services around for miles, so it really wasn't a suitable spot for human beings to live.

After the meeting, I congratulated Titus on his presentation but also sarcastically teased him. I remarked on what a "great job" he did in trying to sell the satellite clinic job where it's apparently cold, miserable, and inhumane. I teased him that we'd never get anyone to go out there if he kept presenting the job description like that.

He agreed but said he didn't want to lie about it or lead someone on; to go to that place, you had to be called.

Just a few minutes later, I was talking to an interesting family that we had met in our language classes, and they had picked up on the fact that this clinic in the discussion was the very place that our family would be going after language school.

The husband, Job, commented that our type of ministry would be a dream for them, and they would absolutely enjoy doing something like that. His wife, Virginia heartily agreed. I encouraged them to really consider joining us in the work there, but he corrected me by saying that he wasn't talking about our main clinic, he was talking about the remote satellite location!

How one family can hear that dreadful work and location description and feel like that was the perfect destination is a mystery to me and was just another insight to see how mysterious and unpredictable God's calling is in someone's life. Job and Virginia would later end up going there and serving for many years and would become some of our dearest friends in the world.

So, what is the deal with finding God's calling? So often, I have been jealous of David, who simply consulted these two mysterious objects called the Urim and the Thummim in the Old Testament to find out if he should do one thing or another.

I don't know how it all worked, but Scripture tells us it clearly gave him the answer on whether he should go to Ziklag or not.

You also see the disciples casting lots in the book of Acts to determine who should fill the space left by the betrayal of Judas. Maybe that was just an immature way to do it, but it seems like God honored that method of determining His will at that point in time.

However, past Pentecost, using the Urim and Thummim as well as casting lots passes out of Scripture as God's people receive the Holy Spirit, which is supposed to be so much better than just getting a black or white answer.

I know the Holy Spirit is way better than rocks and stones as a counselor and comforter, but why do I and others struggle so much with those pesky gray areas? Why couldn't God spell it out to all of us where

He wanted us to serve and invest our lives? It must be part of our growth in faith—a chore but a blessing that God has given us to mature and draw closer to Him.

I love how pastor Tim Keller describes the absurdity of a 20-year-old in college, calling his mom to ask if he should play tennis with his friends. That was maybe a healthy and needed question to ask at 10 or 12 years old, but a 20-year-old college student asking that would cause a lot of worry to a parent.

That mom would think, what are you doing? "Grow up and quit calling!"

Likewise, it's the same way with the Holy Spirit leading us along towards the place God wants us to go. It's time for us to grow up and make the decisions interacting with the Holy Spirit now.

For us, our calling to the Middle East had been a zig-zag run of different inputs and impressions and prayers that led us to that place. But, looking back, it was a beautiful journey of God putting those seeds in our hearts that would prepare us for the work that was ahead.

In the way that most of us naturally find any job or career, Grace and I had opportunities to tinker around in different missional services. We had both made short-term trips before, we had served on a large board at a church and had attended several cross-cultural conferences that challenged us. We read Scripture and saw the repeated calling to God's people to go out and share the news of the Kingdom as part of the fundamental DNA of being a Christian. We often prayed about what God wanted for us in our future as a couple and for Him to clarify His calling.

Others impacted our lives as well. From the very beginning, my parents and her parents faithfully shepherded us and our siblings to church every week as the Bible shaped our lives in many ways. My oldest brother had a huge impact on my spiritual life as I neared college and was finding my place in the world. Later, a pastor in my church took me on my first church trip to Jamaica and spent time discipling me. The Christian Medical Dental Association (CMDA) director in my school further discipled me towards a global missions mindset. The Global Missions Healthcare Conference (GMHC) was very influential for both of us as we were challenged in many unique ways by its speakers. This meeting kept the fire going in our bellies while we went through the long process of getting to the field.

I remember being told by one doctor, "if you don't go overseas directly out of dental school, then statistically you will never go, so don't fool yourself by saying you'll work a little and go later. That's just a cop-out."

That insult stuck with me.

I remember another doctor challenging me with the idea that "Satan doesn't want you to do something bad, he mainly wants you to settle and do something good when you can be doing something better or even great for the Lord."

The Perspectives course on World Missions was very informative to us as well as it opened our eyes specifically to where the need for the gospel and healthcare was most dire. Both needy places were in a geographical position on a map between the 10th parallel and the 40th parallel longitudinally, otherwise called the "10-40 window," where 90% of the unreached people live along with 90% of the poorest people in the world.

Our calling was not what many people imagine. There is this unsaid stereotype where church people assume we must have received some "special" revelation or "special calling" from heaven. Maybe an angel even came down and gave us a sign that we should go overseas to the Middle East.

Honestly, nothing like that ever happened—it was just the experiences in our lives, starting with our parents and culminating in prayer and the Word.

As missionary pioneer, Hudson Taylor, pointed out, no one needs a special calling to share about Jesus and help others because it is already stated clearly all over the Bible as part of the Christian life. Rather, someone needs a special calling, like the kind where you see an angel or hear the heavenly voice if they aren't going to be involved in this type of work. So, there we were.

Speaking the Tooth in Love

One of the best ways we found for learning Arabic was by making mistakes. They usually tell you that the best language learners are the ones who will get out there and use all the new vocabulary or conjugations as much as possible and not worry about if they are correct or not.

If you are not embarrassed about making mistakes, then you eventually will speak enough to quit making them. If you want to speak perfectly and never be embarrassed in public, you will probably keep your mouth shut too much and not get the needed language experience to get past those early errors.

One thing is true in the Middle East—the Arabs will undoubtedly point out to you when you make a mistake in their language. Ironically, they will often encourage you by saying how well you speak Arabic, and the next minute tell you that your Arabic is horrible beyond help.

There is absolutely no grey area with Arabs with regard to them critiquing your abilities. The terrible thing is that we found that minimal mistakes in pronunciation, grammar, or understanding can lead to huge misunderstandings. Some are frightful, but others end up being quite humorous.

The classic Arabic mistake for Christians is using the word for "heart." Scripture, of course, talks a lot about God caring about what is in your heart more than just in your actions, so that is something we talk about a lot.

Whether it's in Hosea 6:6 where God leads us away from legalism in saying, "…I desire steadfast love and not sacrifice, the knowledge of God rather than burnt offerings…," or if we share from Ephesians 3:16-17 about the transforming power of salvation that, "…he may grant you to be strengthened with power through his Spirit in your inner being, so that Christ may dwell in your hearts through faith…," we speak about the heart to our neighbors all the time.

In Christianese, we expand on this idea, and we even have this common category of conversation where we talk about Jesus living in your heart. That's not technically a way of understanding that Jesus taught directly in the gospels, but still, we all usually know what that means.

To say this word "heart" in Arabic, you say *qelb* with a hard "q," which is challenging to pronounce until you have a little experience under your belt. What happens typically is that foreigners mispronounce that word by saying "*kelb*" with a softer K sound.

So it's inevitable that at some point, a well-meaning Christian will tell his interested Muslim neighbor that Jesus lives in their *kelb* instead of in their *qelb*. Sometimes this is followed by them trying to persuade their neighbor that don't they want to ask Jesus to live in their *kelb* as well?

To be kind to the foreigner, this strange request is often agreed to by the Arab, but with unfortunate consequences, because the word pronounced "*kelb*" means dog.

One thing that's sure is over the years many Arabs have asked Jesus to live in their dog. Many well-meaning Christians have shared their testimony to an Arab and stated they asked Jesus to live in their dog as well, which surprises the Arab since dogs are considered unclean. A dog is not quite as unclean as a pig in Arab culture, but it is solidly low on the cleanliness scale, so this is not a compliment to our Lord.

I remember telling a neighbor one day with all smiles as we were about to go on a vacation that we were on the way to a *jenaazi*. He expressed his sympathy for us, which didn't make much sense to me, so I corrected him and told him we were excited and had been looking forward to this for a long time and were bringing all of the kids.

His face clearly showed some confusion, and I noticed he even had some slight disgust with me, so I quickly looked up on my phone to check out my vocabulary and realized that "vacation" was actually pronounced *ajaazi*. Looking up the word *jenaazi,* which I could have sworn was the correct way to say it, I found that it meant "funeral." It took a lot of explaining and correcting to get the proper meaning across, but I never made that mistake again.

Another time in another Middle Eastern country we all were at a conference located outside a large wood. Going into town, we got to go to a TGI Friday's restaurant.

As we walked into the restaurant, they had a huge promotional banner that said, "Try our New Spicy Tennessee Grill!" We were all surprised and thought, what were the chances that we would see a state we had visited celebrated in such a way on the menu this far from the US?

We all posed under the banner and took a family picture because of the absurdity of it. After we sat down at the table, and the waitress brought us our drinks, she handed us a special menu insert that said, "Tennessee Grill."

I mentioned to the waitress using a lot of excitement and finger-pointing that all of us had visited Tennessee like the place on the menu.

She calmly said apologetically that she was sorry, but that Tennessee was not a place.

When she returned, I pulled out a map of Tennessee on my phone and showed it to her to clear up the confusion, eager for understanding to dawn on her face suddenly. Her expression remained like a stone.

She continued to tell us that she was sorry, but Tennessee was not a place. It is only the name of a seasoning, she asserted, just like "Kentucky" spices they put on fried chicken.

She turned and abruptly left the table, and we were shell-shocked, feeling like we were indeed a long way from home.

Chapter 6
THE BUZZ OF THE BALAD

One of my favorite activities during my language phase was to go down hundreds of steps from where I lived into the *balad* or downtown area of the city. There, I was surrounded by the colorful sights and sounds of thousands of Arabs in the capital city as they worshiped at the mosque, sold their food and wares on the street, and carried out business both large and small.

The poor were mixed in with the affluent, and you could smell a different aroma as you walked down each block; freshly baked bread, the sugary sweetness coming out of the baklava store, or a rich cheese-imbued cloud wafting from *knafeh* heated up in the pan.

You could find markets for every kind of spice imaginable or stores containing every movie and computer program for $1. One could observe a fistfight break out in the veggie market (which I did) or discover every type of plumbing supply, electrical supply, or sheep supply you might ever want.

Otherwise, you might encounter some foul smells as the very literal "unwashed masses" rubbed up against you in the heart of the city selling chickens, rabbits, fresh fish (from where?), and all kinds of Bedouin materiel.

There in the *balad*, you could meet all of your earthly needs, whether it was a desire for a brain sandwich, a sugar cane drink guaranteed to increase your virility or $500 in solid gold jewelry, the necessary acquisition for any man wanting to finalize a wedding agreement.

Walking into *Souk Khudra*, the vegetable market, was fascinating as you and hundreds of others in the tight aisles are yelled at non-stop by the salesmen hawking their fresh fruit and vegetables. The first inclination for Westerners is defensive as the yelling feels full of anger like someone wants to hurt you. Still, as you adapt, you realize the excitement and loudness in their voices reflect their passionate belief that their particular commodities are the best you can ever find.

A friend and I once recorded the experience in the middle of this souk, and I would often play it back home and ask people if they could figure out what was going on based on what they heard. Most people would guess that there was a fight nearby, or maybe someone was threatening me. But the only thing I ever got threatened with in those recordings was to make the mistake of buying someone else's tomatoes.

Logic Versus Emotion

This ethos of doing business is considerably different between the East and the West. Overall in the West, we are pretty restrained when it comes to making our point. If I want to convince you that I have the best car for sale or even the only way to salvation, I will convey that information to you in a logical series of statements, hopefully convincing you of the truthfulness of my thoughts. I may use a rhetorical question to help make my point or even a little emotion, but if I yell at you, I will lose the argument. In that case, you will likely write me off as being out of control or out of line.

We even say sometimes, "He's just speaking out of anger, he really doesn't mean it." In the East, the person who wins the argument or debate is the one who is the most passionate about their beliefs.

For example, let's say in a mixed audience of Westerners and Easterners that in a debate, I calmly tear apart by logic all the objections one by one that someone might have to the concept of the Trinity.

For their rebuttal, my challenger doesn't make any line of arguments, but rather yells, "That's impossible—God is not like that!, I cannot believe in three Gods!"

We then poll the audience to see who won the debate. I clearly win in the Westerners' vote, but I completely lose the argument in the Easterners' view.

Why? Because I didn't believe in my argument even enough to back it up with some emotion and passionate yelling. My calmness and control gave them the idea that I probably didn't honestly believe in what I was saying, so the logical ideas were not effective anyway. The other man was raving with passion, so he must have had the better point in their view.

As a result, it is tricky for us ever to win an argument. I often would remember this fact during a discussion and would try to "gin up" some emotion to better make my point, whether it was scriptural or otherwise. My problem is that every time I would purposely act angry to convince someone I believed something, I would start to get mad for real.

One time waiting for a driver to arrive, I realized that he was late yet again. It struck me that I had always chided him about being late with a huff or something, but I had never shown anger. Maybe he didn't think it bothered me.

Thankfully that day, I was not in a rush, so I planned this time to put on an act and get a little angry on purpose so he would know this was a big deal and hopefully not do it in the future.

As he pulled up five minutes later with the usual apologies, I started to let him have it, and the longer I talked, the angrier I got and even went beyond the line and said some things I regretted. We ended the conversation, and I was hot and sweaty and mad even though five minutes ago, I hadn't even really cared.

We made friends, but I realized that it was easy to get carried away with this anger stuff even when you preplan to fake it.

My other problem with trying to get more angry was that my Arabic totally went downhill in those moments. If I could regularly communicate at an eighth-grade level, let's say, I found that when I was upset or someone said something offensive, I couldn't think straight, and my Arabic would degrade to around a second-grade level.

"You're a bad man, a real bad man" was about all I could summon in the heat of the moment or maybe an "eat air!" which was not the kindest thing to say.

Thankfully, I never compared anyone to a donkey, or I probably wouldn't be able to write about it again.

In the *balad*, Grace had found some lovely duvet covers for the beds that we wanted to use to spruce up our apartment, so we put in an order for them and could pick them up the next week as they were routinely air-freighted from Damascus, Syria. The problem was that the Syrian war was beginning to break out, starting in the town of Daraa and slowly engulfing the whole country throughout the fall of that year. So, when we returned the next week to pick up the goods, they still hadn't arrived yet because of the warfare outside of Damascus.

We figured this development was par for the course, uprising, or no uprising, so we just decided to return the next week and see if they had arrived under the "three knocks" protocol.

Unfortunately, a week later, it was the same story, but the owner himself was also getting frustrated with his deliveries not making it on time, which was embarrassing for him. He offered to go ahead and long-distance call his dealer in Syria and get an update.

We listened to him on the phone with this man in Syria, and he literally was yelling at the top of his lungs at this man to get it here quickly. The dealer protested that there was guerrilla fighting along the roads and bombings all around him and that it was so dangerous to get the items to a delivery agent with IEDs everywhere. The owner just continued to yell that we needed the fabrics, and he should just get over it and ship them here as soon as possible.

We weren't sure at first if he was only doing this for our benefit or if this was for real, but it sure seemed real. Maybe the Syrian dealer didn't know how much he wanted it until the shop owner told him with passion to risk his life to get the delivery started.

Man, we thought, we'd hate to work for him, but sure enough a few days later the duvet covers were in our hands, fresh from war-torn Syria with no little amount of guilt connected to them as well.

A Suitable Lifestyle

My favorite part of the *balad* outside of the vegetable market was the *Souk Bedli* or suit market. I didn't have room to bring any dress clothes, and I needed to get a sport coat or something a little dressier to go to church events or dental meetings. While the West is getting casual, Arab men love to dress up and put on a suit and tie for all kinds of occasions, so I headed to the *balad* to find something appropriate.

After asking around, I found this long narrow alleyway that was covered by a menagerie of colorful tarps and roofing materials. Inside, separated by curtains and hastily put up dividers were about ten suit "stores" lined up in a row on the left. On the right side of the alley were about ten tailors sitting adjacent to sewing machines and mostly all smoking and chatting, ready for work.

They watched me carefully as I made my way from store to store, trying to find a suit that fit my style. Most of the outfits had a shiny veneer to them or sometimes even threading that conspicuously went around the borders of the lapel. These were the fashion at the time, but I couldn't help picking out a less shiny, Western style, grey suit. Being a foreigner, I stuck out enough as it was, so I didn't want to draw more attention to myself.

I tried on the coat which was perfect and wanted to try on the pants as well, but there was nowhere around me where I could change. Plus, I noticed that the pants were all just blanks and hadn't been cut and hemmed yet anyway.

The salesman called over a tailor, and with cigarette in mouth, he took measurements on me, held several matching pants up against my side, and then commenced to hem a pair without me ever trying them on.

They served me hot mint tea while I waited, and maybe 10 minutes later, the pants were done. I asked the salesman how much it was, and he quoted me $22. I probably looked shocked initially because it was so low for a complete tailored suit, so to comfort me a bit, he threw in a free tie. One of my pastors, Chris, later purchased a suit there on a visit and proudly wore it as I did mine for many years.

While many parts of the *balad* were humming all day long, it was more usual for shopkeepers outside of the central area to wind down around 3 pm. Many times after finishing up language school and getting the kids home, I would slip out to do some shopping only to find the stores empty or closed.

I once had to go to the backroom and wake up a shopkeeper from his cot where he had fallen asleep before I could buy some desperately needed supplies. At first, I kind of thought of all of these men as lazy for just working from 9-3 every day, but as time went on, I began to appreciate the pace of life in the Middle East. They do just enough work to survive and spend a lot of time with their families and friends afterward.

Many Arab friends over the years longed to go to America at any cost, and they would regularly be applying for a visa, hoping their name would be drawn in the next lottery. To them, a visa to the US was a ticket to paradise and success. They had seen movies, so they knew what America was like with all her money and wealth and excesses, and they wanted a piece of that because they were convinced that all Americans are instantly wealthy.

The process to get the visa is rather complicated, however, and requires an interview where they try to discern if this person is a good bet to give entrance to the US, with many Arab guys looking to get there on a temporary visa and never coming back. I, unfortunately, got dragged into many of these application processes with Arab friends who could get only so far, before the English became too hard for them to understand.

After paying the US embassy about $150, they could get an interview set up there. One neighbor, after completing the interview, angrily told me they had turned him down again for the third time.

I asked him what they had told him was the reason for denying him this time. He said that since he was 24 years old and unmarried with only two days a week of employment, they said they were afraid that he would stay in America and never come back like he was supposed to. Because of that, they wouldn't let him have the visa. He was very upset.

I asked why he was so mad because "Isn't that pretty much what you told me you were planning to do?"

He answered, "Of course, I was never going to come back, but I can't believe they would say that about me!"

However, I would guess that the majority of Arabs I knew who succeeded and made it to the US, returned a short time later, disillusioned about the work required to make it there. One friend told me he had had to work 8-5 every day, six days a week, to have enough money to survive in the US.

I told him that was pretty common and what I had warned him about the whole time, but he wouldn't listen to me before. He would much rather stay home and work a six-hour shift four or five days a week and live without all of the glamorous stuff the US had to offer. I thought maybe he wasn't all that wrong.

Outsiders At Friday Prayer

One of the classic things to do in the *balad* was to take a trip to the old mosque. Out front, there were usually people selling clothes and other things, but on Fridays, they cleared off all of that courtyard as men would come for the Friday prayers around noon.

A pilot friend of mine, Bryan, who regularly stopped over in different locales, made a stop to visit us. I took him down to the *balad* on a Friday so he could get the full experience.

It would be pretty quiet until the time of prayer, but I knew immediately after that all of the shops would be opening up, and the carnival atmosphere of the place would begin. I wanted to show him what the weekly prayer looked like at the mosque from a good vantage point, but also from a place from where we could slip away quickly for safety if needed.

If there was going to be a riot or protest, they often commenced as soon as Friday prayer was over, so the US Department of State often sent us email warnings not to be around the central mosque at that time. Things could get dangerous quickly if they were planning a demonstration or something—and these were sometimes against the US as well.

While we waited for the prayer time to start, we were looking carefully around the outside of the mosque as we people-watched and generally had some in-depth discussions about life here. Some men began to walk over, some holding cardboard pieces in hand so that they could put those on the dirty ground and pray, possibly keeping clothes clean or knees from pain.

We asked some Arabs standing there, and they encouraged us to take a few pictures, and we started to talk with them as they told us about the importance of prayer here on Fridays. We learned this location was one of the most important places to pray in the country, and you got more *hasanat* (points with God) to pray here.

The conversation over, we turned our heads back to the street to begin to exit, and there were already hundreds of men with mats or cardboard set up and ready to pray barring our way. We looked for a way out, and the last passage through the crowd quickly closed as a few more men jumped in the gap and began praying.

We had the strange and fascinating experience of being trapped up against the front wall of the central mosque with no way to get out. Hundreds of men then began the ritual prayer as led by the *imam* (the spiritual leader of the mosque) crying out on the megaphone overhead. They all were praying in unison, facing us directly, going through their series of prayers called *rakats* as we stood there watching them very conspicuously.

Looking at the droll, bored faces, my friend Bryan dryly commented that they looked about as excited and engaged as church-goers back home. It was a good word to me as I can easily judge my neighbors here for their "checklist" of duties they must do to earn God's favor. But, *how am I living before God?* Am I just checking the boxes, too, or am I thrilled by the foolishness (to the world) to which the gospel propels me?

It was a little scary to be there, but it was amazing to see it take place from the front. As they completed their prayers, sure enough, a small protest broke out as people stood up and quickly pulled out Syrian flags from all over and began protesting. Thankfully it was very peaceful, and we were able to make our escape, a little embarrassed but also grateful to have had the experience.

Chapter 7
TICKET TO RIDE

The standard protocol handed down to us by our sending organization was firstly to live in the part of town where English was not widely spoken and secondly not to own a car during the initial phase of language learning. It is thought that driving a private vehicle insulates you from other people and takes you away from many opportunities to use your Arabic and to see life through the eyes of most of the population who could never own a car themselves.

We agreed with this principle and followed their guidelines and were probably better off because of it. Still, coming from a two-car family in the US, I don't want to undersell how hard an adjustment it was to make. Having three kids in a big city where we often had to get around from one side of town to another or bring large amounts of groceries and goods from one side of the town back to our apartment was difficult.

This experience was before the days of Uber, Lyft, and Careem, so if we had far to go, we had to rely on the taxi service and flag down someone on the street. Our family learned the ins and outs of taking taxis, including checking that the meter got restarted and negotiating your price before you sat down in the car. I enjoyed riding around and getting to meet interesting people every day without having to worry about navigating the crazy traffic around us.

It was harder for Grace, who had to sit in the back with the kids and pretty much remain silent, but for men, it was a great way to practice your new language and hear some new perspectives.

Over the years, I was driven by taxi drivers who happened to be accountants, engineers, and the occasional dentist as well, because unemployment was so high in many of these job markets. The general unemployment was around 19%, but dentists were famously 50% unemployed at the time, so they had to find some way to make ends meet.

As our first year neared the end, we started some paperwork with our clinic to receive residency visas prior to our move up to Manara, and these would be annually renewed each year we remained there. We had seen others in my language school showing off their residency cards as people slowly started to receive them as the year passed on. We would look at them with relish, passing them around the class and secretly jealous that we didn't have this coveted documentation that would open up so many doors.

When those beautiful cards finally hit our hands after multiple trips to the department of social development, department of the interior, and the lawyer's office, we knew what this meant—we were official residents and could finally buy a car.

As a foreigner, you could buy a car and avoid paying customs, which would cut the price of the car in half. The only problem was that you had to wait almost one month for the paperwork to go through.

We initially signed a contract on a car with one man, and as we neared the end of our month of waiting, he called to tell me that he had sold it to someone else for more.

He was really, really sorry but more money was more money, and that agreement he had with us was less important. I realized that this was a good deal for him, as we had signed something promising to buy it after the paperwork went through. While we waited, he went ahead and raised the price and put it back on the market and was able to sell it for more, knowing that he had it sold either way.

The next time we tried it, I went through a used car dealership that our clinic often worked with, and the owner promised not to sell the car out from under us while we were waiting on the paperwork. As a result, a month later, we were the proud owners of a silver Mitsubishi Pajero for $14,000.

Foreigners couldn't buy anything more than five years old, so this was the oldest car we could find of this type. I knew my work would take me into rural areas where I would likely need four-wheel drive, so the Pajero (which is called a Montero in the US) was a good fit for family and work.

It wound up being very dependable and fun to drive throughout our entire time in the Middle East.

While we had waited for the car paperwork to go through, Grace and I had gone through the process of getting driver's licenses. Like most processes in the Middle East, it wasn't hard, but it was time-consuming and illogical to our minds.

We started the first day by going to the department of the interior to fill out the paperwork using our new residency visas. The paperwork is pretty much mind-numbing in addition to being in Arabic, so we paid $1 to one of the many men sitting at desks on the side of the road to fill everything out for us. We followed the recommendation of our friend, Job, who came along with us and had just completed this process himself.

Job then led us through the interior ministry getting various stamps on our paperwork. We got one stamp from a desk on the main level, then a trip up to the third floor for a stamp, back to the main level for a signature, and finally a trip down to the basement where we could get final authorization.

He had spent hours previously trying to figure all of this stuff out for himself, so we were grateful that we could learn from him and speed up the process.

The man we turned the papers into at the end told us that he couldn't get to them until tomorrow because he had a lot of computer work to do, so we thanked him and said we would return the next day.

The next day we returned to the same office in the basement and found the man again busy on his computer and smoking.

We sat down—I at a chair intimately beside his desk and Grace sat across from him. He told us that he had never gotten around to getting the paperwork done yet, and we could just come back later.

We pleaded with him to go ahead and do it for us then because we had taken yet another trip across town, and we had three kids at home, and it was hard to manage care for them.

He sighed a little and went and got the papers from another room. I noticed with surprise as he left that the only thing on his screen was not work-related, but pornography. He didn't seem to care at all that I knew.

He returned, and in a couple of minutes, all the paperwork was stamped and approved.

On the third day, we were then able to get to the DMV outside of the capital and procure our driver's licenses. Like the previous ministry of the interior, the department of motor vehicles was comical in the amount of bureaucracy that was present. At least, it created a lot of jobs for the people living there.

Thankfully, at the first desk we came to, the man there was very familiar with our clinic because he had family who had received treatment there. He called over a *sheb* or young man to go around with us and navigate all of the procedures required to get a license.

There were about seven different buildings in the complex, each having 1-20 windows you could approach for service. He literally would take us to window five in building three for a stamp, and then we would go to building five, window seven for a signature. Then he would return us to the previous window in building three for them to look it over and stamp over the signature. The next stop was building seven and the eye exams for both of us, which we passed basically by reading the "E" at the top of the chart. Then it was subsequent visits to many of the other buildings to check for tickets and who knows what else.

It was so funny to us that we started counting as we went on. When the hot licenses finally issued out of the printer, we felt like we had accomplished something. We had gone to 19 different windows over the few hours at the DMV—which had just been the final day of a three-day-long process.

Life in the Fast Lane

Driving in the capital and later in the countryside was freer than the type of driving we have in the US. Usually, there are no lines on the road marking off the different lanes on the highway; rather, you just kind of make your own lane as best you can.

In this case, it was nice having a large car, because you could fairly easily negotiate the traffic because of your size.

When everyone came up to a traffic light, then the lanes would multiply further as cars would pull off right and left onto the shoulder and median. This movement created more lanes of vehicles ready to jet away and fit back into the smaller number of lanes at the first sign of the upcoming green light.

Circle intersections were also very popular in our country, and we used to joke that it was a game where you tried to get to the interior of the circle, kiss the middle and then make your way out before your exit came up.

Sometimes, and very commonly outside the capital, you might see cars coming full speed down the wrong side of a divided highway. In fact, I once came upon two vehicles bearing down on me, going the wrong direction while I was in my regular right-side lane. There was nothing to do but hold on, and one passed me on the right while one passed me full-speed on the left.

If you missed your exit on the interstate, it was common and acceptable just to stop and back up until you got back to the turn that you had missed. Other times you might get behind an old Bedouin man going about 30 mph down the interstate, or conversely, a Black Cadillac Escalade would blink their high beams at you as they zoomed up from behind going 100 mph.

My friend Ron used to joke that driving all depended on the ancestors of the people. Some used to drive camels, and now in automobiles would plod around too slowly and get in your way. Others had groomed Arabian horses and always driven too fast and recklessly. Finally, some families had only driven donkeys, and they were the ones notoriously going on the wrong side of the road.

Surprisingly, I can't say that with all of that lack of regulation, I saw more car accidents than I usually witnessed in the US. I decided that it was because everyone drives very defensively.

Without driving laws or at least driving laws being enforced, you always had to assume that everyone was going to do something stupid, so you constantly were watching out and not able to relax. As a result, it seemed like the system mostly worked. I occasionally had a car or two rub me on the side as we were negotiating our unmarked "lanes" on the highway, but a little "rubbing is racing" as they say, so it wasn't a big deal.

Shortly after we got a car, I went out one morning on our street and noticed that a side window had been broken out. Nothing was missing except a Bible Atlas that had been in the back seat, and some loose change. We filed a police report, and finally, a neighbor woman came out and said that she had seen the man that broke our window while she was praying around 4:30 AM.

The police were familiar with the description of this man and said two other cars had broken windows in the area as well. I got a call that afternoon that the man had been arrested and I was to come down to the police station to write out the damages.

The primary damage was the window which cost $28 to fix, so I was mostly mad the man had broken it to steal a $15 Bible Atlas, which I would have handed him if he wanted it.

As I walked into the police station, they led me around a maze of corridors and rooms until I finally got to the captain who was in charge of the case. He sat behind a big desk opposite some chairs, and I noticed two men sat on the floor on opposite sides of the room. It looked like one man was facing forward waiting his turn for something, and the other man was maybe cleaning the wall or floor because he was turned away from me. I wasn't sure what else he could have been doing in that awkward position.

After I signed the police report, the captain informed me that the man on the floor facing out was the one that had burgled all the cars last night. Unfortunately, this man was a drunk looking for money, and he already had a long rap sheet and could never pay anything back. They were going to put him in jail for a few nights.

I now realized then that the reason he was on the floor facing out was that his hands were handcuffed behind him to the radiator attached to the wall. As I looked a little closer, I saw the other man had been handcuffed face-forwards laying in a half prone position connected to the radiator on the other wall.

Those fellows were just gonna hang around in there until they got transported to the jail, I figured. I couldn't believe what I saw with new eyes, and it certainly opened my mind up to the workings of the criminal justice system. Those conditions would likely make the front page in the US for police brutality, but here they had found a quick but harsh solution for being out of room.

Eye Contact Pros and Cons

In addition to some road rule differences in the Middle East, another huge difference to us was the social aspect of driving. I usually tend to zone out in the car and enjoy music or podcasts and go into autopilot. I found out quickly that no one did that in our new country.

One day a friend told me that he had seen me drive past him at 10:30 by the roundabout and then again at 2 pm at another place. It struck me as odd that he had seen me that clearly twice and knew some of my movements through town that day. I hadn't seen him at all.

Then I started to watch other drivers as I drove. Everyone else was driving and looking at all the other drivers and pedestrians in the eye. People on the street were also looking directly at me as I drove. Every driver I passed in oncoming traffic was also looking at me straight in the eye as we drove past each other. It was kind of unnerving, but explained why they always saw you drive past—they were always watching.

I never figured out the cultural reason why this happens exactly, but as I started looking at drivers, I started to see my friends around town as well. It's just never something I had done before because it takes more energy and focus.

Eye contact while driving in a car also carries another obligation about which I learned. If you saw a hitchhiker on the street or a beggar asking for money, it was best not to look at them unless you wanted to respond to their needs.

One time I glanced very briefly at an old Bedouin man who was trying to flag down a ride. He caught my glance and walked over to the car, and I figured that he would saunter up and ask me for a ride. To my surprise, he opened the door and hopped in, saying thank you.

Another time a beggar kid came up to the window yelling for money, and I looked at him to tell him I had food but no money. He got really upset that I wouldn't give him money and harassed me until the light changed and I got out of there.

I was riding around with my friend Titus, who had spoken before at the language school, and we passed a man trying to hitchhike. He made some moves towards the car as we passed by, speed unchanged.

Titus asked me, "Why did you look at him? Were you going to give him a ride?"

I retorted, "No, he just looked interesting, so I was watching him as we passed by."

Titus explained to me that because I looked at him, he took that as a signal that I had agreed to give him a ride. Then as he walked towards us, I had left him in the dust, which was very rude.

I was perplexed on how this had happened, so I asked Titus what was I supposed to do in the future?

He said to keep people that you are not able to help in your peripheral vision and never focus on them. It's weird to say, but this became my habit in driving.

If I couldn't help a person with something, I never looked at them directly because I didn't want to obligate myself. Gangs of kids I passed by on the street gave me less trouble as well if I never looked them in the eye. Beggars you couldn't help were best declined by staring straight ahead and maybe clicking your tongue and nodding your head up for a "no."

As I changed my driving behavior in these social ways, things were better, and I got annoyed less often. It felt weird and cold to put people in your peripheral vision and not look at them, but it was better than attracting every one of them to the car

Chapter 8
A PROFESSOR IN CASE

Also, during the period when we were in the capital, I wanted to get to know as many national dentists as I could. My senior director had some concerns that our visas through the clinic may not last forever, so he had directed me to keep my options open for getting visas through other means like part-time work.

As a result, I decided to go to a national dental meeting and try to bump into some people and make connections. Years before, I had actually met a local orthodontist here that was doing braces on my director's kids, and since that was my own specialty in the US, we had hit it off a bit and stayed in touch by email.

Seeing him at the meeting, I was able to tell him that I was now full-time in the Middle East, and he immediately told me he would love to have me consider work in his practice. It would be good work for me, and it would boost his practice having an American orthodontist join him. I was excited to pursue that opportunity for sure.

Sitting down for one of the lectures, I grabbed the last empty seat available in the back and introduced myself to two female doctors who were on either side. By God's providence, one happened to be an orthodontist who was actually the Dean of the local College of Dentistry, and the other happened to be an Associate Professor of Orthodontics in the same College.

What were the chances? 100% if God wanted me to meet them.

M is for Miraculous

We enjoyed a full day of dental lectures that were given surprisingly in English. Throughout the day, I got to know them reasonably well, and they got to hear my story.

As we departed, the dean told me that if I was interested in teaching Orthodontics at the university, I should call her and set up an interview. They would be happy to consider having me there as part-time faculty if I was interested.

As time went on, I quickly found that working in private practice for income as a foreigner was pretty much impossible. Even though the orthodontist that offered me a job had some high-up connections, the visa I had only would let me work as a volunteer in either a hospital or university setting. So, although he knew the right people, he kept getting his efforts blocked because other professionals were jealous of him having an American possibly come work with him, and they felt threatened by the competition.

That led me to pursue a part-time job at the university. The problem from the beginning with that position was that they would surely want me to work there more hours than I wanted. I knew they would want some consistency with the lectures and education of their residents. Still, I made the trip there to see if anything might be able to work out.

Talking to Grace, we had decided with my upcoming load of work and travel for the clinic at which we were about to begin working, that I ideally just wanted to volunteer at the university only two days a month.

Preferably it would be a role where I wouldn't have to spend hours preparing lectures at home every week. If something like that was impossible at the university, which it surely was, maybe I could work there one day every week at the most, but that would take me away from some direct ministry opportunities.

As they introduced me throughout the dean's office, I felt a little bit like a novelty, being the only foreign person in the whole place. We were all dressed in formal business attire, which is standard in the Middle East for professionals, and I was glad I had my new suit. The dean and associate professor I previously had met at the dental meeting were already seated in the dean's office waiting for me.

They rose as I entered and served me the traditional coffee and some dates, and we exchanged pleasantries and caught up a bit. I told them that

I was interested in only a very part-time position because my principal obligation was to the clinic. Still, I would love to serve the university and help train the residents in orthodontics as best as I could.

The dean told me that she was a little bit familiar with our clinic and had met some people who had gone for treatment there before. She surprised me by asking me, "Now what is the English word for what you call yourselves? It starts with an 'M'."

I was like, "Do you mean *m*edical doctors…or hu*m*anitarians?"

"No," she said," it is a word with 'M' like *m*iss…"

I interrupted her and said, "Oh, you mean *mutatua*! (volunteer). Yes, we are volunteers. I enjoy volunteering all around the world!"

I quickly whipped out a card I remembered was in my wallet, which had my name and listed me as a volunteer for a previous project.

They were very intrigued and commented that the US was famous for sending out people like me. I also showed them my visa card which said on the back my purpose for entry was *mutatua*. We had finally figured out that mysterious "M" word.

She then told me that she had discussed it with the associate professor, and they would like to offer me a position at the university, but they were afraid it might not be what I wanted. They wanted me to work at the university every other Monday as an adjunct professor and teach the orthodontic residents in their clinic as they regularly saw patients. They didn't have any lectures or other positions open but would love me to simply spend time with the residents doing this hands-on work.

I couldn't believe it—it was exactly what we had hoped for. *Thank you Lord!*

I enjoyed all of my time working at the university. However, like some of what we had experienced with Rae's kindergarten previously, the typical calendar frustrations still occurred. Thus, I would show up to work only to find out that the university closed for an election no one told me about or for the King's birthday or for Muhammad's birthday or something like that every time. It felt like Muhammad must have 2 or 3 birthdays every year.

So, organizationally, once you got up to the college ranks, I learned that things were pretty much about the same as kindergarten, at least in terms of scheduling.

Rote Memory

The style of education mostly present in the Middle East uses rote memorization to teach students the material they need to know. I had never really been exposed to this method personally, other than sight-words or spelling class, because in the US, our teachers wanted us to know the answer and *why* something is the right answer.

Ultimately the question "why?" is the critical difference between these two educational systems, as one system ignores the question, and the other system emphasizes it.

What this results in is that the cream of the crop academically in the Middle East are those who have amazing memorization capacity—a so-called photographic memory. These people rise to the top and can get into Medical and Dental school, which are two of the hardest professions in which to enter. That's because they score well on the end of high school examination, whose score ultimately determines your future job and destiny.

It changes yearly, but for instance, a 96 score or above means you will be a medical doctor, and 95 means a dentist, 94 a pharmacist, 93 means a civil engineer, and so on.

Could you score a 98 and then decide you wanted to be a dentist because that is always what you had dreamed of doing? Theoretically, that could happen because you achieved above the qualifying score, but practically it was impossible because the pressure from your family and society would push you to do the profession that was the highest on the scale whether you were cut out for it or not.

I remember a friend of mine dearly wanted to be a dentist, so he knew that on the end of high-school exam, he not only had to get a 95, he had to score a 95 exactly. If he scored below a 95, he would be a pharmacist or engineer, and if he scored a 96 or more, his family was going to make him become a medical doctor even though he dreaded doing that profession. I was looking forward to training him and working with him in the dental clinic. Unfortunately for me, he got a 93 and became a civil engineer.

In my experience with these memory masters, I was always impressed by their abilities to not only remember the answers given in a book but also where they found it. I still remember asking one resident early on how he would adjust a particular orthodontic appliance.

He proceeded to rattle off to me the textbook answer, including the page number and place on the page where the answer was found. I had a sinking feeling in my belly, thinking *how can I even begin to teach this guy anything? He already knows it a lot better than I could even explain it myself.*

I then asked him to apply that knowledge to the current patient in the chair, whose situation wasn't exactly ideal. He had absolutely no idea how to do it—and I still had a job.

Ultimately, I think there are religious underpinnings to these two styles of education. I became convinced over time that Islamic thought cannot persevere in a system that asks a lot of whys, because there are not a lot of satisfying answers. As I studied this religion for myself in my formative years, ultimately reading through the Quran twice and logically progressing through it and asking all of the hard questions, it finally fell apart.

For Islam to remain in power, no one must ever ask why to all of the hard questions, but must take all of the dogma purely by faith and assent. Local friends universally told me that they had asked their local *imams* some difficult questions about Islam and the Quran and had been told that they would not answer those questions. One *imam* told my friend if he even continued asking questions about God, he would go straight to hell.

I consider our freedom in Christianity to be a unique and blessed position where we can ask all of the difficult questions about God and not be afraid. Followers of Jesus who follow the Bible are not afraid to test it out as the only source of truth and see what it says and if it stands.

If Christians have doubts as they process certain doctrines or teachings, they are welcome to seek out for themselves these answers and make their faith their own. We can't just believe it because others have said so. I feel this gives us a vibrant and dynamic faith that can be tested, endure doubts, and as a result, absorb the Bible's teachings in a way that yields rich application to your life.

Another interesting thing to me about graduate education was that it was becoming more and more about money and status every year and less about excellence or result. This evolution is probably something that has equally happened in the US as well, but I got to observe it first-hand on foreign soil first.

A few years before I started working there, I was told there were traditionally 150 dental students at any one time in a four-and-a-half year dental program that immediately followed high school. When I got there, we enrolled over 200 students, and over the next few years, the enrollment grew to over 400 students.

Growth is a good thing, but when you don't add any faculty members to compensate for the growing student body, and the patient numbers are not drastically increasing, it's not a good thing. Thankfully, the program expanded to a five-year degree program (in the US it takes eight years to be a dentist), which gave the students a little more time to cover their core biology and science courses and then complete some practical dental work the last year.

Yet, there were still times where one student would be doing a filling on a patient while 15 other dental students stood around them in a circle, watching how to do a filling without ever doing it themselves.

As a result of the increased student numbers, many of the graduating dentists could not find a job and that helped explain the 50% unemployment rate for dentists. If the student actually could find a job, they were grossly inexperienced and were literally "practicing" dentistry.

I was happy to avoid many of these issues and ethical concerns because I was only teaching orthodontic residents in a three-year specialty program for Orthodontics that came after the completion of dental school. We only took four new residents every year throughout my time there, and that never changed.

Faith Encounters

Other than being another avenue for getting a visa, I looked at my work at the university as being another way that I could connect with people and introduce them to my life and faith.

A study at that time had shown me that 90% of people living in that part of the world had never even met a Christian before in their life, let alone heard anything true about Jesus. I was, therefore, excited to spend a good amount of time there with students weekly as well as professors who I taught alongside.

One thing I was always sure to be asked when I met a new resident or professor was, "Why in the world did you move here from America? Wasn't the pay better in the US?"

"Of course it was better," I would say.

"Wasn't the living better and more comfortable in the US?"

"Of course."

"So why in the world are you here?" They couldn't possibly comprehend how someone could ever leave money and comfort as I had. It was what they were all striving after.

I was able to answer that question in many different ways, depending on my audience, but I always made it clear in the end that I had come ultimately because of my faith. Then, according to how they responded, I usually could tell if I had an open door or a closed mind to continue talking with them about those subjects.

One particular student from the Gaza Strip showed particular interest in my story and wanted to have lunch with me and talk about it some more. I was excited to do just that and was surprised as we ate to find out that he was a Christian!

There are only 1300 Gazan Christians in the world, making up 0.02% of the population of Gaza. What was the chance? But, I quickly found out that he was part of one of the small communities of Palestinian Christians who lived in Gaza and who were said to be "between two fires." They were being persecuted by the Jewish government that ruled over them and also loathed and pressured by their Muslim neighbors.

We had some powerful conversations, and while his faith was more political than heart-felt, he invited me to come to his house and have a Bible study with him and some of his friends who were Muslims.

I enjoyed the times I got to spend with him and his friends. I got to share with them the reality of my faith, and they opened my eyes to see what was happening among the young people during that time in the midst of the Arab spring.

I remember they surprised me by popping open beer cans during one of my times with them. In surprise, I asked one of them, "I thought you were a Muslim?"

He jokingly responded, "When I drink, I am a Christian."

I wasn't convinced this was orthodoxy, according to any religious teaching.

Christmas Tree 101

During the Christmas season, I took the opportunity to ask Anwar, one of the more friendly professors, what he thought about the birth of Jesus. My friend Benjamin had previously told me that an excellent conversation starter for him had been to ask people during Christmas time why they don't celebrate Christmas.

The virgin birth of Jesus is clearly described in the Quran, albeit with some minor changes, and is a point of agreement between Christians and Muslims. So, I asked this professor that very question, and he surprised me by drawing me close in and saying that he was actually considering celebrating Christmas that year.

He said every year, he had a growing interest in the Christmas story, and he asked me to tell him more about what the Gospels said about the birth of Jesus. We had some good conversations over those weeks about faith, and I wasn't sure where it might lead.

One of my favorite things to share around Christmas in the Middle East was the meaning of the Christmas tree. It's interesting that in the US, we all have decorated trees everywhere, but we don't ordinarily know what in the world this symbol of Christmas stands for and from where the idea even came.

Learning that I was a Christian, one of the first things they usually asked me during a Christmas conversation in the Middle East was if I had a tree at my house and what did it mean. I learned I needed to have a good answer, and initially, I only knew a few fragments of information myself about it, so I studied on the subject.

It seems that the full, clear history of the Christmas tree is hard to dig up, but there are plenty of sources I found that give us hints and ideas from where it might have come.

First, we can learn that the early church often gave Jesus the name "Evergreen." This moniker makes sense because in the midst of death and winter, when everything is brown, the evergreen tree stands out even brighter just as Jesus alone brings light and life into a dead and broken world.

Isaiah 11:1 says, "A shoot will come up from the stump of Jesse; from his roots a Branch will bear fruit." This prophecy describes Jesus, and from this tree stump that everyone thinks is dead, new life comes again.

Secondly, I found that in the Middle Ages, there was declared a Feast of Adam and Eve that occurred on December 24th. During this feast, it was common for Europeans to find a large evergreen tree in the woods and decorate it with red apples and other fruits. These trees were referred to as "paradise trees," harkening back to the time when Adam had eaten the forbidden fruit and brought death to the world. The following day of Christmas then celebrates the incarnation of the Second Adam, the "evergreen", who was the baby destined to die to take that penalty of death upon himself and free us from our sin.

We have sources that indicate that somewhere around the time of the reformation or shortly afterward, people in Germany began to dig up these "paradise trees" and place them inside their homes. The German tradition of circling the tree with strands of shortbread cookies then began representing the host or the body of Jesus in a similar way to how it was received during the sacrament of communion.

While Easter has long reminded Christians of the "cup" of communion by focusing on the cross, Christmas has long commemorated his incarnation and taking on flesh through the "bread," and even the Christmas tree was connected in this way.

In the 18th Century in England, we know that people lit candles around the Christmas trees that now were commonly being brought into homes. Each lit candle represented a particular loved one who had passed away and now was in the presence of the Lord.

As electricity came into being, these lit candles disappeared and were replaced by Christmas lights, just as the apples were replaced often by red balls in modern times.

All of this history gives quite a bit of information to share about the Christmas tree and honestly turns it into a helpful discussion about my faith, and this was part of what I was sharing with Anwar over the weeks of Advent.

Finally, one day, he waved me over to the side of the clinic to speak privately with me. I wasn't sure if he was going to try to sell me drugs or what, but it felt like that kind of situation.

Looking around to be sure the coast was clear, he moved in and asked me, "Where do you think I can find a Christmas tree?"

"A Christmas tree?" I whispered.

"Yeah, a Christmas tree. I think I'm ready to buy one," he said.

"Well, okay," I answered softly, "I know a guy down on the valley road who I bought a good one from. He can help you out I'm sure."

Thus was concluded my first "illicit" Christmas tree deal. The first one's free, but they always come back for more, so they say.

Selling a Christmas tree to this man had not been my real goal, but I hoped that it was symbolic of something resonating deeper within him.

A few months later, Easter was approaching, so I got several opportunities during break times to answer his questions about the meaning of that holiday. It is particularly offensive to Muslims because they think it directly opposes the teaching of the Quran that says Jesus did not really die on the cross.

One morning as I came into work, Anwar pulled me aside and said he wanted to talk to me about something and ask me what I thought. I told him to go ahead, and he shared with me that he had been having visions and dreams about Christianity, and he didn't know what to do about it.

I asked him to share with me what he had last seen in his vision.

He said he had dreamed last night that he was in a church. As he saw himself there, he noticed that he was in the front of the church on his knees. He heard someone saying the Lord's prayer, "Our Father who art in heaven, hallowed be thy name…" and then he realized that it was him saying the Lord's prayer, and he didn't know how he knew it.

He said as the dream went on, he saw himself continue to recite the Lord's prayer until the end. At that point, he realized seeing himself in that church, that in the dream—he had become a Christian.

He turned to me and asked, "What do you think it means?"

I was ecstatic and tempted to tell him exactly what I thought—that God was obviously giving him a dramatic call to faith that must be heeded.

Wanting to hear it from him first, I held myself back a bit and said, "How did you feel when you realized in the dream you had become a Christian?"

He paused and said, "It felt really good. Like it was natural."

"Then, I think you need to realize that God is trying to tell you something very important. He wants you to follow Jesus with all your life now," I said.

He looked at me and nodding, basically agreed, and said he would definitely be thinking about it.

Our work schedules never matched up again after that time. I had noticed that someone definitely overheard one of those religious conversations we had right before the schedules got switched, but I don't know if that was just coincidence or not.

Regardless, I kept in touch with him outside of the university, but sadly I never heard him during my time in the Middle East make a clear decision to make his dream become a reality.

I had a few other memorable residents and professors that I had contact with, which was always icing on the cake, although the results were not always positive. One particular foreign student spent a lot of time with me, and we met outside of school hours to converse about many spiritual topics.

When it came to a discussion on sin and especially sexual sin, I wasn't starting really heavy-handed because that is an area of life that is not discussed commonly, at least with foreigners like myself.

On the outside, with all of the separation of men and women and strict rules concerning how they communicate, it seems like sex is not a big issue in the Middle East. He surprised me by telling me that one of the things that disgusted him most about his society was how rampant sexual sin was.

I was a little taken aback, but he insisted that the Arab world had more sexual sin than the West. He said that Arabs know all about our sexual sin because we don't hide it, we put it in all our movies and everywhere else.

He told me that Arabs just cover it up inside the family or inside the house, where no one can ever witness it or find out. He insisted there was incest, rape, and illicit sex going on all the time, and it was just covered up because of shame, which made it all worse.

He found the teachings of Jesus challenging but inspiring when it came to men and women and especially dealing with your enemies. Ultimately, he found it too hard in some ways to lead a life like that.

He kept coming back to issues of money and prestige as the driving factors of his life. He just wanted a little Jesus on the side to blow his mind every now and then and wasn't yet ready to make him Lord. He told me that maybe after he had enough money and a wife, he would be ready.

Most of my experiences at the university concluded with something along these lines. It made me wonder if I was doing anything other than just increasing the judgment that would come upon these people on the last day because now they had more responsibility for rejecting the teaching of Christ. I have to trust Him to be the one who opens hearts and introduces me to the people that He has appointed to faith.

No one can know Him if their "name has not been written before the foundation of the world in the book of life of the Lamb who was slain," according to Revelation 13:8. So, I can hope and pray that small seeds will grow, just as they also once grew in my own heart. How many people who spent time pouring into my life, left despairing after they witnessed my own immaturity and lack of interest in the gospel?

PART 2

A JOB TO DO

Chapter 9
A PLACE ON EARTH

*And the world cannot be discovered by a journey of miles,
no matter how long, but only by a spiritual journey, a
journey of one inch, very arduous and humbling and
joyful, by which we arrive at the ground at our own feet,
and learn to be at home. —Wendell Berry*

We didn't know it initially, but tamarisk trees are fairly common in this part of the world. As we started a study of Genesis when we got here and saw the tamarisk mentioned there (Genesis 21:33), it made sense that we should look for one.

What we found was that they are deep-rooted trees, often found in well-watered parks, providing great shade wherever they are, but also taking many years to grow. You can't expect instant shade, but rather you plant them for the benefit of others who will enjoy the results later.

Abraham's Tamarisk

When God promised Abraham that he would inherit the promised land and become a great nation, Scripture tells us that as the pieces started to come together, he went and planted a tamarisk tree. By faith, he knew God's promises were something to bank on, so he acted for generations to come because he knew there would be generations to come.

As we finished up our full-time language school and culture learning in the capital, it was time for us to move to Manara and begin work at the clinic, at the place on Earth where we felt God had specifically called our family from the beginning.

We hoped to emulate Abraham by putting our tamarisk tree in the ground here as we began our work. We did that symbolically, hoping that by God's grace, these small steps in language and relationship would yield deep roots and large shade in years to come. But we also did this literally by planting a tamarisk tree outside our house immediately after we moved to our new town.

How we ended up with a house that had a yard in the first place was a true gift from God. Some Arab-Americans were returning to the US for their kids to get launched into college after coming back home for them to learn Arabic and culture themselves. They had built a stand-alone house with a walled garden and now were looking for a family to rent this house and take care of it for them as they left.

They came to our clinic and asked if any Americans would be moving in town soon to work at the clinic. We were the only ones that fit that description, and some of our friends had known this family. Our medical director and his wife also had put a good word in for us.

So now, after all of our troubles with our little apartment in the capital city, we had the opportunity to live in a stand-alone house for reasonable rent. My pastor Chris was with me at the time visiting us when we got the chance to go and look at the house for the first time. We were amazed that a place like this was available in our little dusty rural town.

Chris looked at me and said, "You'd be crazy not to take it, but never put a picture of this in your newsletter."

He thought it wouldn't fit the normal picture of a hovel that Americans liked to think volunteers should live in, but he thought it was clearly a God-ordained thing that we could live in a space like that.

We then made the big move from the capital city, fitting all of our belongings in a single truck that we hired for the move. We purchased several additional furnishings before we left, part of someone's "kit," as we called it. We obliged an English couple that was moving back to the UK and trying to get rid of their stuff.

We left behind our dear friends, Benjamin and Valerie, even as they were receiving a new couple to help get accustomed to the strange and wonderful culture and language of the Middle East. We were not the greenest ones anymore.

Arriving at our new home, we were happy to have some extra space finally, and our hearts were touched when even the pastor of the local church came out to help us move our things. The pastor was a special man who had a heart for refugees and lost people from the majority faith living around us.

As normal as that might seem to us, I couldn't say that it was a regular point of view for most Arab Christians living in the Middle East. After enduring centuries of persecution and being barred from many freedoms we take for granted, wanting their Muslim neighbors to join them in heaven is often the last thing on their minds; this man was different.

As we began to attend his small church, we were blessed to have a group of fellow believers to be around weekly. Even though our Arabic wasn't good enough to begin with, we soon learned the Arabic songs and could follow most of the preaching. The pastor was humble and took great pains to translate things into English for the foreigners working at our clinic and in the town.

A Picture Worth a Thousand Words

It was summer, so as we settled into our new home, I quickly began work on an irrigation line to help water the new tamarisk tree as well as some other trees that we began to plant outside of our house.

We planted three or four fig trees and peach trees as well as a pomegranate tree and several palms. Digging in the soil with my hands made me feel alive again, even if the neighbors would just sit there next door and watch me, never wanting to do work like that themselves and never offering any help.

I hoped at least I was putting on an entertaining show for them. They made it clear they had never seen a doctor doing any work like that because it was below his station. I should hire Egyptians to do the digging and yard work they said, but I would never give up this kind of joy by paying someone else to do it.

One day as I was out in the yard putting the last touches on the irrigation system, I heard the sound of breaking glass towards the front. I froze and turned my head towards the front wall, and scanned the area.

Suddenly I saw a rock fly through the air over the wall and land harmlessly in the yard, but a second later, another rock found its mark in one of the glass lanterns perched on top of the wall— "Crack!"

I started running towards the front, even as I noticed a broken second lantern. I jumped up onto the wall holding myself up with my arms while my legs dangled a few feet off the ground.

Three boys were standing there in the street, rocks grasped in their hands.

I shouted at them, "*Aib aleikhum*!" telling them that shame was upon them.

They froze and looked at me with big eyes. I'm not exactly sure how I thought about it, but I pulled my phone out of my pocket and snapped a picture of them with the rocks still in their hands.

The rocks fell to the pavement, and I asked them, "Where do you live?"

They told me they lived a few streets over and pointed across a rocky field that was in front of the house.

"I want to talk to your parents. Take me to your house."

For some reason, they agreed and nodded, and I walked around to the gate in the wall to exit the yard.

I looked down and realized I was only wearing flip flops, and I knew that they weren't ideal for crossing the rocky field, but I also knew if I returned to the house to change shoes that my quarry would flee and I'd lose my chance. So, exiting the yard, I started walking after the boys.

Things were pretty normal, but the boy in the lead started picking up the pace a little bit and put some space between the other two lads and me.

As we began to cross the rocky field, he started looking back to see how I was progressing. It was hard to keep up with them in the flip flops, but I was trying to hide it as much as possible whenever he looked back. However, the further we went, the more I couldn't keep up with the pace.

As the distance between the lead boy and me continued to increase more and more, he looked back as I stumbled once in the very middle of this rocky field, and then he took off like a bullet.

The other two kids seeing this move immediately looked at me and bolted as well. They knew I had no chance of catching them in these flip flops.

I followed them in the direction that they had gone, but I wasn't sure if they had run in a false direction, trying to throw me off, or if they had simply run for home.

Discouraged, I knocked on the door of a nearby house. As a man answered the door, I pulled out my phone, showing him the picture, and asked him if he knew these boys who had broken two of my lights. He looked the picture over with fascination.

By God's grace, in the photo these boys had been captured very clearly and red-handed holding the rocks. It was evident by the looks on their faces that they knew they were in trouble.

The man told me that he recognized one of the boys but didn't know where he lived. I thanked him and went up the street to another house. Seeing someone on the road who wondered what I was doing, I went up to him and told him what had happened.

The man looked the picture over carefully and told me that he thought one of the boys was Abu Asher's son, who was one of my neighbors living two houses down from mine. That didn't make sense because the boys didn't head that direction at any point in the chase.

However, the man at the next house agreed. He said I should go tell Abu Asher what had happened and show him the picture. He would take care of everything.

Wandering back in the direction of home, I made it over to Abu Asher's. Accusing someone's son of doing something like this is pretty confrontational anywhere, but especially in the Arab world, so I took time talking to him and even received an offer of tea from him as we visited.

Once the pleasantries were over, I pulled out my phone and showed him the picture and told him what had happened. I asked him if that wasn't his son in the picture.

He stared up and down the picture for a few seconds thoughtfully and then calmly said, "No. That is not my son. These boys look like some of the *miskeen* (poor) boys who live over by the ravine. Maybe you should go over there and ask around the refugee families. Better yet, forget about it because you'll never find them again."

I thanked him for his time and departed dejected, feeling like this endeavor had all led a dead end.

I called up my landlord's family and told them what had happened. The landlord's brother told me that it was probably hopeless to find the boys, but that we should at least turn in a police report with a printed version of the picture so that if anything else happened in the future, it would already be on file.

He offered to drive me on over to the police station and help me with the report, and I gladly took him up on it after printing out the picture on an 8 x 11, which is the only size I had.

The police received me with honor and escorted me into the office of one of the sergeants charged with filing reports. It was a simple room with an empty jail cell in the corner, and he beckoned us to have a seat while he readied a new blank sheet of paper, cradling a cigarette gently in his mouth.

I described as best I could the events as they had happened, and my landlord's brother who spoke fluent English and Arabic filled in all the blanks. The sergeant wrote out everything slowly by hand, filling out an entire page. He then asked me to sign my name at the bottom of the report.

I initially hesitated since I couldn't read any of the details in the handwritten Arabic, but they both encouraged me to go ahead and sign to finish the report.

Lifting my photo, I then told him that I had brought a picture of the boys, and the sergeant's eyes brightened up. He took the photo, looking over it with extreme interest, and immediately called over two other officers.

They asked me if those were the exact same boys who broke the lights, and I confirmed they were the ones and excitement just filled the room as they yelled over to others, and more and more officers filled the room.

At one point, there were around ten police officers gathered around the picture, passing the photo back and forth with excited interjections and various pointings; they greedily looked at every detail of the large photo in amazement as if something like this had never happened before.

Finally, one of the police officers looked at me and said, "I recognize the smallest boy in the picture and know where he lives. Come with me."

My landlord's son and I hopped in the police cruiser and started to make our way through town to the section of narrow streets and houses near where I lived. He came to a stop in front of a small house, and as we looked out the window of the car, a little boy stuck his head up over the wall in front of the house.

We all recognized his face from the picture immediately, and that same face turned white as a sheet and dropped from view quickly. He had recognized me as well, now coming to his house, not in flip flops like last time, but seated in a police car.

The officer told me he could handle everything from here, so we left him as he was invited into the house by the boy's parents and we walked the short distance back home.

I thought it had been an exciting day and that we had accomplished something, knowing the policeman would probably take care of everything now. I had learned a lot about the culture in the process, but I didn't realize there was more to come.

The next day, my brother arrived on a visit from the US, and after picking him up from the airport, we headed out for a few days of travel. We wanted to show him the country and then take a short excursion to do some scuba diving.

One day as we traveled, I received a surprise phone call from the police, but at that point, my phone Arabic was not that great, so I really couldn't understand what they were telling me.

In-person, you can pick up on a lot of body language, but on the phone with someone who is not used to speaking slowly with a foreigner, it can be really hard to understand.

He confirmed that I was the one who had turned in the report, and it just sounded like they were wrapping up the case with the boys, and I thanked them for their help and assumed they were making sure they took care of everything.

A couple of days later, as we headed back up to Manara, I received a phone call from one of my colleagues at the clinic. He said there were several families that had arrived, and he asked me if I had recently pressed any charges with the police against some boys or anything like that.

I told my friend I hadn't pressed any charges that I was aware of, but I had gone to the police because of some boys who had broken out the lights at my house.

He informed me that, apparently, I had signed a police report that pressed charges against three boys, and those boys had been expelled from school as they now awaited a court date.

"What?" I said, "I had no idea that is what I signed."

He said the parents were there begging that I would give mercy to the boys and let them go back to school because they had already missed two days.

I was flabbergasted as the reality of what must have happened filled my mind. I told my colleague I would go to the police and take care of it as soon as I got back. Pulling up in front of my house an hour later, a crowd of people met me.

Getting out of the car, three men, who were the three fathers of the boys came up to me, beseeching me and groveling before me all at once to give mercy to their sons.

I recognized immediately that one of the very men talking with me was my close neighbor Abu Asher, who had just a few days before looked at the picture and denied that it was even his son at all.

They told me over and over how sorry they were and that the boys had just been playing an innocent game of soccer, and they had broken my two lights with the soccer ball.

I corrected them once, saying they had intentionally broken them with rocks, but I couldn't sway them from this accidental soccer ball story, so I just let that part drop. They were predictably trying to avoid the shame of the incident.

As the group gathered around me in a circle, I told them that God had forgiven me for my many sins, so I was very happy to forgive their sons this sin of breaking my lights.

I told them I would go then to the police station to get their kids back in school and drop the charges that I had unknowingly pressed.

I hopped back into my car and headed over to the police station with the other families following me in their vehicles like a tiny caravan weaving our way through town.

Once we got there, I was ushered back into the same room as I had filed the report, and some seven or eight police officers were there with me and a dozen people related to the three boys.

I informed the policemen that I had forgiven the boys and wanted to drop the charges, and the three fathers insisted that they would fix the two lights that day. We all agreed that the police could just do away with all of this trouble because we had reconciled.

The station manager was then brought in, boasting several medals across the front of his uniform and some epaulets on his shoulder.

We then explained everything again to this austere man, ready for him to take care of the matter for us expeditiously. To my surprise, he didn't make this go away quickly as he scolded the boys and their fathers over and over for what they had done to a foreigner like myself.

I insisted that I wanted to drop the charges and just let them repair the lamps, but he yelled, "You can't drop the charges! I'm pressing the charges!"

He informed us to come back the next day at 9 AM to the civil courts, and the case would be heard then.

Immediately a sense of helplessness and discouragement fell on the men and their sons as we all realized this was going to continue. I apologized and said I had done all I could, and they chided me for filling out this police report, but I countered that my landlord's family had insisted, and it wasn't my house, so I just followed orders. We all left that day feeling bad and wondering what would happen the following morning.

Dressing up in my *balad* suit and tie the next morning, I asked my brother if he would want to go to court with me, but he demurred and wanted to stay at home. He was still recovering from some stomach issues he had picked up from eating Bedouin bread, among other things during our trip.

My landlord's brother came with me again to help translate, and we arrived at the town hall on time. I was ushered in again to a large, well-appointed office complete with flags in the corner of the room and all of the gaudy decorations that indicate prestige and respect. A man behind the desk rose as I entered and came around the desk to shake my hand.

He introduced himself as the mayor of Manara, and as I took a seat, I realized they were pulling out all the stops to show me respect by first letting me meet the mayor. He served me tea, and then he yelled to the bailiff, and the three boys and their dads walked into the office.

He had the three boys stand in front of his desk, and he began to tear into them, berating them for their actions against me. The mayor was passionate, and as he came to the end of his diatribe, he told the boys to look at me.

They turned their heads, and he said, "Look at how he is dressed. Suit and tie, he is probably a millionaire from America, but he left that and came all the way here to help our people for free. And what do we do for him—we break his lights! This is the greatest shame!" He called the bailiff again, and the boys then were marched out of the room.

I wasn't sure what was going on exactly, but my landlord's brother was grabbing my arm, amazed. He said he had never seen anything like this himself, but they were really honoring me so much by doing all of this.

We had tea with the mayor at that point, and we all talked about life in Manara and what we did and who we knew for the next thirty minutes. Around that point, the mayor told me he wanted to give me a tour of the prison, which was in the adjoining building.

It sounded interesting, so I agreed, and we stood as he led all the other men and me out of his office and down the hall.

As we walked into the prison, he brought me up to one of the jail cells and slid to the right a metal slot in the front of the door, which would allow you to look into this completely enclosed cell.

He gestured for me to look in, and I did, only to see the three boys sitting on the floor of this dark room.

He laughed and nodded his head, excited that I got to see what had happened to the boys in their solitary confinement while we had had tea.

Opening the door, he let the boys out and charged them never again to do anything like that to other foreigners or me. The police chief pledged to add our house to the neighborhood patrol route to ensure we didn't have any other trouble. Then the fathers all signed a sheet which stated if any other damage occurred, they would have to pay 5,000 dollars, which was about one year's pay.

It was all very dramatic and intended to deliver a giant effect, and they were not disappointed, because I was overwhelmed by what had happened. As I drove back to my house, some men were on top of the wall, already replacing the broken lanterns.

Walking into our house and telling the fresh story to Grace and my brother, they were amazed as well. My brother, with his usual tongue-in-cheek encouragement, told me, "Well…this is basically why we all sent you over here, to get your neighbors arrested by the police and get their little boys put into jail and traumatized. Good job."

Some good did, however, come out of the whole event. As the big feast, *Eid al Adha* was soon approaching, and I took the opportunity to go to each of the three families and bring them some sweets and make peace with them as it were. I had really good visits with all of them; we were reconciled, and the "incident of the lanterns" became the way that we got to know all of our neighbors as this was a big event in our neighborhood.

For our remaining years there, we enjoyed a good relationship with my neighbor, Abu Asher, who would often have us over to eat. He never ceased pointing out his son, who he had previously denied knowing, always calling him "the little criminal" with a laugh.

Except for one other minor event that happened on the day of 9/11 (which is 11/9 in the Middle East) when our garage got egged, we never had trouble with any of the neighborhood boys again. We figured everyone in our community knew not to mess with us.

Basket of Summer Fruit

Apart from dealing with the criminal justice system that one time, living in our house in Manara was a blessing and gave us the ability to get R & R when we weren't working at the clinic or in rural villages. If our ministry had required using our home for hospitality, it wouldn't have worked, because we had too nice a house for that dusty town. As it was, no one knew where we lived except for foreign visitors who we often invited over for dinner or housed while they were passing through.

All of our work and contacts were made outside of the home at the clinic in the patient rooms. If not there, almost always we met people out of town in their own tents or villages, so our home served as a perfect place for our family.

It was often our custom to take vacation in the summer because Ramadan was often not a very good month for doing ministry except at the feast at the end.

I remember after one of these trips in the summer, we returned to our home in Manara to see the fruit trees heavy and laden with ripe fruit. Gathering figs until you couldn't carry any more and looking forward to our first pomegranate harvest since planting that tree three years ago, we were reminded of a picture God gave.

When the prophet Amos in chapter 8 of his prophecy observed abundant ripe fruit, God told Amos that the time was ripe for His judgment on this earth and that destruction will be real and devastating. Thankfully, He also promised in chapter 9, that despite that destruction, he would restore and bring in a harvest of His people in the end. Our garden was often refreshing to my soul and a regular reminder of Bible truths and stories.

We enjoyed our house for a good four years before the landlord called and informed us that he was bringing his family back to the Middle East. He said that the young kids had forgotten Arabic, and they wanted to inculcate the culture back into them.

He wasn't going to come back himself, because he told me he could never live outside of the US again. He thought living in the Middle East was so backward and primitive. But, he was going to bring his wife and four youngest kids to live there again, so we needed to make plans to move somewhere else.

It was sad to lose our quiet, peaceful home, but I was also getting tired of cleaning it and taking care of all the repairs that were necessary when you managed a full stand-alone home. We said goodbye to our tamarisk tree, fruit trees, the grave of our pet bird Noel and a host of good memories with our kids as we moved into a three-bedroom apartment on the main street of town, which was all we could find at that point.

Chapter 10
EAT, DRINK AND BE MERRY

*O*ne of our favorite things to do and a real privilege that comes with Arab culture is the opportunity to visit friends and neighbors and to receive visits regularly. It's not overly disturbing to anyone's schedule like in the West, rather it's expected of people, and that's why they have the salon at the entrance to every house, always ready for a visitor.

One of our first memorable visits was to the house of a dentist, Fawzi, with whom I had made friends in the capital. He and I had serendipitously first met on the airplane during a previous return trip to the US when I was traveling by myself.

We had exchanged pleasantries, as one usually does with a stranger, but he seemed intent to change gears and get some work done. That was fine with me because it was late and I was fatigued.

Just as I was stretching out and preparing to go to sleep on the plane for the night, he pulled out of his backpack a textbook titled *Cosmetic Dentistry*. I was a little miffed at the Lord for making this such an obvious hindrance to my plans for sleep, but I obeyed what the Spirit said and propping myself back up into the chair, I asked him the obvious question, "So are you a dentist?"

That had led to about a seven-hour discussion that moved from dentistry to Christianity and the Bible, and we spent several hours just reading through the Gospels together to see what they said. He was excited, saying that he had never had the opportunity to learn about

Scripture before. In the end, I gave him my Bible, and when I was back and in his town, we would routinely try to get together.

One particularly memorable time, he had invited Grace and me to have dinner with him and his wife, who had already heard a lot about us at that point but had never met us. He immediately shared with me the bad news (at least to us) that they had won the visa lottery and would be moving to the US in a few weeks, leaving everything behind, including his ability to practice dentistry. So, this was the last time I would get to see him on this side of the pond.

As we settled into their house and sat down, his wife began the usual serving of coffee and dates. She then left the room to return to the kitchen. He then pulled out his Bible, which was thoroughly marked up on every page, and he told us he had read through the New Testament three times now.

The problem he said was that his wife had seen it and had told her brothers about it. They had recently come over and threatened him with bodily harm unless he would stop reading the Bible. To Fawzi, receiving this visa to move to the US was a gift from God, because he felt like the walls were closing in on him a bit as he explored Christianity.

His wife reentered, and he visibly hushed up as she served us tea and some bread. After she left, he quickly resumed his questioning about certain parts of the Scripture until she would return, and then we would turn back to ordinary types of conversation.

After the business of dinner, which was very delicious, but not a time when conversation ever occurs in the Arab world, they escorted us back to the living room.

We were stuffed, but he asked if we wanted some fruit, and we declined. But still, he turned his head and told his wife, "Go into the kitchen and cut up some fruit for us."

As soon as we all saw she left the room, he turned back to us with an expectant face and asked suddenly, "Quick, tell me about the Holy Spirit! I don't understand it exactly."

We gave our best quick answer, trying to explain the Holy Spirit as a person of the Trinity and what His role was in our lives before she reappeared with a plate of fruit.

It was torture as we tried to put away some pieces of fruit because we had already eaten so much, but we did it to show respect, and we had barely passed that test before Fawzi barked to his wife, "Go back to the kitchen; bring us sweets and coffee."

We were dying at that point, but as soon as she left, we knew why he had said that because he pried us with a few more quick questions about biblical teaching before she returned.

We left that evening, excited about what we had shared, stuffed to the gills with food, and also saddened that this level of subterfuge was necessary between a man and his wife because of his interest in the gospel. That certainly wouldn't be the last time we experienced that emotion.

What if God Was One of Us?

At the season of Christmas, visits to your Christian neighbors are a common thing. Happily, our Muslim neighbors always wanted to visit us, just as we would visit them during *Eid al Fitr* after Ramadan or the great feast of sacrifice, *Eid al Adha*.

Eid al Adha is when they celebrate Abraham's willingness to kill his own son. While Christians typically emphasize how God was providing a lamb for Abraham during that episode, our neighbors mainly talked about what a great sacrifice Abraham had almost made, and they call on themselves to also make a sacrifice to God to please Him.

This sacrifice is largely manifested by slaughtering an expensive sheep. All I can say is that it is an extremely bloody event as they sacrificially slaughter thousands of these animals in one morning, one for each family. It gave us even a little sense of maybe what it was like back in the days of the temple.

Our neighbors always shared some with us after hosing the blood off the driveway and down our street. Thankfully, it was also a great opportunity to share about the real Lamb of God who had been slain.

During Christmas, however, Jesus is not known as a lamb, but as the humble One. The One who was incarnated as a weak babe into a poor family.

This idea is an extremely hard concept for Muslims that God could humble Himself in this way. They feel like no normal king would give up his throne or do anything that even smells like weakness, so Jesus must not be God and King, just a prophet.

But on reflection, Jesus is no normal king, and only a truly great and mighty King who had no doubts about His authority and future standing *could* step down to save us. A lesser king would be too fearful of losing his status. In the end, the humble infant and mighty King Jesus has ended up bringing more glory to His name and more citizens to His kingdom through the process of stooping down to us.

Since Christmas is the time when incarnation most fully comes to the forefront as a model for us, one feeble attempt I made to follow in Jesus' pattern was to decide to dress like my neighbor when he came to our house for Christmas.

Abu Asher had never failed to dress in traditional Bedouin *thobe* (robe) and *keffiyeh* (headdress) for every visit he ever made to our house. This time, I reasoned that to best welcome him, I would be like him and put on my full-length Bedouin *thobe* with a checkered keffiyeh on my head.

What a surprise it was, when for the first time ever, he showed up in Western clothing, decked out in coat and tie to help me celebrate my holiday. This misstep necessitated pictures of the two of us, dressed like each other and both failing in our comical efforts to contextualize ourselves.

During our Christmas program at the clinic, we used the example of how a famous authority figure got out of his limo during the heavy snow that year to help push a car stuck on the ice. The news and TV stations just ate this up, and everyone was celebrating how this famous person was just like one of us!

We proclaimed to all our guests that we had even greater news: the King of Kings became one of us; Jesus stepped into time to redeem his people, he came to us when we couldn't come to him.

It was a very moving presentation, and who Jesus is was clearly proclaimed. Though our personal "incarnation" efforts may fail, it is great to witness about the one who came and will come again.

His Eye is On the Platter

Many times as we worked among the Bedouin, they would invite us to visit them after our work and any other time for that matter. I quickly learned that culturally, work was never an excuse to get out of a visit. Receiving a call or personal invitation to come for tea, I could protest that I had patients to see or a meeting at the clinic.

But, they seemed to look at me as if saying, "So what?" and just kept inviting me.

The only thing that universally works is if you are out of town. If that's true, then people will give up on their invitation and agree you can't truly come without any shame coming upon you.

Unfortunately, though Christians should never do this, what I observed from talking to other local friends was that people would tell you they are out of town when they are not.

One friend of mine got mad when he asked his uncle to come to visit and found out that he could not because he was away on work in another city. Five minutes later, he saw him walking down the street in town. The uncle could never say he was too busy; he had to lie and say he was hours away.

Many Bedouins in my experience would grab my hand after work and lead me out the door, insisting that we come to his tent to visit and eat with them. On one such occasion, a dear old Bedouin gentleman who owned a large farm and much livestock had his wife and daughters preparing a meal for our dental team who had worked in their village all week.

As we arrived after work and reclined in their tent, they put down before us a vast platter of lamb and rice, which is the foundation of all the favorite dishes for the Bedouin and widely found throughout the Middle East.

What makes these dishes special and unique are the different creamy and flavorful sauces created for it, some made from goat milk. The sauce really makes the dish. If it is too goaty, it doesn't taste right, but if done well, it was one of the favorite dishes of my family and especially for my son David.

The most honoring presentation is when the whole intact head of the lamb is cooked in situ, right on top of the large tray. Rising up, out of the mound of yellow rice, you see the open jaws of the lamb with all of its teeth, complete with tongue and eyeballs protruding from the skull.

A famous story we heard about a woman who worked with Bedouin many years ago described how she once was blessed by a Bedouin family by receiving a meal like this one. As a special gesture, they offered her the eyeball, which is the most honorable part.

With all eyes watching, she knew she would have to eat this thing. After a long time, she finally choked the eyeball down, swallowing it whole and drinking a lot of water.

Understandably, it was such a gross and hard experience that tears started running down her cheeks from the process. Mistaking her tears for thankfulness and gratitude, the Bedouin family felt highly honored.

Later on, after returning home, to her credit, she bought a sheep head and practiced eating the eyeballs so that she would never again come close to bringing shame on her hosts or embarrassing herself. In the end, she found the tongue was actually worse than the eyes.

A female colleague used to teach us essential ways to get around or at least to mitigate some of these cultural food issues after we arrived. She warned me once to always drink goat milk, but always after asking them to boil it. This treatment would kill the bacteria in the milk and keep you from getting brucellosis or "Maltese fever," which is a common ailment of the Bedouin shepherds.

She also told me to drink it down while biting my teeth together to filter it and try to breathe through your nose. It didn't make much sense to me until a Bedouin family I was caring for brought my dental team some fresh goat milk. Clenching my teeth together, I drank it down sip by sip to honor them and then easily removed a solid pinch of goat hair from the front of my teeth. It seemed they don't filter the milk very well.

This woman also told us to be careful of what you ask about or show interest. She herself had once asked a Bedouin with a camel how the milk tasted because camel milk is highly prized among the Bedouin and thought to cure many illnesses.

Without a pause, the Bedouin man began to milk the camel into a metal tin held on his shoulder. He then presented the milk to her and insisted she find out for herself.

She said that hair and other things from that end of the camel were floating around in the freshly squeezed camel milk, but holding her breath, she drank it down.

Seeing her drink it that fast, he quickly milked it again and presented it to her, but she insisted that he give it to his children for their health, and after initially demurring, he agreed.

Spoon Feeding

My friend, Dr. Ron, once told me about a visit he made with a mutual friend where their hosts were serving a big meal. This friend of ours hated eating traditionally by hand because you get so messy from it, and often people will take choice bits of meat out of their own licked and nasty hands and put it into your hands to honor you by giving you the good portions.

Spying a large spoon hanging up in the rafter of the tent, he quickly asked the *bedouiyya* hostess if he could borrow it for his meal. She readily handed it to him, and he began to eat, now beaming with pride about the spoon he had while everyone else was having to eat by hand.

As the meal finished and everyone else was about to go outside and wash their hands, he simply handed the spoon back to the Bedouin woman with a great thanks for letting him use it. She took the spoon and greedily licked it clean on both sides before promptly hanging it back up "clean" in the roof of the tent and walking away.

The moral of the story is that when you are in a foreign land, it may actually just be better for you to go along with the customs of that place if they are not breaking any ethical boundaries. When you try to adopt or force Western priorities into Eastern settings, you may end up worse.

On one occasion, our lamb was complete with tongue and eyeballs, and our dental team was adventurous and wanting to try this delicacy in the traditional way with their hands. One of our team members at that time was actually a Messianic Jewess who followed Jesus but still maintained her Jewish identity by following the Old Testament laws about only eating kosher food.

We had pretty much navigated every hurdle so far in the trip to help her eat according to conscience. Despite her initial scruples, she had been willing to try the lamb and some of the tongue as well, and overall the whole meal was just delicious.

As we sat back fully satisfied, one of the men asked me to inquire of our Bedouin host from where this lamb came? Was it one of his own flock, or did he get it from the market?

I asked the man, and he was delighted to let us know that he had prepared for us one of his personal lambs to honor us. He said, in fact, they made this meal in the most honorable way from a very young lamb, which he had boiled in its own mother's milk.

To him, this method was considered the ultimate way of preparation. As I translated his description to the group, the jaw on the Jewess woman just dropped as she realized she had broken this strict prohibition from the Old Testament that no one had to think about anymore in the Western world.

She quipped, "Oh well, I guess there's no way I can even pretend anymore after eating a lamb boiled in its mother's milk. I'm clearly saved by grace alone."

What Would Muhammad Do?

So why is it so traditional to eat many Arab dishes by hand? According to tradition, Muhammad always ate with his right hand using no utensils, so this is still how the Bedouin prefer to eat this food, being Sunni, who desire to follow the practices of their prophet.

Sunni Islam is the largest sect of Muslims, making up 85% of its population. The word "Sunni' translated means "practices," and it refers to this group of Muslims whose full understanding of Islam is slanted towards wanting to copy Muhammad in all of his practices. In all manners of life, they are practically asking themselves, "What would Muhammad Do?" and looking to their book of traditions, the *Hadith*, for the answers.

When I first encountered this emphasis on what Muhammad did, it was fascinating, to say the least, and enlightening to understand why things worked in particular ways. It explained all kinds of behaviors like why Sunnis use their right hands for greetings and food, why they honor brushing your teeth with a *miswak* (stick) and not a toothbrush, why they dunk flies that land in their drinks and why they throw stones at a lizard. All of these disparate behaviors can be explained simply by a story from Muhammad's life and practices, as written in the Hadith.

Yet, it also made me question how we as Christ-followers are any different from them. I mean, don't Christians wear the WWJD bracelets and Muslims just wear WWMD ones?

I think for me, the difference has essentially boiled down to externals versus internals. Most of the Muhammadan practices that I have seen emulated by Arabs concern what we are doing in public or private life that people can witness. In other words, if I am wearing the WWMD bracelet, anyone around me can observe if I am true to it or not.

You'll either see me praying in the right way and at the right times or you won't. You'll listen to see if I name my child Abdul Rahman or Muhammad, or you'll notice I use a non-Quranic name. In all ways, an outsider can generally see if I am sticking with it. In this sense, the Quran and the Hadith are really a return back to classic Old Testament rule-following.

But following Jesus is a lot more complicated because he took honoring God to a whole new level with His teachings as we find them in the Gospels. True, the Old Testament definitely hints at this "heart level" of obedience a lot, while still emphasizing the external laws that the Jews had to follow. But, when we get into the New Testament, we see that God is intently interested in the heart more than anything.

Even if we do the right things, it doesn't honor God unless we have the right intentions. Jesus and the apostles draw out the, "I desire mercy and not sacrifice, the knowledge of God rather than burnt offerings" (Hosea 6:6) idea from the Old Testament and solidly double down on it as we are called not to hate, nor lust, nor covet.

These things are mainly unobservable to the public, but God always knows our hearts and desires and wants us to give those to Him fully. In the Gospels, it's almost as if we're told we can keep all the rule-following and external obedience stuff that we are happy to give God. Jesus prefers to have all the things we don't want to give Him. If we give Him those things, we have genuinely made Him Lord and offered Him our heart.

If we submit to the externals, that may be a step forward in obedience and initiating a liturgical submission with our lives before God. Nevertheless, in my opinion, we can still carry out a lot of those things out of duty and not out of gratitude and stay distant to God.

It especially can feel like duty if you perceive your upcoming judgment before God in the Quranic tradition as being a grand scale of judgment that measures out the righteous things you have done versus the sinful things you have done. If the righteous deeds on that scale outweigh the wicked things, you may go to heaven according to Islamic teaching. Yet, because you can never know until you die, you tend to become a slave to duty.

Moreover, there are a lot of social benefits to following the externals, because we can get a lot of praise from men because they are observing all of the good things we are doing and praising us or honoring us for those actions. If men and women are praising our external righteousness, surely that makes us feel better about our chances at the final judgment. The sad thing is we've already received our reward in full if we do these things for human praise (Matthew 6:1).

What makes the difference to me as a Christ-follower is what Jason Hood has described as the "cruciformity" aspect or cross-shaped obedience in his excellent book on *Imitating God in Christ*. I'm convinced this difference is the crucial element of obedience that makes the WWJD slogan different than the WWMD slogan.

Jesus is always calling us into obedience, but it is especially pointed towards ways that only God can see and know about and ways that often require suffering and not the praise of men. As Hood points out, Paul was teaching, "my way of life in Christ Jesus… everywhere and in every church," which he further describes in 1 Corinthians 4 as a life of weakness, foolishness, dishonor, hunger, and persecution, among other things.

Sure, I can brush my teeth with a stick, dunk my flies in my tea or even honor my wife in public. Still, I must really examine myself to see if I love my wife as Christ loved the church, make moves to help the widow and orphan and sacrificially trust God with my life.

The White Tent

One of my most memorable Bedouin visits in all my years was taking part in a Bedouin wedding way out in the desert. We had worked for some time in this village and without knowing it, just happened to time it perfectly to be there when a prominent village man and woman were having their wedding party. Graciously accepting the invitation, we headed immediately after work to one of the assembled wedding tents to take part in the festivities.

After enjoying some good food and conversation, we were then invited to continue the party by traveling by truck around the village and taking part in the general merriment. It was quite a scene as we got in the bed of a white Toyota truck that had been donated to this village by the government because the people were mostly poor shepherds.

Almost immediately, another white Toyota pulled up and then another and then several more until there were about fifteen identical white Toyota pickups all ready to go. We drove around in circles for a while, stirring up the dust and driving all through the village honking our horns and waving to the people, some of who were still in their tents and not in the back of one of the many pickup trucks.

Finally, we got out and transferred into our car to drive over to the wedding where there promised to be music and dancing. As we arrived in a cloud of smoke, dusk was rolling in, and we observed a giant wedding tent set up with a partition in the middle. That partition would serve to separate the men from the women throughout the party. Strangely, we also noticed a small white tent that was off at an angle to the side, not many meters from the large party tent.

As the celebration continued into the night, I had my first chance to learn the traditional style of dancing with the Bedouin men. We naturally held hands, and each moved in step, side by side, snaking around the tent as we were led by the first gentleman who was wielding a sword and a large smile. It was quite fun, but I certainly hope no Bedouins were filming me because I struggled to stay in sync with the other *thobe*-wearing shepherds who had done this dance a million times before.

I couldn't help being intrigued by the small white tent set up a stone's throw away from the party tent, so I finally inquired what the purpose of it was. They informed me that during the party, the groom and the bride go into the tent to consummate the marriage. Then, they return to the party brandishing their white bed sheet between them marked with blood to prove the new bride's virginity as well as the now official standing of the marriage.

As the reality of that sunk in, I couldn't imagine the pressure that must have put on women. Most of these marriages were arranged by the parents, and the thought of having sex for the first time with a man they barely knew a few feet away from a roaring party with all of their relatives was intense. It definitely felt like it was still biblical times around there with some of the customs.

I wasn't too sympathetic about the men's part to play in this ritual, but I mentioned to my friend how incredible I found this ritual with regards to what a woman or girl, sometimes as young as 12 years old, had to go through with a near stranger. He quickly confided to me that most men would bring a knife with them into the white tent and if the girl is too scared, he will just cut his thumb with the knife, sprinkle the blood all over the sheet, wait a few minutes and then return to the party with his new wife.

I was glad to hear that this optional "way out" was available and seemed to be widely used. The plight of the female in this part of the world was not always a high consideration, and we took pride in addressing their underserved needs as much as we could.

Chapter 11
MINISTRY TO THE GENTLER SEX

What do a disabled woman, a Sudanese refugee, a Bangladeshi cook, and an Indonesian rape victim all have in common? They were some of the regulars Grace sat with, smiled with, and shared with every week in our new home town.

These aren't exactly the people we are used to meeting with back home, but they were exactly the kind of people with whom Jesus would meet. They are also the kind of people God is drawing to Himself. Being on death's door or in crisis and away from the normal societal pressures at our clinic, they have the chance to consider another path where Jesus calls us to rest easy in His work and not our own.

Because of the cultural taboo related to cross-gender relationships, any personal contact I had with women was purely in the professional setting. This phenomenon would have customarily meant that outside of talking to women at dental visits, I would not have been able to get closer into the deeper lives of women in that part of the world.

But, as a result of being married to Grace, who heavily engaged in friendship with many of these women during our time in the Middle East, I got to peek in and learn about the lives of many women. I could start to understand what their lives must have been a little bit like because of her ministry to them.

Although I often felt like I was doing a helpful service for many of the women with their dental care, I found that they always preferred her to me. A glum and bored expression on their faces as they visited the dentist would suddenly transform into an excited smile and instant joy if I told them that I was the husband of Grace. Their cold and nervous stares would suddenly brighten into big smiles when they thought of Grace and all of the fun activities they got to do with her at the clinic.

By marriage, I then suddenly grew in their regard, and they would be friendly and kind to me, if only for the sake of honoring her. I always likened Grace to being similar to a cruise director, planning all of the daily activities for various women, while I was only known to them as the guy with the needles. No wonder they liked her best.

The Bird Lady

One older woman she worked with quickly came to be known in our home as "the bird lady." She was a refugee from a war-torn country and came to our country with nothing except failing health and the ability to sew.

Grace often did art therapy and other creative activities with the women to bridge the barrier between East and West and build relationships with them. The Bird Lady initially would never want to participate in any of these events; she refused to join in with the other women. Slowly, over the weeks with nothing else tangible to do, she began to participate. Her creative juices started flowing for maybe the first time in her long life, and she quickly jumped into drawing, but everything she created was an absolute mess.

Many of the Bedouin women that Grace worked with had almost no basic eye-hand coordination in the use of tools. Many of them had never used scissors before and would hack away with uncontrolled zig-zags destroying hard-to-obtain colored paper from the capital city.

Otherwise, when trying to draw between the lines and fill out a child's simple coloring book, the result was often a disaster. I have seen many four and five-year-olds with more patience and skill in staying within the lines than these Bedouin women possessed. It was apparent they had never had an opportunity to develop these skills growing up and to just be kids.

They were called on at very early ages to shear sheep and milk goats and do the heavy labor of staying alive out in a hostile desert. Their dirt-crusted hands and tattooed faces revealed the history of a hard life without much free time for any pleasures and no opportunity for creative outlets.

Whatever age we usually guessed these women to be, on inquiring, we often found that they were ten to fifteen years younger than their appearance suggested. Desert life was difficult indeed and took a toll on their bodies.

As time went on with gentle instruction from Grace, many of these women developed a new love for the arts, and their faces would light up as their world became bigger and more colorful. The Bird Lady was no different; she slowly increased in skill and found that she loved drawing birds and sewing bird images more than anything else, hence the nickname that stuck to her. It didn't take long for her patient room to quickly get wall-papered over with all of her creative output, and we received several bird drawings and stitchings to take home.

Her husband was in appalling health as well, having Type-2 diabetes and uncontrolled sugar levels over 700 mg/dL when we met them. He started to get insulin and learned how to give himself injections, but his health did not improve dramatically.

They had a daughter Aida who became a friend. This relationship developed even though she was hostile toward Grace's faith and very afraid that her parents might, in weakness, start to believe.

There is a strong idea within Islam that a person can change faiths very quickly, just by whispering a quick confession, so we had to be careful about our interactions with people close to death. We didn't want others to think that we were sneaking in to get them to confess a rote Jesus statement at the last moment of their lives and seal them in as Christians before they died.

Their whole idea of faith itself is quite different than Christianity because there is an emphasis on the external confession and change in loyalty more than on a change in heart and mind, which was our primary concern.

Often to the Muslim, belonging to the group takes the emphasis over believing something particularly as an individual. When children are born, the father will quickly whisper in the baby's ear, the *shahada* or testimony of Islam, "*There is no God but God. Muhammad is the messenger of God.*"

It is vital that this statement is the first thing the baby will ever hear and puts them firmly in the Muslim community.

To the Muslim, everyone on Earth is born Muslim; it's just whether or not you will continue in that way or deny your natural faith and convert. Because faith in Islam is the default and requires almost no extra commitment on a person's part, I think this is why converting out of Islam is feared to be so easy.

I've had Muslim friends, looking out for my best interest, ask me to recite the *Shahada* with them. If I were to simply say those eleven words out loud, in their minds, I would instantly be Muslim, and they could put me in that box and know that even though I was outwardly Christian, I was now covered by the Muslim testimony on the last day.

I felt like had I done that, they would put up with my Christian faith and no longer listen to it, knowing that I was now genuinely a Muslim in their eyes and in the eyes of God.

This understanding of faith becomes transparent when you consider one of the fundamental Islamic missionary strategies. To expand Islam throughout the world, Muslims have often been financially supported to move to other countries, marry the women there, and have children. All those new children and families, by definition, will be Muslim. No part of the strategy concerns convincing people of the truth of Islam or instructing people in the Quran or Hadith.

This method is in stark contrast to Christianity, where Jesus taught us that while going and baptizing, *teach everyone to obey* all that He commanded us. In other words, make other disciples who not only know information, but who truly believe and submit to what Jesus taught with their whole lives in faith. It would be a pretty hard sell for Christians to raise support to go overseas and impregnate non-believers.

Toward the end of our time with the Bird Lady, Grace learned how very jaded Aida must have been when they were looking together at pictures on Aida's phone. Grace saw pictures of her husband dressed like an ISIS fighter. A lot of time, love, and knowledge was shared between Grace and the Bird Lady, but unfortunately, she passed away without us having much hope for her eternity. Once the mom had passed, Aida and her dad quickly returned to their home country, where we learned by social media, he also quickly succumbed to his diabetes.

Jameela

In the country where we were serving, the love and energy poured into people like the Bird Lady was often not returned or at least not revealed to bear much fruit. Still, we felt called to be salt and light where we were and to be obedient in sharing with people the love and hope we had in Jesus.

Ours was not the job of changing hearts—only God can do that—but of proclaiming the message of love that we knew. Still, it was great encouragement when you got to see God doing something right in front of you instead of wondering what the point of every effort was. Jameela was one of those hope-building interactions that Grace had along the way.

Jameela brought her dad to the clinic because his prolonged cough made them suspect he had a deeper disease, and everyone said ours was the place to go. They were called back to the small offices where they met a doctor. While they waited for the x-ray and sputum test results to come back, she picked up a small book, the *Injil*.

She knew the Quran said this is Holy Scripture, but she had never seen it herself. The doctor offered to pray for them, and they did not refuse—they felt they needed all the help they could get as refugees.

When the results came back, they were negative for her dad, but then the doctor asked if she herself had any problems. She mentioned to him the painful remains of her teeth, the result of being struck with a soldier's rifle butt as they were trying to leave their war-torn country. That was when they contacted me—he asked me to do a consultation and confided to me that she may be a good candidate for long-term treatment.

After examining her, I mentioned that if she could stay in our town for at least a month or so to get the remaining bony fragments and roots of teeth removed, I could make her a denture. She said it was probably the only chance she would have to get married since a marriage contract is often signed or denied based on a two-second look at a woman's face. Her dad agreed to it.

She roomed with some other women we knew and I began the process of getting her broken teeth out. Grace invited her to sewing class, and she loved to get together with her and sew. But, when it came to spiritual things, she did not want anything to do with it, and she told Grace she did not want to hear any more. Grace graciously complied.

Thankfully, the Jesus movie was playing in the dental office, and after several visits, she actually had watched the entire thing. One time when watching the part when Jesus was crucified, she teared up. She told me in the dental chair that it seemed so unnecessary that they would inflict that much cruelty upon Jesus.

Grace invited her to go to a women's Bible study, and finally, she began to attend. She suddenly got very interested and would even go back to read the big Holy Bible that she asked for to learn more about the passages they were studying.

One night, an older woman was teaching the study, and afterward, she grabbed her shirt and pulled her aside. She told her she was ready to follow Jesus, but since it was a different religion, she felt she probably wasn't allowed to start a new religion.

The teacher told her that the last thing she needed was a new religion, rather she needed a new relationship. She told her that following Jesus was about relationship, not duty. Jameela gave her heart to Jesus that night.

After her treatment concluded, and she tried out her new smile, she packed up and told everyone goodbye. She confided that she had originally thought that all the Christians she met were pretending to be nice to her, putting on a good face just to deceive her. After a month, she realized our behavior was genuine because we couldn't fake something like that for so long, and that realization had been a huge eye-opener for her.

She honestly didn't know what she was going to do now. She came with no plan to meet Jesus here, but she had, and He had changed her; now, she was really scared to go home.

We prayed for her and her family's salvation, and we prayed that the Spirit would let her live such a different life among them that she would earn an opportunity to share when they asked her what was so new about her.

Kino

Many of the women patients we saw at the clinic were factory workers from other countries who would come over and do the jobs that the nationals didn't want to do. The wages were low, but to these people, it was a lot of money, and they could send it back to their home country to provide for their parents or families.

One of these women that became a fixture in our lives was from Sri Lanka. When she arrived, she was thoroughly sick and clearly would have died without any treatment. In all, she stayed a very long time with us before she was healthy enough to leave.

She already claimed to be a Christian but had fairly weak faith and understanding. She and Grace bonded as she loved sewing and was extremely good in language. Kino learned Arabic while in the clinic and could then translate for other factory workers to the doctors and us.

Grace spent a lot of time discipling her, and a key part of that was encouraging her to share her faith. She held her faith very privately and quietly but at the same time, had a lot of giftings for knowledge, language, and networking, so she could have a big impact for God's kingdom.

She was very well connected with many of the other female patients and could play the guitar, which was certainly unusual for our area. As she readied herself to leave the clinic and return to her home country, Grace tried to encourage her to go out as a witness.

We stayed in touch with her through social media. A Korean worker was able to connect with her back home and bring some things to her and meet her in Sri Lanka. This relationship continues and has been a memorable one for Grace along with many other dear women she cared for along the way.

Chapter 12
DENTISTRY AT THE CLINIC

One of the tried and true stories that we often used in health teaching is the story Jesus told about the four friends and the paralyzed man from Luke 5:17. This paralyzed man and his friends have sincere faith in Jesus being able to heal. They really go to extremes digging through the roof and lowering their friend to the ground in front of Jesus. They know all his physical needs can be cured perfectly by a word from the Master's lips.

To the surprise of the onlookers, Jesus totally ignores this obvious outward need and forgives him of his sins instead—prompting the Pharisees to react strongly. It's only after this declaration of forgiving sins that Jesus goes ahead and heals him physically as well. This physical healing proves the legitimacy of the spiritual healing.

Physical or Spiritual?

We often met patients that know precisely what their needs are physically, but they are sometimes startled or reticent to hear about their real spiritual need. This story is an excellent example of the need for both types of healing and shows that Jesus is holistic; He doesn't neglect one for the other. Because of that principle, we can't act any differently as doctors who are trying to follow Him as we care for our patients.

Nicely, this narrative also begs the question about how Jesus has the authority to forgive sins. If all sin is against God, then claiming the right to forgive someone else's sin is to claim deity. This assertion of Jesus is a central question and truth we longed to share with our friends and patients.

Although we tried to focus our efforts on addressing both our patients' felt needs and spiritual needs, a lot of spiritual learning had to go on in our own hearts in the process. Sometimes the culture impacted the way we did our work, or occasionally our own sin was the biggest obstacle to carrying out our purpose. Regardless, God was good, and despite many crazy and interesting situations along the way, I think we were able to love many patients holistically at the clinic despite our human weaknesses.

The Dream Team

As I began to practice dentistry at the clinic, my personal limitations became very evident. I enjoyed the work I did and the interaction with people, but running a dental office also requires a lot of other skills and talents that I didn't have. It was often lonely working by myself, and for every patient I saw, which was very enjoyable, I spent at least that much time filling out paperwork, cleaning instruments, cataloging treatments, buying supplies, and other tasks.

Not to mention that I operated at a plodding pace without a dental assistant. I also hadn't cleaned teeth in years and had forgotten exactly which scalers to use where. As a result, treatments could take a long time, and if I needed to do a cleaning, I hated it. Honestly, the patients probably didn't get the good thorough care they deserved from a dental hygienist.

I remember a few colleagues told me I gave the most gentle and quickest cleanings they ever had. They meant it as a compliment, but I realized it was probably because I wasn't doing a great job and leaving some calculus (calcified dental plaque) on their teeth. All these facts pointed to the reality that I hurriedly needed to assemble a dental team.

God answered my prayers for a dental assistant very quickly when I met up with Max one morning for coffee. He had been recommended to me by a colleague, but he had no history of working in a dental office, let alone practicing as a dental assistant.

The meeting went well, and the coffee was tasty, and in the end, I offered him the job if he was interested. There wasn't exactly a long line of people waiting for that type of work, and it was a volunteer position as well, so I was thankful he was even interested. It ended up being one of the best decisions I ever made because Max became a gifted dental assistant and a very dear friend with whom to share the work of many years.

I was equally blessed by God to meet a compassionate and enthusiastic dental hygienist named Ruby soon afterward. A friend literally waved me over during their Skype call and said I should talk to this woman who had been evicted from another country and was looking for a place to serve.

We chatted for a while, and I liked her personality and passion, so I asked her to send me some more information. Based on our conversation and her *Curriculum Vitae*, I asked her to join Max and me on the dental team.

Finally, I would not have to do any more mediocre cleanings, and we added a talented female element to our dental team, which was very important in letting us practice on both men and women in the dental clinic.

Once the "dream team" was assembled and our capacity for serving patients was greatly expanded, we quickly came to find out that the culture and language were still going to impact the way we provided dental care for the patients. The mechanics of dental care would not change; a cleaning was still done the same way (much better by Ruby), and an amalgam (silver) filling was still an amalgam filling on the other side of the world. What does change is the interaction with patients versus the way we treat them in the West and the treatment plan we create for patients as we try to get them into a good state of oral health.

Jesus, D.D.S.

We had the luxury of not trying to make obscene profits or cover ridiculous overhead expenses as we practiced dentistry, so we got to relax and enjoy a healthy amount of dialogue with patients in the chair before and after any treatment that we might need to render. This investment of time helped us to get to know them and their backgrounds and to perform a thorough exam to understand all of their dental needs.

Many times in the West, we are simply too busy to spend this much time because the production needs to be high enough to cover our office costs. Thankfully, we found that labor and dental materials in the Middle East are often only a quarter of the Western costs.

I had already learned in my training that dental caries (cavities) were the most prevalent disease in the world. That sounds like an opportunistic line for a dentist to quote, but my time overseas certainly strengthened that premise.

People in the US are addressing dental needs with high-level dentistry like implants and orthodontics among those who can afford it down to extractions, dentures, and common fillings for even the poor. But in the Middle East, the level of care was abysmal and the dental needs were overwhelming.

There, no regulated presence of fluoride in the water exists for dental health. What the Centers for Disease Control has labeled as one of the most significant health breakthroughs in the twentieth century—fluoride in drinking water—was not helping the people I treated at all.

Equally essential and disastrous for people's health was the absence of the cultural ideas of prevention, which I previously addressed. People were always reacting to problems with their teeth when they were in great pain after decay had gone too far. They were never nipping things in the bud when the issue was small and quickly addressed.

Similar to patients in the West, many of my patients were frightened and nervous as they anticipated the sharp needle that might be required to remedy their problems. Often, seeing the condition of their teeth, I guessed they would indeed have to endure no small amount of pain and discomfort to get things back in a healthy state.

We understood and believed that a great way to address their anxiety and to provide them with the best blessing for their care was to pray for patients. In dentistry, we are often waiting for patients to get numb from the anesthetic, so we will go and work on another patient in a different treatment room or maybe leave and get a cup of coffee.

For us, we always used this downtime for Max, Ruby, or me to talk and ask people about spiritual or other needs they might have. It is true that for many people in that part of the world, the only chance they ever have to ask an open question about Christianity is in the privacy of a treatment chair. There, no one is eavesdropping, no one is suspicious, they are merely getting needed dental work done, and maybe a spiritual conversation happens in the process.

In our time praying with patients, almost none of them were Christians, but I would estimate that a good 90% of them would allow us to pray for them in Jesus' name. Looking back, I feel like these times were essential to cement the doctor-patient relationship, calm nerves, and, most importantly, open the door for the Holy Spirit to move in these people's lives. There was no doubt after these encounters that we were available for them in regards to both their dental and spiritual needs, and that was nice to have that clearly out in the open.

Regarding treatment plans that we created for patients, the bar was much lower than in the West. This difference was mainly related to patients' home care and income. While a painful and deeply decayed tooth might regularly be treatment planned for a root canal and a crown back home, we often needed to extract teeth like that after consultation with the patient.

True, a procedure like that in the US might cost $2000, while it was only $200 in the Middle East. But in our neighborhood, people were often making $400 per month. Moreover, a tooth with a root canal treatment might be a good investment in the US, but I quickly realized that in the absence of home dental care, most dental treatment lifespans radically decreased.

A study in our town showed that only 50% of people even owned a toothbrush, and most of those were shared by entire families! A survey we conducted ourselves among our patients revealed very similar results.

I had been to several impoverished countries providing dental care in the past. I had always felt good about placing white composite and glass ionomer fillings because when I left a week later I had never seen any problems with them. It was a geographically successful treatment you might say.

Now, living long-term with the people I was serving, I was able to follow up on my work over the years in areas where there were low levels of hygiene. It's just anecdotal, but while a white composite filling might hold up for ten or fifteen years in the US, the same filling would only last two to four years where we were serving.

These white fillings slightly constrict over time, which gives a placeholder for invasive bacteria to infiltrate and restart decay. It might not be long before the person is complaining about pain in the same place that was treated a few years ago.

Silver or amalgam fillings, despite some negative anecdotal stories back home, look really good after examining the research. Thankfully, they put up very well with lower levels of hygiene and stand the test of time because they slightly expand (or creep) as they age, sealing out harmful bacteria. These can easily last twenty-five years and were my preference if it was in a non-esthetic area where they could be placed.

I figured if I was doing this work to glorify God, I wanted to do it in a way that would bring the patient the greatest relief from their dental problems for the longest time. Otherwise, two years later they might find themselves in pain again and remember that their tooth had been treated by that Christian dentist who put in a filling that didn't last. Being privileged to be Jesus' hands and feet among these people required that my work be done with as much excellence as I could render.

The Language of Tooth Doctoring

Before I give the illusion that we functioned like a cleanly operating machine, it should be clear that my dental team and I probably made about every mistake along the way until we found our groove. These were language mistakes, as well as cultural mistakes.

For one, in the US, I think it's pretty common to comfort patients by saying something along the lines of, "I'm sorry if that stung a little" or maybe even, "I'm sorry you got dry socket" if a patient came back in after a complicated wisdom tooth extraction.

The problem I found with that apologetic language is that it admits fault and doesn't convey compassion when used in the Middle East.

So, if you comfort a patient at all by saying *asif*, "I'm sorry," you're actually communicating to them that you did something wrong to cause it. Instead of sympathetically comforting patients about their dry sockets, I was confessing to them that I had done something wrong that caused it! This sentiment was not the type of communication we wanted.

Simple instructions to patients also took time to figure out. One time, I was treating a Christian woman who had tutored me in Arabic, working on a tooth far back in the upper arch. It was hard to see and hard on my back, so I told her I needed to lower her head a bit more to complete the filling.

She exclaimed, "Dr. Adam, I hope you don't normally say that. Never tell a patient that you will lower her head!"

I had been saying that for a long time actually and who knows how many patients I offended by telling them I would "lower their head." At least I always told them I would "raise their head" too when it was all over.

After that interaction, I simply described every body movement by referring to the dental chair, i.e., "I need to lower your chair," and everyone seemed happy.

On a lighter note, we did have quite a bit of fun switching around Arabic words with English words when talking to other Western volunteers. Fortuitously, the Arabic word for a tooth is *sin*, and the word for filling is *heshua*, which sounds a lot like Jesus' Arabic name "*Yesua.*"

This similarity led to a lot of fun double entendre discussions about dealing with people's *sin* or removing decay and giving them *Yesua*. Our claim to fame was that we were the only department that literally removed *sin* from people as we followed our motto of "Giving the Bedouin a Reason to Smile."

As I mentioned before, we tried to emphasize praying with every patient that walked through our door who wanted prayer. However, the simple act of asking a patient if they wanted to pray was one of the hardest things we ever had to communicate. Only a minority of patients didn't want to pray, but in their shame/honor culture, they could never say that directly to a doctor or person helping them.

Many times I would mention a short story from the Gospels or discuss the power that Jesus' name had over disease or demons and then inquire if I could pray for their illness in that same power. The person who didn't want to pray would then say, "I don't understand; explain that again." At that point, I would know that either they didn't really want to pray but couldn't say that or possibly they really didn't understand the question and might want to pray.

I wouldn't know for sure, so I was inclined to explain it again in a more straightforward way or alternate manner. After finishing my second explanation and inquiry, hopefully, the person would consent.

However, if the patient didn't want prayer, they would generally do one of two things. Either they would thank me for my kindness and care and tell me they were now numb and ready for the treatment, ignoring the question altogether. Or, they would turn to my dental assistant Max and ask, "Do you know what he's talking about?" and play dumb. Either way, in that situation, I would finally know they didn't want to pray.

Many of the patients who wanted to pray had a hard time understanding the circumstances of how to pray initially. I imagine having a Christian ask you to pray would be somewhat surprising anyway in that cultural context, but if you consider the differences between Muslim prayer and Christian prayer in practice and language, it really gets complicated.

In Arabic, there are two keywords used to describe prayer on a daily basis. The first word, *salah*, denotes prayer in general but has different connotations between Muslims and Christians. To the Muslim, the *salah* prayer necessarily would make them think of reciting memorized prayers in the mosque or at home, completing their multiple *rakats* on their prayer mat.

To the Christian, *salah* is just the simple word for prayer in general, whether it is memorized or extemporaneous in church or at home.

Having been in a church and hearing it said many times, I made some early mistakes of asking patients if they would like me to *salah* for them or with them. One gentleman agreed, quickly got out of the chair and walked out the door. Looking behind him, he asked if I was coming, and I realized I had inadvertently invited him to go with me to the mosque to make *salah* prayer.

After several mistakes and strange looks using the *salah* language, we quickly turned to using the other word for prayer, *dua'*. *Dua'* prayer is not something you usually hear used among Christians, although they would certainly recognize it. But for Muslims, it is the prayer of supplication or appeal that often can come following completion of *salah* in the mosque or any other time during the day.

Because this prayer does not have to be made at a specific time or location, it was a better descriptor of the type of prayer we were offering to patients. *Dua'* prayer is really a cry of the heart and an extemporaneous appeal to receive help from God with your circumstances.

After years of praying *dua'* with patients, I realized that one of the most significant differences between Islamic and Christian prayer is between these two types. Christians, at least in my protestant tradition, pray in the *dua'* style 90% of the time, while reciting a prayer or liturgy 10% of the time.

Muslims are exactly the opposite. Most of their prayer time is consumed with reciting memorized prayers over and over. If they make *dua'* prayer at all, it does not seem to occupy much of their time or prayer bandwidth.

Praying *dua'* prayer as they do with eyes opened and hands raised was a special privilege we enjoyed with many of our Muslim patients. God honestly already knows our needs before we ask, but it reminds us of our need for God and dependence on Him for life, health, and everything else. Using Jesus' name is truly powerful and has often been the most important thing we ever provided for our patients in combating the challenges in their bodies and their lives.

Coals on Top of Your Head

Handling the needs of a wide variety of dental patients that you couldn't hand-pick led to a lot of joy overall, but sometimes it was very challenging for the heart as well.

I previously mentioned that we moved out of our rented house in Manara with the tamarisk tree because the owners returned from the US to take up residence in the Middle East again. What I didn't describe then was the terrible ending we had with those landlords who demanded around $3000 of made-up damages after we had moved out, leaving it spotless by Western standards.

We had freshly painted many rooms and had replaced both of the broken bathroom vanities and mirrors that they had left us with new. I had landscaped the entire yard as well as planting many trees and installing an irrigation system. We wanted to leave it better than we found it and be a blessing to this family as they returned to the Middle East. We were also planning to help the wife, in particular, transition back to living there because we knew her husband was often away for work and we wanted to be a friend.

Sadly that didn't work as I received an unexpected call from the wife late one night after they arrived. I couldn't believe she called me directly and not through her husband. She was cursing me and calling me a thief and liar, and I couldn't figure out what was going on. I tried to talk nicely to her, but she couldn't control her rage and I finally just hung up the phone as she was in full scream and I was in a quandary as to what in the world had happened.

The next day, as I went over to talk with the husband to find out what they were upset about, I quickly found that the demands were not coming directly from him as much as it was the result of his wife. She was demanding that he rip out all of the toilets and sinks and repaint the whole house because we had damaged everything. The husband, with frustration, told me that he had already spent thousands replacing other random items. However, I knew there was not any problem with any of those things when we left.

We were a bit broken-hearted, expecting to receive a kind thank you from them when they saw the excellent state of the house we left behind and instead were crushed to be the target of screaming and cursing.

Finishing up my discussion with him and heading out, she revealed herself finally, peeking out of the kitchen door. She began yelling, calling me a thief and an infidel and accusing me of stealing her prayer rug and refrigerator. She told me I'd go to hell, and they soon were going to put a report in to the police about me so that it would freeze any travel out of the country until I paid everything in full.

It didn't help to point out to her the refrigerator sitting right there in the kitchen, as it was more about emotion than reasoning at that point. Even her husband and son were apologizing to me for the way she was screaming and insulting me. I still, to this day, have never been talked to that badly by anyone in my entire life.

I asked an older Arab friend to help me with the situation, and he quickly intervened and agreed to meet with us all together. After meeting with the landlord, he said that a lot of women, when they are threatened with their husband taking a second wife, try to bankrupt them. The woman's goal is for the husband not to have any remaining funds available to pay for a second wedding, which is relatively pricey.

As long as she can keep him paycheck to paycheck, he will never have the ability to get a second bride, so my friend thought this was a classic case of her trying to prevent this outcome. She was putting a lot of pressure on him to rip everything out and spend all of his money replacing everything needlessly, and he, in turn, was trying not to lose all his money by putting pressure on us to pay him money in damages for problems we didn't cause.

That made sense, but still didn't make me feel better about the situation and how personal it had become. My Arab friend confirmed that the landlord had threatened him as well that I was going to be placed on a police travel ban until I paid everything in full.

My Arab friend said that the other problem was that we were a ripe target for this type of extortion because we were not part of a tribe. This landlord wouldn't dare extort money like this from another Arab because their tribe would get involved and put pressure on his tribe. Attacking foreigners in this way led to no such worries.

My friend told me to give him a day, and he'd take care of it. Right there, he pulled out his phone and began to make calls to members of the landlord's family. When it was all done, he had talked to two or three members of the landlord's tribe that he knew and explained to them how the landlord was unfairly demanding money from a foreigner who came all the way to the Middle East to treat their townspeople for free.

He asked them if this is how we Arabs are supposed to repay those who care for us in such a way. Basically, he was playing the shame game and spreading the word throughout this tribe to get the pressure put back on the landlord. It didn't take too long as a few days later, we were notified by the landlord that he was backing off most of the complaints and just agreed to take a small damage deposit as a compromise.

We took the deal and were amazed yet again by how the tribal system worked and how different this culture was from ours. I would have never thought to start calling the relatives of a man with whom I was having a dispute.

We were thankful that this experience was not one that happened to many of our friends or even to us again, but was an unfortunate end to this particular rental arrangement.

It was no little surprise, therefore, when I saw the landlord's wife a few months later walk into my dental clinic holding the hand of her nephew. I froze at the sight because I thought I would surely never see her again and thought she had some kind of nerve to come in here and ask for help after the way she had treated me.

She had caused me many sleepless nights as we had gone through the process of dealing with their complaints and worrying about the police issue regarding their rental house. But somehow, the Spirit calmed my heart and reminded me of truth from Scripture, and I was able to remain relatively calm, remembering whose I was.

Romans 12:21 says, "if your enemy is hungry, feed him; if he is thirsty, give him something to drink; for by so doing, you will heap burning coals on his head." I received supernatural help to help me internalize this teaching, and it was enough to help my heart welcome them for the sake of her nephew, who had a painful tooth.

She didn't say much the whole time, and I completed my treatment of her nephew as she sat by herself in the reception room with her head down, avoiding any chance to look into my eyes in the treatment room. As they left, I found out that her husband had returned to the US after only two months, leaving her with her four young kids to raise by herself. She never apologized for anything—that elephant remained hauntingly in the room—but she did thank me for helping her nephew and departed quickly with him tightly in hand.

I'm not exactly sure what the best explanation of "heaping burning coals on his head" would be in this instance. In the Middle East, we often accept blame or responsibility by saying, *Ala rasi*, which means "It's on my head." So, in that sense, it would be placing blame or shame on the person by absorbing their curse at you and returning a blessing.

C.E.B. Cranfield, in his classic commentary on Romans 12, agrees in saying, "by thus ministering to one's enemy's need one will inflict upon him such an inward sense of shame as will either lead him to real contrition… or else, if he refuses to be reconciled, will remain with him as the pain of a bad conscience."

The Israelis Strike Again

Other dental visits and experiences were more light-hearted than that one but equally challenging towards developing the virtue of patience in my life. One denture patient in particular, a man named Gazi, was so excited about getting his first set of dentures. He only had a couple of wind-blown front teeth remaining, which I had to extract and give time for healing. He just couldn't wait as we went through the process of making impressions of his mouth, recording his bite, trying in his new teeth, and finally delivering the final dentures to him.

I kept telling him throughout the whole process that dentures are terribly hard to get used to, and he wouldn't be able to eat with them very quickly at first. I was pretty concerned with how excited he was getting because I always think dentures will be extremely disappointing for people, especially your first set after having real teeth. However, he still had a broad toothless grin across his face every time he saw me.

Finally, the big day arrived, and he received his dentures the way a small child heads to the Christmas tree on Christmas morning. He was bubbling. I adjusted them, and they fit reasonably well, and he was still excited, although a few times, his lower denture popped up, and I could measure some concern on his face.

I told him to expect some sore spots and to come back over the next days, and I could adjust them. I exhorted him not to wear them all of the time because now his teeth were like the stars, they always come out at night.

As Gazi started to come in day after day, he began complaining, not just about typical sore spots, but about how the dentures felt and worked.

He couldn't bite into hard things as he used to, and the lower denture just moved around back and forth.

These were the exact things I had warned him about before he got them, but he just insisted that I had made him a lousy denture. Apparently, a properly-made denture would stick in his mouth like implants and let him eat steak and bite into apples easily like he previously did with his natural teeth.

At that point, he started asking me to make him another set, which I, unfortunately, had to refuse. It was actually clinic policy only to make each patient one set of dentures during their time of treatment.

I find that some patients will deal with adapting to dentures and do well with low expectations, and others will never entirely accept them— he was definitely in the latter group. Aside from the policy, I knew in my heart I couldn't make him a new denture that would fit any better than this one he already had.

Every time I saw him around the clinic, he would point to his mouth and say, "New denture?" and I would quickly nod my head back and forth in annoyance. He tried to wear me down or even shame me by having other doctors call me and ask me if I would make him a denture, but my Western mind resisted these efforts of shaming, and I persisted in my denials.

This bargaining happened for at least a month until one day, he strutted into my dental clinic, holding his lower denture in his hand. I looked at the denture resting on the palm of his hand and observed it had broken in half. He told me he was so very sorry, but his denture had fallen out of his mouth while he was crossing the road.

According to him, we all knew it wasn't a suitable denture anyway, and after it fell out of his mouth onto the street, a car had run over it, breaking it in half. Now the only thing I could do was make him a completely new one. He almost had a twinkle in his eye as he told me his bad news.

I told him to leave it with me, and by the end of the day, I had repaired it and called him up to get it. He was crestfallen as he saw the denture again wholly restored to its original, pristine condition because I don't think he ever had really worn it. It fit very well, and he was surprised I could fix it like this after breaking into two pieces. Shortly after this repair, Gazi was discharged from the clinic and returned to his country, disappointing denture in hand.

That wasn't the last I saw of Gazi, because almost a year later, he returned to the clinic for several months for some follow-up care. He came into my dental clinic one of the first days he was there, and I quickly witnessed that he didn't have any dentures in his mouth.

Gazi told me that he was so sorry, but he had been visiting inside a school one day back home, and he had taken his dentures out and put them on a table in the school.

At that moment, he explained, the Israelis had launched a missile strike at the children's school to blow it up.

He had run out of the school and barely escaped with his life, but sadly the dentures I had made him had been blown to smithereens, collateral damage from an Israeli Delilah missile strike.

I looked into Gazi's dark brown eyes as he stood quietly, waiting to see my response. He was here in a new year and on a new visit, and I told him I'd be happy to make him a new set of dentures. I'd had a long respite from his daily demands at that point, and I have to admit that the creativity of the story alone had won me over. It's still the best dental excuse I've ever heard.

One of the drivers for the dental team also helped in my sanctification. He was always late, but no matter what, he would say he was only five minutes away.

One time, I called him as the entire dental team with guests was waiting on him so that we could do some community dental work in a village. Not surprisingly, he told me he needed five more minutes.

Fifteen minutes later, I called him again, and he was still at home, but he insisted he would be with us in five more minutes.

Finally, he showed up some 45 minutes late. We quizzed him about why he would keep lying to us like that. He was supposed to be a Christian, and we expected him to be on time, but at the least, to be honest.

I asked him, "When you told me five more minutes, did you know you were lying?"

He responded, "Of course I knew, I hadn't even taken a shower yet at that point, and I needed to shower and eat breakfast."

"Well, why didn't you just tell me you were going to be 45 minutes late? Then we could have all gone and done other things instead of just standing by the road waiting for you!"

He coolly responded, "Dr. Adam, you wanted me there on time, didn't you?"

147

"Of course," I replied.

"Dr. Adam, I respect you so much that I am even willing to lie for you. That's why I said I would be there in five minutes."

I had found out in that encounter that the honor/shame culture was potent even among Christians, and they sometimes valued that even above telling the truth.

I didn't get to experience too many things on the medical side, but I'll never forget Dr. Ley one time commiserating with me about the frustration of understanding the culture with regards to medical and dental care.

He was one day trying to do an ultrasound on a little kid who wouldn't stop crying. This little boy had been brought in by his mom, who was wearing a black *niqab* that thoroughly covered her body from head to toe, only revealing her eyes through a small slit in the front of her veil. Because the boy wouldn't hold still at all, Dr. Ley was about to give up trying to conduct the ultrasound.

Understanding his body language, in a flurry, this *niqab*-dressed woman suddenly whipped out her entire breast and stuffed it into the mouth of this toddler. The kid was instantly satisfied with milk, and Dr. Ley was able then to thoroughly conduct the ultrasound and get a proper diagnosis.

When they left, we realized that no one had seen the face of the mom, but everyone had acquired an excellent display of her breast, and this was deemed entirely appropriate in the culture.

Was the breast merely a medical device at that moment? Apparently, it wasn't considered to be sexual during breastfeeding, or we certainly would have been "seduced" by her, which was not allowed.

We were never sure, but we continued to be surprised by different instances like this one, which would make us rethink how much we really understood the culture.

How Much Land Does a Man Require?

It was a Thursday, and I went down to the dental clinic to treat a long list of patients for the clinic. One patient, I remember in particular that day was a Sudanese man. This frail man eagerly desired to see me to have a filling in one of his front teeth, which greatly bothered him.

As I escorted him to the dental clinic, one of the nurses whispered to me that the doctors felt his AIDS would probably kill him in the next week or two, so don't do anything unnecessary. Even this whole dental visit was unnecessary, they said, but he had eagerly requested the appointment, so they brought him, and I took him.

Tolstoy wrote a fabulous short story, *How Much Land Does a Man Require*, in which he cleverly reminds his readers how much property is ideal to have. It doesn't matter if a man or woman accumulates a great farm or a considerable plantation or vast acres of timber or enormous swaths of the prairie. In the end, the only amount of land we need is about six feet worth. Enough to dig a hole to place your coffin because all the rest you've gathered will simply stay behind.

It's good for us to contemplate our own demise like this story forces us because that helps put everything in focus. We can best see the essential things we should aim our lives and our work at in light of what will be left at the end. In the end, the only thing that endures is relationships, because the only eternal things we deal with are God and the people He has created.

The realization hit me that it really didn't matter how good my filling was or how long it lasted—what would last is how I could love him, share with him, and the way I cared for him. I prayed with him, talked with him about why I was there, and placed an esthetic filling on that front tooth that made him very happy as he reflected on it looking in the hand mirror.

In the end, the filling only lasted two weeks, but that was long enough. He had heard the gospel countless times, but sadly to my knowledge, we're not aware of him ever following Christ before he passed away.

This experience reminded me of the reality I have with all my patients, that they are all dying men and women. Even while loving them through excellent dental care is paramount—that work will always reach its end, but the love of Jesus will not. We must continue to press on and share that eternal hope.

Chapter 13
SICKNESS UNTO ... LIFE?

We all know consequences from the fall of humankind that ultimately were redeemed in some form or another. For instance, we may look at murder or suicide which indeed never occurred before our first parents sinned and likely we can all recount stories of how God has taken some sinful situations like these and brought resurrection or rebirth out of them.

As we are all intuitively aware, the same is true of sickness and disease. I imagine bacteria and viruses were swell chaps before the fall happened, working in perfect harmony with the human body as well as other creatures dwelling on the Earth. Now, post-fall, they are transformed in our consciousness into entities that only evoke fear and pain and death.

Thankfully, although infirmity and death abound in our world today, God is not constrained to work only through pleasant things but even through these bitter things in our lives.

I don't want to go too deep theologically with this example, but we may look at the outside of something like an orange and only imagine the bitterness of the peel that we see on the surface, but nothing is too broken or unredeemable for our God. He can redeem us from the external bitterness of any given situation and in fact, bring fruit into our lives from it. He does that by first taking that bitterness on Himself.

Dorothy Sayers explained it well when she alluded to God being like a physician, who doesn't just offer us the bitter tonic of medicine that will cure us of our disease, but, "He had the honesty and the courage to take His own medicine."

God never just expected us to hurt and suffer alone, but being a loving creator, He first drank deeply of the bitter medicine Himself before offering us the cup. And consequently, He is making all of the bad things come untrue, including disease.

When I moved to the Middle East, I thought I had a relatively robust understanding of the place of medicine and dentistry in God's kingdom work. Over the years, I found that I kept getting challenged with people and needs and brokenness in ways I had never been challenged back home.

These experiences certainly had the cumulative effect of making me look at sickness and disease differently. It made me step back a bit and reconsider my meta-understanding of where and how the medicine of missions fits in, so I'll try to unpack a few of those issues here.

Sickness Through Jesus' Eyes

Thanks to Tim Keller and other Bible teachers over the years, I think I had a useful framework for understanding the brokenness that came from the curse mentioned in Genesis 3. You could say that four overlying circles of relationship were broken on that day as depravity took hold.

Initially, a theological break happened in the inner circle between man and God. That intimate relationship was broken and humankind now cowered before its creator.

Further, an ontological break occurred in man himself as his rationality and psychology left perfection. We see the results today in all things from illogical arguments to school shootings.

Next, a break ripped apart a larger circle that connects humans in relationship to each other. Marriages, friendships, and family relations have suffered ever since. Adam blamed Eve, and Cain murdered Abel; and it has continued unabated.

Last, even the biggest circle relationship between humanity and the entire creation broke apart. We are often at odds with the creation for which we were designed to care; from the weeds in the garden to pneumonia in the hospital, there are so many things wrong in our world that are a result of Adam and Eve's sin. It's certainly not the way it was supposed to be.

Despite these woes, the good news is that they will be eradicated at Jesus' return. Revelation 21 tells us, "there will be no more death or mourning or crying or pain."

Naturally, we in healthcare will be out of a job. Until that day, medicine and dentistry intersect well with the outer circle of brokenness; some fields even try to take on the mental and interpersonal brokenness. I am convinced that altogether they are a premier way of bringing God's kingdom into this world in a real, tangible way.

As Christian healthcare professionals, we can daily address these felt needs that our neighbors and friends have. But being Christians, we also necessarily should be the most holistic practitioners in approach, because we acknowledge the underlying brokenness that exists in all of our patients' hearts, separating them from their creator.

If that core imbalance is not addressed, then we know we may have eased our patient's physical symptoms for a while, but we have not taken aim at all the circles of brokenness to make them whole again. If we believe the Scripture, then clearly Jesus teaches that the physical is intimately connected to the spiritual realm.

In Luke 13:11-16, Jesus heals a woman who had a "disabling spirit." After telling us about this spiritual problem, the passage explains she was bent over with a physical challenge and could not straighten herself.

Jesus laid hands on her, and she straightened up and was freed from her disability. He then explains to the crowd that she had been "Satan bound for eighteen years." Jesus seems to drift back and forth between the spiritual and physical without any pause.

But this description is undoubtedly just superstition written by an unlearned fisherman, right? No, this passage is actually found in the writings of Luke, a physician himself who often goes to great lengths to investigate and explore details and medical nuances of Jesus' life and ministry.

My neighbors in the Middle East, like Jesus, would naturally assume the link between spirits and illness. Sometimes my wife and I would see their young kids sick and would ask them what illness they had. More often than not, they would tell us that they had fallen asleep during the jinn hour and were sick because of the jinn.

The jinn hour was between 2 and 3 PM, and you would never see any kids outside of the houses during this time. Even if you did stay home, apparently you should not fall asleep or the jinn would come and make you sick.

It was just assumed that if someone got ill, there was a prima facie spiritual reason to blame. For ourselves and our medical colleagues back

SICKNESS UNTO … LIFE?

home, this diagnosis seems ridiculous, but when we look to the Scriptures, we see this challenging perspective spelled out over and over.

Another distinction Jesus and the disciples often make is to connect disease with an opportunity for repentance and the growing of our faith. In James 5:14-16, the brother of Jesus completely mixes these two categories when he inquires,

> *Is anyone among you sick? Let them call the elders of the church to pray over them and anoint them with oil in the name of the Lord. And the prayer offered in faith will make the sick person well; the Lord will raise them up. If they have sinned, they will be forgiven. Therefore confess your sins to each other and pray for each other so that you may be healed. The prayer of a righteous person is powerful and effective.*

Confessing our sins to each other may not be the first thing we naturally do when we are sick, but we are encouraged to do just that. Sickness here is seen as an opportunity to draw close to God and examine our hearts for any secret sin or wrongdoing that might lie there unexposed to our consciences. We might not find any hidden sin in our lives as we look deep during a time of illness, but we certainly shouldn't miss the opportunity it affords us.

We are also called to invite leaders in our fellowship to pray for us and "anoint us with oil." While this seems like a wholly spiritual connection to illness as well, in another light, it may genuinely be mixing the physical needs with the spiritual.

Xpeo is the common Greek word used to describe anointing in the context of worship and that word is not used here. Instead, *aleipho* is used, which has more of a connotation connected to anointing someone as medical treatment.

If you remember in the parable of the Good Samaritan, he "binds the man's wounds with oil." In that time, there was a connection between oil, anointing, and healing, and this is the sense we get from *aleipho*. We don't know if elders carried around a first aid kit, but it makes me suspect they were practicing some primary medical treatment in combination with their prayers for the sick.

When our categories of spiritual and physical needs get intertwined so clearly in something as nasty as disease, it reveals that God is bringing good even out of these terrible circumstances. Jesus told His listeners that when the Tower of Siloam fell, it occurred not because the people in it were evil, but as a general call to repentance. Likewise, the sicknesses we deal with in our lives are often pointed reminders of our sinfulness and his willingness to forgive us if we just turn to him.

One of our most memorable patients at the clinic was a woman who had been admitted for diabetes. She did not want to stay there at all; she just wanted to get her insulin and be discharged back into the desert. But we had enough experience to know that this plan wouldn't work because uneducated people need hands-on training to be able to check their glucose and administer the correct doses of insulin. Otherwise, they will show back up with worse problems the next time after they overdosed or underdosed themselves.

After some days passed and she was getting the hang of checking her blood and giving herself injections, her attitude was completely transformed. She was very excited to be there and began to listen to the Gospels and learn for the first time about Jesus and the forgiveness He offered.

I'll never forget hearing her call out when it was time for her to be finally discharged, "I thank God for my diabetes! I thank God for my diabetes!" She grabbed us and told everyone that would listen that had she never gotten sick, she would have never had the opportunity to hear the gospel and follow Jesus, and she was the most grateful patient for her disease.

There are countless other facets of disease that I think would shatter our expectations, but one much repeated in the Gospels is that our illness can be for the glory of God. I should clarify a bit. Does God have to work something good out of all our sicknesses? I would answer a resounding "no!" to that question.

I went to a conference during my time there where the speaker stated, "If a good God allows suffering, it has to be for the sake of a benefit that outweighs the suffering or He is no longer a good God." I wrote the quote down because it felt immediately wrong to me, but I needed some time to think about exactly why.

The reason this idea is rubbish is that it sweeps under the rug the initial cause of suffering and lays it all at God's feet. As I mentioned earlier, all suffering and death is a result of our sin which broke up the circles of relationship. God certainly can act this way in bringing good out of bad circumstances, but He doesn't have to. Otherwise, we are placing ourselves in the position of putting God on trial, when we are actually the criminals.

I love Elisabeth Elliot's sentiments in *Through Gates of Splendor* when she recounts the aftermath of her husband's death in the jungles of Ecuador. She recalls how many people told her during her grieving that she shouldn't worry because God was surely going to do something great out of this tragedy; her husband Jim didn't die for nothing.

She began to really resent this line of thought and would rebuke people because she knew that whether God did something amazing afterward, or whether nothing positive ever came after this tragedy, God was still good and He would be glorified either way. If God wanted to be glorified by Jim's inglorious death, that was up to Him.

As it played out, some amazing things did occur because of the martyrdom of Jim Elliot and his four friends, and often, that is also what we happily see in Scripture.

John 9:1-5 describes a man born blind and paradoxically states that "this happened that the works of God might be displayed in him." After a lifetime of suffering from blindness, this man glorifies God with his broken body as Jesus opens his eyes and makes him whole again.

Soon after, in chapter 11, verses three and four, the sisters of Lazarus approach Jesus and press Him to come, pleading that their brother is near death. When Jesus hears their request, He says, "This illness does not lead to death. It is for the glory of God, so that the Son of God may be glorified through it."

Shortly after that, we learn this illness did in fact lead to Lazarus' temporary death, but also one of the most astounding miracles as Jesus raised him from the dead. The Son of Man was glorified, and death did not hold Lazarus, at least at that point in time. Jesus' perspective is the long perspective, and I think Him stating "this illness does not lead to death," sums up a lot of the understanding a Christian healthcare worker must have as we interact with our patients.

Praying for the Sick in Jesus' Name

In addition to a biblical perspective on disease overall, a biblical understanding of prayer for healing is also critical for the Christian healthcare worker as well as the individual Christian.

In past years, colleagues trained in the West would simply deride the idea that prayer has any place in the practice of the healing arts. Any data supporting that notion would be dismissed as a placebo effect or some psychological persuasion or hypnotism. However, study after study out of Duke University has concluded that the patients who receive prayer with their treatment are undoubtedly receiving better outcomes. Patients who are prayed for by their doctors, dentists and healthcare providers get statistically more significant results time and time again. Nevertheless, the praxis of doctors is not becoming more inclusive towards prayer even among those who are Christians.

The importance of healing prayer should not be surprising to the Christian, especially in light of Jesus' healings and even the James 5 passage already discussed. Still, it is critical to distinguish between types of healing prayer, because the Scriptures seem to make a distinction as well between prayer for yourself as an individual and prayer for others corporately.

An individual mandate towards prayer is really the focus of the James 5 passage as he encourages the sick to go to God directly with their needs for healing and also to "drum up" prayer partners to help as it were. The impetus is clearly on the sick person in that situation to take the action.

The Old Testament gives us a first example of an individual's responsibility when it discusses the life of King Asa in 1 Kings 15:14. Clearly, Asa was seen to be a godly ruler as we learn, " ... the heart of Asa was wholly true to the Lord all his days." Yet, at the end of his life, like many of the kings, his heart shifted somewhat. When he was dealing with illness, God was not the priority for his healing.

2 Chronicles 16:12 gives us the sad account,

> *In the thirty-ninth year of his reign Asa was diseased in his feet, and his disease became severe. Yet even in his disease he did not seek the Lord, but sought help from*

SICKNESS UNTO ... LIFE?

physicians. And Asa slept with his fathers, dying in the forty-first year of his reign.

In contrast to seeking God, he actually did something terrible. He went to the doctor first! I see a lot of sweet Bible verses often hanging up on the exam rooms of Christian doctors I visit, but I have to admit I've never seen this passage on any of those walls!

King Hezekiah gives us a contrasting response as recorded in Isaiah 38:16-17. When he is deathly sick, he turns to the Lord with prayers for healing and even sees a benefit from his experience with illness.

O Lord, by these things men live, and in all these is the life of my spirit. Oh restore me to health and make me live! Behold, it was for my welfare that I had great bitterness; but in love, you have delivered my life from the pit of destruction, for you have cast all my sins behind your back.

Hezekiah turns to the Lord first for his healing and even has the big picture perspective that God had done something positive out of the negative experience of disease. For this attitude he is praised and considered one of the very best kings of Judah.

If an individual Christian seeks medical help or advice from us, these passages seem to indicate we are doing them a disservice if we do not redirect them back to the Lord in some way and include prayer in that process. Otherwise, we are complicit like Asa's doctors in condoning the false narrative that all their health needs can be fully met in the profession of the healers.

How we serve our patients can be a bedside prayer, a reading of some meaningful verses, or a challenge to seek the Lord in confession. Regardless, our medicine must be holistic, involving the spiritual with the physical if we want it to be beneficial to our patients and biblical.

During our tenure we observed many miraculous answers to prayer with our patients. One of our doctors would pray boldly in Jesus' name for people who requested prayer. Following the prayer he would often ask if they were now better and sometimes the ailment was completely gone at that instant. It was a reminder to me to pray in faith and not with doubts.

More often we saw answers to long persistent prayers on behalf of our patients and families. These long-sought answers reminded us we had to pray and persevere like the widow persisted with the unjust judge in one of Jesus' parables.

While James stresses the individual role, it indirectly suggests a corporate role for healing prayer when it suggests elders praying for the sick is a godly endeavor. This idea is assumed as it seems like prayer circles are often spending 70-80% of their time petitioning God about someone's sickness, injury or health concern.

This assumption got strongly challenged for a season while we were working at the clinic. My good friend Job, who is actually responsible for a lot of my changed thinking on these issues, surprised us with a challenge to prove from Scripture that we are supposed to pray for the sick.

We were at that point praying every Thursday for all our patients by name to get better and felt like we saw a lot of good results from that. On the other hand, the patients that did struggle with chronic disease were encountering the gospel more times because of their longer therapy, and many of them were understanding God's love for the first time.

So, he questioned as the devil's advocate, when we pray for their quick healing, could we possibly be doing the wrong thing? Like the one patient who told us, "I thank God for my diabetes," it is possible that their illness is the best thing that could happen to them because it was extending their opportunity for repentance. Should we keep praying for quick healing of these sick and possibly rob them of God's blessing?

Well, at first the answer to these questions seemed obvious—of course, we should pray for them! But he chided us and asked us for verses that supported that idea, and we assured him we would get back to him with plenty to support the argument.

The truth is that as I personally pored over Scripture, I was starting to sweat a little bit because I couldn't find any direct imperative or teaching that said to pray corporately or even individually for other sick people. There was James 5, but I knew Job asserted that passage emphasized the individual praying for their own infirmity.

3 John 2 was a relief to finally find when John says, "Dear friend, I pray that you may enjoy good health and that all may go well with you, even as your soul is getting along well." Job bristled on hearing me quote that verse. However, he admitted I had something, while I had to admit it was a little weaker than I hoped.

I also found Mark 9:28-29, which talks about Jesus' disciples failing to cast out a demon. They asked Jesus why they couldn't drive it out, and he told them that "this kind can come out only by prayer." It seems like they had forgotten that option, and Jesus was now admonishing them to pray for this possessed sick boy.

There are, thankfully, many examples of Jesus healing the infirm and caring for the sick. If sickness is the best thing for people, then when the paralyzed man came to Jesus, Jesus would have simply left him paralyzed and told him that was the best thing for his life. But because Jesus healed people, He showed clearly that His will is for the blind to see and the ills of this world to be healed.

Scripture seems to conclude the matter by telling us in 1 John 5:14, " ... if we ask anything according to His will He hears us." It was Jesus' clear will to heal all those with infirmities, so we must pray in that direction ourselves if we want to be heard.

We as a group concluded, that while it's not explicitly stated over and over, we observed healing and praying for healing to be part of God's kingdom work and an instrument of undoing the curses of the fall. We would engage in that work physically through treatments and spiritually through prayer.

That conclusion was not surprising, but the pleasant surprise we found in the process of searching the Bible for prayer commands is we got to explore what indeed gets emphasized in corporate prayer. Far more often than healing prayer, Jesus and the apostles are concerned about praying for the faithfulness and spiritual strength of people in and out of the church, rather than only their illnesses.

For instance, praying against temptation is a common theme as we are likely familiar with praying, "lead us not into temptation, but deliver us from evil."

Jesus prays for Peter in Luke 22:32, saying, " ... I have prayed for you that your faith may not fail."

Paul in Romans 10:1, exclaims, "Brothers, my heart's desire and prayer to God for them [the Jews] is that they may be saved."

Over and over the saints are praying for the people to be "filled with knowledge" or to have "spiritual wisdom" or to "abound in love". This understanding didn't stop me praying for the sick following these studies, but I have certainly seen a big difference in how I pray for the sick and others in my circles.

I am far more concerned now about praying for people's walks with God and that they may find themselves drawn to a more intimate relationship with God following their illness than about merely feeling better. In the way I want to integrate the spiritual needs with the physical needs as I treat patients, I also feel like this is a more holistic type of prayer I can offer for them.

Going to the Sick for Jesus' Kingdom

Driving for hours towards the South, we once traveled as a dental team to do some community health work in a small village that was stricken with poverty. This place was extremely remote, but after news got out that we were there, many people traveled to us from even more remote desert places because they urgently needed dental care. One woman, Sharifa, came twenty kilometers to see us, and she arrived dressed to the nines, even wearing high heels which were preposterous since we were in the middle of a sandy desert.

After assessing her needs and getting started, this woman in her early twenties suddenly had a seizure as I was giving her anesthetic.

It started like other seizures I have seen, but quickly she curled up in a fetal position and began crying for her mother. She voided her bladder and was crying like a baby for a minute as urine ran down the chair and across the floor.

Suddenly a change came over her, and she looked at me with anger and started trying to strike me as she spoke in this weird low voice that was not anything like her usual timbre. My assistant pinned her arms as she writhed and cursed us in this unworldly speech that gave me the shivers.

It didn't last long, before in a flash, her muscles relaxed, her eyes changed and she became what I could best describe as a seductress. She transitioned from murderous rampage and now started beckoning me to her with a sensuous facial expression and a repeated curl of her tongue and reached out trying to grab me towards her. At that point, we all were simultaneously struck by the fact that this was demonic possession.

I've seen the movies and heard stories, but nothing had prepared me for that experience. There was no way I could now attribute this event or excuse it as merely acting or consequences of some medical condition.

As reality struck, the energy in the room began to feel very oppressive, even as she struggled even more to seduce me by making sensual actions no female Arab would ever dare to do in her right mind.

Max and I quickly got out of the room and let Ruby and the female assistants hold her arms down as we all prayed for her in the power of Jesus' name.

Over the next five minutes, she then cycled back through the different manifestations. First, the crying baby, then the wrathful imp and finally the seductress all took their turns. Then her eyes relaxed once more; she looked at us again, and we all knew she was back.

She asked what had happened and after telling her, she reported to us that these seizures and manifestations had occurred for some time. *Thanks for putting that down on your medical health history sheet,* I thought to myself!

Her husband told us that he had taken her to a sheik when she was having seizures at first, and he had made some incantations over her which seemed to help for a while. Then the seizures came back, so he had brought her to a second more powerful sheik who had sacrificed an animal and had called a jinn to take away her seizures. This process too had worked for a time, but again they returned, and the last time he had driven her some distance to see a third very powerful sheik who had done a really powerful incantation over her because he was in congress with stronger jinn.

To our team, this confirmed the cause of what we experienced precisely. Three trips to the local sheik witch doctors had opened her up to three competing demon possessors. However, when I once proclaimed this assertion to a believing colleague, I found out I was misguided.

I was told that after seizures, sometimes patients documented in the medical literature will experience hallucinations, and that was simply a post-epileptic hallucinatory manifestation. What we had seen was not the result of demon possession, it was only normal sequelae that sometimes occur following seizures.

I asked what was considered the medical cause of this phenomenon, and learned it was unknown. The good thing is that when it happens now, we have this long diagnosis for it. Suffice to say, this did not persuade me to abandon my first diagnosis.

I looked it up and it was called postictal psychosis in the medical literature but always occurred from two hours to one week following a seizure, after the patient had recovered. It didn't fit our circumstances at all. It did show me that all of us like to use titles for things we don't understand to give us the delusion that we control things more than we do.

We don't understand the spiritual dimension much at all, but if we can call something a post-epileptic hallucinatory manifestation, that sure makes us feel a lot better than saying a demon was on the loose. Our non-Christian colleagues would laugh at us if we purported that nonsense. We certainly want their respect, right?

As a Christian healthcare worker, I was then learning that we have to call the spiritual side of things as it is, even if we don't understand. The end result may lead to mockery, but in truth, we will have a more comprehensive and correct understanding of disease and illness in the context of God's kingdom.

As His people, Jesus is sending us into places which are far from the good news of the gospel to peel back the damages of the fall and push His kingdom agenda forward. He has actually "passed the baton" to us now if we believe Scripture and understand our place in it correctly.

> 'Peace be with you. As the Father has sent me, even so I am sending you.' And when he had said this, he breathed on them and said to them, 'Receive the Holy Spirit. If you forgive the sins of any, they are forgiven them; if you withhold forgiveness from any, it is withheld.' —John 20:21-23

The Father had given the proverbial baton to Jesus before the incarnation and now He is extending it to us. Because Jesus took on flesh and stepped into our world, we now have this possibility of reversing the incarnation and interacting with the divine. With it comes His peace and His Spirit and His power which is certainly humbling of which to be a recipient. To be the source of forgiveness and light to others is undoubtedly powerful and also a huge responsibility.

Are we up to this task? By ourselves, we certainly are not, but happily, God's story is one of equipping His saints, step by step, to take on this work.

We see this pattern continue in the book of Acts as Jesus' disciples start emulating their teacher after He has ascended to heaven. Jesus had very early in his ministry healed a paralytic man. It was one of His first miracles and showed His desire and authority to heal physically and spiritually. Now in Acts 3, the narrative reveals to us how Peter and

John, still trying to get their legs underneath them after Jesus' departure, likewise heal a paralyzed man in the temple.

There is also a parallel story that occurs later in Acts 9 I saw pointed out by Peter Leithart in his book *The Four Gospels*. Arriving at a house where a sick girl had passed away, Jesus and the disciples had encountered a mournful group of people. Jesus raised this little girl from the dead in the Gospel accounts by merely saying, "*Talitha*," which means, "little girl" and telling her to get up.

Now we see Paul the apostle coming upon a servant of the church, Tabitha, who has died prematurely. Interestingly, not only does he raise her from the dead, just like Jesus, but he calls her by name, "Tabitha." It's not only the same miracle but merely a difference of one letter.

These passages let us see that the disciples now filled with the Spirit are starting to do all the very things that Jesus had been doing. Mysteriously, Jesus had told them before the crucifixion that He must leave so that the Holy Spirit could come. According to Jesus, this advent would be better for them.

Can you imagine thinking that we're better off now that Jesus is gone and not present with us? In God's timing and purpose, they were now seeing that they were actually better off not having Jesus present with them. As Jesus had taught, they were better off having the Spirit within them, and this seems to encourage them and us to carry on in the same pattern and the same power.

> *When Jesus had called the Twelve together, he gave them power and authority to drive out all demons and to cure diseases, and he sent them out to proclaim the kingdom of God and to heal the sick....So they set out and went from village to village, proclaiming the good news and healing people everywhere. —Luke 9:1-2, 6*

Healthcare workers are one of the many types of workers that have some way to intertwine Word and deed ministry directly through their skills. This ability helps us serve in countries in the 10/40 window. We may have no entrance point into people's lives or countries until we can help meet their felt needs first. This mixing of Word and deed ministry comes out of the pattern we see in the work of Jesus.

It is a challenge to us in the healing arts but also a privilege to be His hands and feet in a very practical way to so many. As we practice our talents, we are pushing back on those circles of brokenness that all humans have and trying to bring resurrection and hope back into many of these shattered relationships.

Sometimes by meeting these felt needs of the outer circles, we get the benefit of introducing people to their greatest need, the reconciliation of them to their creator which is the most inner circle and where dynamic healing finally occurs.

Chapter 14
SECURITY MATTERS

"Suffering produces perseverance; perseverance character; and character hope." Romans 5:3-4

One year, a carpenter friend used some of the extra olive wood from our trees and fashioned a sweet gift for us for Christmas. He turned a lonely piece of cracked olive stump into a beautifully polished cross, patterned throughout with undulating ebony lines.

One thing you quickly learn about olive wood is that if your olive tree is watered consistently and never stressed, then the wood it produces is pretty much worthless. The wood is too soft to carve and is not attractive, just a dull yellowish-brown color. However, if the tree experiences times of stress or drought and yet manages to survive in the harsh climate, that olive wood is beautiful and valuable. Dark ridges and lines denoting each hardship of the tree's life mark the wood throughout and leave it extremely hard and durable for all kinds of use.

The same of course is true of us as God's people. As we live more and more in troubling times and lean on Him for our survival, He will more and more mark us throughout. The places in our lives where we feel we have weakness; in them, He will show his strength and carve something beautiful out of it. We were the beneficiaries of His love and comfort many times as he met us in weak times living in the Middle East.

Fear of the Foreigner

People have commonly asked my family and me, "Have you ever been scared of living in the Middle East?"

I don't know what people normally picture in their minds. Probably, it is the usual depictions on the news broadcasts of terrorists and madmen hurling weapons of death at innocent people. By God's grace, we never ran into those people in person. Despite being in a volatile place to live, notably through the times of the Arab Spring, I have thankfully only genuinely been scared one time while living there and I usually share that story with them.

I was staying in a medium-sized town of about 50,000 people, and because it was Friday, the Muslim holy day, work was over early, so I decided to take a walk into town to look through the outdoor marketplace and do some shopping. I'd been there a few days before with my friend Dr. Ron who lived in this village.

Since I pretty much knew which direction to head, I just started walking into town without bothering to get a taxi or anything. Lots of people were out and about, kids playing with sticks in the dirt, people sitting around talking and visiting, and pretty much everyone watched me, the white foreigner, as I walked from the outer sparsely occupied area where I was staying into the more densely occupied town.

After walking around fifteen minutes, I reached an intersection and made my best estimate of where to go. It had been easy to see which direction I should take from a distance, but now that I was amid multi-storied apartments and buildings, my perspective was less clear.

As I continued to walk, it slowly happened that the people and activity I had been observing before quickly diminished. In fact, after trotting down one street for a while, I realized I was the only one even on that street. However, that didn't last for long, because as I went on, I soon passed a lone person leaning against the wall in what seemed now to be a pretty empty section of town.

After some way, I soon perceived that this man had ceased leaning and had begun walking behind me on the same street. I kept looking for signs of grocery stores or a marketplace and saw a sign up ahead on a building, but was disappointed to see that the store was closed.

That's right I realized—it was the Muslim holy day here and unlike back home, they actually close their stores on their Sabbath day. Still, I thought I must be getting close to the market and should go ahead and see for sure.

Now, as I took a glance behind me, I noticed two men walking behind me instead of one. *Surely they weren't following me—there would be no reason to follow, but rather they were likely just heading the same direction,* I thought.

To be sure and clear myself of any unfounded worry, I took a sharp left turn onto the next street I reached. *No one would turn off the main thoroughfare to go left if they were heading into town. They would surely continue heading straight, and then I could keep my walk unmolested.*

Unfortunately, as I watched behind me, I noticed that as they reached that intersection, they also turned left behind me. At the next road, I again took a turn, this time a right turn onto a smaller road and started to pick up my pace slightly, realizing that my "test turns" had now actually put me onto an even more remote and desolate road than before. Glancing back behind me, I thought I had probably lost them for a second until I now noticed three men taking that right turn behind me. Now I was worried—there was no way this was a coincidence.

My eyes darted for any sign of life up or down the street. The distance between my followers and me was slowly decreasing as well, and I saw nowhere to escape as the walls built up around this small road hemmed me in more and more narrowly. *Why had I gotten myself into this? Had I forgotten I was in the freakin' Middle East when I started this walk?* I had let my guard down after long periods of living among these kind people, and now I was in trouble.

The road was quickly coming to a "T" intersection up ahead of me, and I had to choose right or left. I chose left, and to my amazement, as I turned, I saw a small little store up ahead on the left side of the street that had lights on and looked open!

As the three men behind me had noticeably been drawing closer and closer, I decided that if I had to face them, I would rather do it at the store, because at least the store owner would provide some protection to me according to their culture.

I entered into the front entrance of the tiny store and turned around to face looking down the street in the direction of my pursuers. As I watched them also make a left at the "T," I knew that I was essentially calling their bluff. Either they would have to continue walking past me and act like they hadn't been following me, leaving me in the protection of the store;

or they would now show themselves and confront me inside, despite the presence of the store owner. I fired up some quick prayers to the Lord to protect me and in His mercy to let the men pass by. However, as their eyes scanned back and forth across the street, they quickly spotted me, and the three men made a beeline to the store and drew up in a semi-circle around me.

"Where you going?" the formerly leaning man spoke to me in broken English.

In my mind, I knew that giving them my real intention of wandering about town to find some stores was not a wise answer because it would betray the fact that no one else knew where I was going and that no one was particularly looking for me. So in that split second, I decided on a new destination, to which I knew I would be grateful to arrive.

"I'm going to my friend Ron's house here in town," I told them.

There was a pause as the man thought. The others continued to look me over with no expression.

"Do you mean Ron, the doctor?" the ringleader then responded.

How did he know that Ron was a doctor? Had he been to his clinic as a patient or something? I couldn't say for sure. Would this knowledge be a blessing or a curse?

"Yes, Ron, the doctor," I responded.

A smile slowly eased across the man's face. "I know Ron," he said. We all go to church with him."

Muslims going to church? How could that make sense I reasoned? My breath started coming back to me now, as I thought about what had happened. Wait, these were Christians!

"Why then did you all start following me?" I exclaimed in relief.

The man responded, "I saw you walking through town, and you looked lost. So, my friends and I have been following you so that no harm would come to you. You really shouldn't be walking through this part of town by yourself, you know. We just wanted to keep you safe."

So, I've always been happy to say that the only time I ever felt imminently unsafe in the Middle East was when I was being chased by Christians who were trying to protect me.

That said, was there always a low background noise type of fear about our location?

Well to that, I would absolutely answer," yes," because I regularly marked that when we left the country, it always felt like we could finally relax in a true way. We didn't feel it or see it day in or day out, but when we were out of it, that's when we could tell we were continually living in a low-level tension with our surroundings.

Living in a constant low-level security risk area doesn't mean you can't do your work well or have a meaningful ministry or even enjoy a great life as a family. In fact, I think we were able to do all of those things well, and we were blessed as a family to be there and stay there. But what it does do is raise everything a notch in intensity.

I may say something to my wife in a moment of frustration that is not godly and she may rightly respond to me with criticism or anger. Those things which generally you can brush off in a relationship can escalate quickly in that context.

It is always taking a little bit of your energy to be there and be aware of your surroundings and monitor the news a bit more and watch your kids. This energy expense gives you a little less margin to tackle the other things you have to deal with and can affect your sleep considerably as well, not to mention the 4 AM mosque call which doesn't help that issue either.

I don't remember experiencing a terrible amount of angst about our living conditions until we went through several series of informative meetings about security concerns and protocols that we needed. We encountered various meetings like this whether it was through our clinic or our organization and the goal was always to give us better awareness about our surroundings and about how we can mitigate some of the dangers.

If you're not worried about security issues beforehand, you will certainly be more concerned after these types of talks, at least with our personal temperaments. Even though that's the downside, it would have been unkind and unfair not to let us understand more and learn more to protect our family. That desire is ultimately what led us to take a course on surviving kidnapping, which was considered the biggest threat to us in the area in which we lived.

True, we ultimately trusted God with our security in this life and the next. But, we felt a responsibility to at least learn some reasonable means for dealing with issues, if only for our kids. Oliver Cromwell once said, "Trust God and keep your powder dry," and this pithily explains my understanding of that interconnection.

Kidnapped!

The kidnapping seminar was going along pretty well, and we were learning about the details surrounding other kidnappings that had gone on in our area, so we might be prepared for how to handle a situation like that if it arose. We enjoyed good fellowship with our instructors and it reminded me of being back in school, attending lecture upon lecture in a very relaxed setting.

They were outlining some of the things we should consider in a hostage situation when, suddenly, out of a corner door, four blackly clad men busted into our classroom carrying automatic rifles and shouting, "*Allah Akbar!*" The suddenness and unexpectedness of it scared me to death. They pushed us and demanded that we get on the ground with faces towards the floor and they went around tying our hands behind our backs with zip-ties.

After the initial few seconds of the invasion that felt like minutes as it happened, I realized in my consciousness that this must all be staged and planned as a part of the course. I mean, what was the coincidence of getting kidnapped during a kidnapping course? I knew that Grace had done some training like this beforehand as well which had involved her being kidnapped and driven in the back of a car.

As I laid on my face on the floor, I took comfort that everything going on around me was fake. But that knowledge I had in my brain couldn't make the reaction of fear and anxiety boiling up in my body diminish as we went through the kidnapping scenario.

A masked man got in my face and yelled at me to get up. I chuckled a little bit out of nervousness to his request, and he lit into me with a barrage of cursing that I couldn't believe. It made me again question whether this kidnapping scenario was real or not, because I had only been cursed in that way before by my landlord's wife, and this was supposed to be a Christian security trainer. Are Christian security trainers actually allowed to swear at you like that I wondered?

I wiped the smirk off my mouth but found out unfortunately that my natural response to a fearful, anxious situation is apparently to smile and chuckle to relieve the tension, which put me in horrible standing with my captors.

After they blindfolded us, they led us downstairs in a line to a dark holding chamber. The man I had chuckled at before told me if I smirked or laughed again, he would kill someone of the group. I pressed my lips firmly together for a few seconds but really couldn't help it—I chuckled again.

Suddenly he flew into a rage full of cursing and vitriol and grabbed a girl who had also been kidnapped along with me. In truth, she had been crying uncontrollably ever since the kidnapping commenced.

He took her out of the room, and I heard a gun discharge, and there was silence. He then walked back in and asked me as I kneeled on the ground in the dark if I thought that was funny. I was able to say a dull, "no sir" this time. I then felt a small trickle of water hit my head and start to run down my shirt into my clothes. I thought that he was urinating on my head until I realized the water was not warm. I sat wet in the dark until the simulation was over.

The kidnapping training was memorable and helpful because I think if I went through the real thing in the future, I would at least know some pointers about how to conduct myself better and hopefully how not to get someone else hurt.

I had pretty much failed this time around. It gave more reality to the possibility of it happening and gave us some tools for us to make our captives realize our humanity and see us as more than merely objects.

The primary adjustment we had to make to our kidnapping training as the years went on was a change in strategy regarding the actual kidnapping event. When we went through the training, they recommended not fighting your captors or doing anything hazardous to get away, because most deaths occur at this point or the point of release at the end. If you can stay alive through the kidnapping phase, the data showed that 95% of kidnapped people are eventually released and live out their days.

That changed with the uprising of more radical groups within Islam who believed that the goal of kidnapping was not to extort money but to give them a political and public weapon against the West. As they employed their techniques of video beheadings, the rescue success rate of kidnap victims in our area was approaching zero. This sudden reversal necessitated a change in strategy.

We were now to do everything in our power to avoid being kidnapped since if we were kidnapped successfully, it would likely be our death sentence. So, now we needed to do anything we could in the first 60 seconds to make the kidnapping unsuccessful, regardless of how risky.

For instance, if you were pulled into a car and restrained, you may only have one opportunity to make a move. A valid option would now be

SPEAKING THE TOOTH IN LOVE

to throw yourself on the driver or stick shift and try to cause a wreck. Not usually ideal with a bag over your head and without a seatbelt, but now this new action had become the logical choice.

With my dental team, our official security protocol evolved as well. We no longer surrendered as the first option. Now, we maintained some simple weapons near us at all times and transitioned our security slogan to be, "If you can't run, fight to the death." It was never an especially catchy slogan, to be honest. Even though it never caught on too well, it succinctly illuminated the rapid transformation of our security situation.

The Hopes and Fears of All the Years

At Christmas time, we would often try to have a particular time set aside when we would gather with patients and villagers. They would celebrate with us the joyous occasion of the advent and generally were pretty understanding because the story of Jesus' birth is included in the Quran as well as the Bible, albeit with a few changes.

It was always an excellent opportunity to be ourselves and very open about the hope we had in life. Sadly, not all of us could let our hair down, because it was also a time we had to be cognizant of the security environment around us.

During these gatherings every year, the whole village was out of school and work, and the *shabab* (adolescent boys) would inevitably look around for Christians on Christmas day because they were always hoping to get a gift. I don't know if some well-meaning Christians had indeed given out presents at one time in the past or if these boys had just seen that in the movies, but they would unrelentingly harass you on Christmas trying to get something free out of you because they knew you were a Christian.

One year as we gathered a large group together on Christmas morning, I got assigned guard duty. It was a pretty lame job because we met in an area surrounded by a fence on all sides and at the front gate sat two police officers. I was at the left corner gate and stood around watching the perimeter. Like most years, the young people found us meeting together on this holiday and started walking by and shouting and begging for Christmas gifts through the fence. I said a few words to them but mostly ignored them because there was no valid answer they would accept.

As time passed, the numbers of *shabab* grew until they had around 25 young boys and young men gathered outside my gate. They obviously enjoyed my gate better because the police would just curse and threaten them at the center entrance and I'm sure a foreigner was more attractive as a target at which to hurl insults.

After they saw I wasn't going to let them in, they began to call me names and say that all Christians were infidels and going to hell. "Only Muslims know God," they yelled at me and so on and so forth for twenty or thirty minutes.

Finally, the efforts of the young men began to coalesce, and they started chanting outside the gate as a unified group, "Let us in! Let us in! Let us in!" The chanting then evolved into them all holding the gate and pushing on it back and forth as a group as they continued the chant. I still felt pretty immune to everything and was chalking this whole event up as being another fascinating cultural experience.

Suddenly, I heard and saw the center stabilizing bar at the bottom of the gate break; at that point, I knew I was in big trouble. I pulled out my cell phone to call the front guards for help, and I saw the young crowd continue to push the gate back and forth as a pulsing throng, now encouraged by the damage to the bar. The only thing currently holding the two gate doors together was a thick chain fastened together with a lock in the middle.

I wasn't sure if my message in Arabic was getting through to the Arab guards when I had to hang up because to my horror, I saw the arm of the lock break. A little hand swiftly shot through the hole in the gate door and removed it from the chain. The chains dropped heavily to the sides of the gates and both enormous gate doors now swung slowly inward towards me with a loud creak until they were both lay completely open. The left door came to rest on the fencing on the left side of the enclosure.

Twenty-five young men stood opposite me, finally unrestrained and staring, but to my surprise, something was still keeping them from stepping through the open entry. I was surprised they hadn't already run in like a herd of buffalo and disrupted our gathering.

Not knowing exactly what to do, I yelled at them with as much authority and anger as I could muster and asked them from what tribe they belonged. A few of them, shocked, looked back and forth at each other, and a couple of the boys told me their tribe name was *Bani Zaalan*.

I then asked them, "Does the *Bani Zaalan* tribe normally break gates and try to harass people on their holy day?"

For a few moments that seemed to drag on like minutes, there was silence as the boys looked at each other. I thought that perhaps I had stunned them from doing any further damage by holding the weapon of shame over them.

Unfortunately, the moment passed quickly as one older boy reached down and picked up a rock and hurled it at me. Immediately there was a clamor as these young boys started yelling and looking around for stones to throw at me. These airborne missiles, mainly small-sized, started zipping by my head and hitting my body. I took quite a few sharp hits in the abdomen and realized in that moment that if I got hit in the head, it could actually be quite lethal.

I ran and sought the protection of the left gate door that was hanging ajar and leaning against the side fence, because ironically while hurling rocks at me, they were still respecting property lines and refraining from crossing the boundary line of the gate. I could pretty much protect most of my body except for my lower legs which protruded around the corner of the gate door and took a lot of the beating from these winged stones.

At that moment, the police officers arrived brandishing their guns and shouting curses at the youth. The boys dropped their rocks and scrambled to get away from the "real" guards as fast as they could as they ran flat out into the desert in all directions. The frightful situation was over, and presently, several men gathered around to assess the damage to the gate and relieve me from my duty.

Grace and the kids had fortuitously stayed at home that morning, so I returned to them with quite a Christmas story to share. My now bruised and blood-marked legs were an eye-opening testimony to the kids. With all the danger of the morning over, I relaxed a bit and sat down to open some presents with my children. I reflected that it should be a source of joy to get to suffer some for the sake of the Name on Christmas day, not that I ever wanted to do it again unnecessarily.

Suffice to say, that after that morning, I resigned my Christmas day security post forever and just offered to pay the salary in the coming year to hire nationals to do the guard work for us. It didn't make cultural sense to place a foreigner at odds with locals—I feared it could only lead to more dramatic problems in future years now that this precedent had been set.

Frogs in Hot Water

After living for a while under low-level threats, it is amazing how people naturally can adapt to their situations. We saw that intensely with the calm reactions of children to things that would be horrifying to most kids back home. We also detected those attitudes in ourselves over time, because things that would have shattered our risk threshold earlier didn't trigger much reaction later in our experience.

One night on a trip back to the US, there was a terrible thunder and lightning storm that passed over us. My kids had not been used to much storm activity like this one in their lives because of the abbreviated rainy season we had in the Middle East.

As the thunder boomed menacingly outside and sudden flashes broke the darkness of night, they were afraid and came to us terrified and seeking comfort. I don't know why, but the first thing that came to my mind was to tell them, "Don't worry kids, this thunder is just a bunch of noise like the bombs make back home—we'll all be fine." It then dawned on me what I had said. I turned to Grace and confessed, "I can't believe I just comforted our kids by saying the thunder was only like bombs! Who does that?"

Another time I was in the car with my son and one of Job's boys and we were driving some visiting guests around our town for the first time. Suddenly, a loud repetitive detonation was heard in the distance. It sounded like a jackhammer, except a hundred times more powerful and the ground seemed to shake several times.

My guests were quite startled and asked me, "What in the world was that?"

Before I could reply, Job's son in the backseat piped up and said somberly, "Oh, it's just some more of that Russian carpet-bombing."

I was thinking, *what have we done to our kids when encountering the terrifying noise and reality of carpet-bombing is just another droll occurrence to them?*

The only time we ever felt the need to evacuate, we actually tried to turn it into a small family vacation. We quickly packed our "go bags" that were ever-maintained into the car and headed out of town. I think the gas masks being passed out in town among some of our Korean co-workers made us realize it might not be the best time to be brave.

From my limited study on chemical warfare, I knew that it was the kids who often succumb to its lethal effects well prior to any adults. I didn't want one of my kids to have to act like the canary in the cage and be the alarm that guarded my welfare.

Ultimately with situations like this one, Grace and I had reasoned that if we overreact to a security threat and leave when it wasn't necessary, then we may feel silly and a little ashamed around our peers when we get back with our tail tucked between our legs after they had stuck out the difficult situation. Yet, if we under react to a security situation and stay in order to be tough, we might regret it for the rest of our lives, especially if it led to the permanent harm of a weaker family member.

So, in this case, we opted towards the former idea. Perhaps, if it was just the two of us on our own, we may feel encouraged to stick out the situation, but we didn't want hindsight to be an ever-present reminder of our stupidity.

We were blessed to have the situation ameliorated just two days later. A political "red-line" was crossed, threats had been uttered, but no actions had been taken by the powers that be, so the crisis was quickly averted.

The kids really enjoyed their time away and we did a lot of fun activities together and acted like it was no big deal in front of them. The younger ones just assumed it was a spontaneous vacation trip. We would put them to bed and then be glued to the television and cell phone for the rest of the night to get an update about the situation back in our town. When the commander-in-chief of one side finally backed down, we were glad because we knew we'd be heading home.

Two other times we found out that there had been threats against our work, but it didn't lead to an evacuation of any kind. The main reason for us persevering in those situations was because we didn't know there was a threat until after the fact.

In one instance, government agents told us that they had averted a threat by intercepting text messages and patrolling our area with undercover officers. An attack never came on the date indicated in the text messages and we hadn't known about it anyway.

Another time we did recognize that there was something peculiar going on in our neighborhood, although we were never informed about anything in particular until after the fact. Armed personnel carriers showed up and patrolled the whole area where we worked back and forth for several days. Police officers were on high alert and patrolling around the clinic area. If we inquired, they just told us that there was no problem, they were keeping us safe.

Later, agents revealed to us that they had clear intelligence of an imminent attack being planned against us. We were thankful for these efforts provided by our host country to protect us and prevent these threats from becoming a tragedy. However, we did wonder why we were not informed and instead left to continue work as usual, acting as bait to entrap the terrorists who had threatened to come.

In a following incident, a group of colleagues with our clinic was under increased caution because they were providing health care in a remote area filled with political unrest. We all received alerts not to travel on a certain highway that connected that town to another. It wasn't a concern to us because it was not in our proximity, but for our teammates, it meant they were severed from food supplies and other resources.

Honestly, we all received alerts like this one all the time and in all my experience in the country, I had only seen one with my own eyes that truly had been important and related to a really hazardous situation. Therefore, most of us got the feeling that the embassy was just trying to cover themselves by doing all of these warnings and they were generally considered to be overreactive by some people. That said, we still always observed the warnings just to be sure, but there was a little bit of alarm fatigue among us and our friends. You can only cry wolf so many times and still get the same reaction from the people you are trying to protect.

This mindset led our group of colleagues and friends to make the decision to travel the forbidden highway in order to get groceries and other supplies. Their trip outwards went normally and further confirmed their suspicions that this alert was just another overreaction like many others.

However, following their shopping spree as they returned on this highway back to their village, they began to be concerned and uneasy. They observed small fires being lit in the distance along the highway they were traveling on as the sun began to set to their west. Finally, as they drove on into the darkening sky, they realized the highway ahead was completely blocked by a truck parked across the roadway.

Slowly coming to a stop behind this large truck, another vehicle quietly pulled in behind them. A few seconds later a third vehicle approached on their left side blocking them in on that side and that is when they realized they were being trapped.

The driver of the car hurriedly hit the gas and squeezed their vehicle off the road to the right, just seconds before a fourth car could pull up and block off their escape. As they departed the highway onto the rocky and sandy surface of the desert, a huge rock the size of a watermelon sailed through their back window glass, shattering it into hundreds of sharp pieces that rained down over the five passengers in the car. People suddenly emerged out of the looming darkness and were angrily shouting on all sides for them to stop. The driver brilliantly avoided all the people and other barriers and was able to maneuver the damaged car back onto the roadway ahead of the blockade.

As they headed up the highway, praying and praising, they were relieved to see police vehicles up ahead at a gas station. Pulling in, they quickly observed buses, trucks and other personal vehicles bearing similar evidence of abuse from the marauding crowd they had encountered.

Initially, they thought their report of the incident would incite the police to go quickly and take care of the villains. Yet, the police said they couldn't do anything about that many people because it was connected with the uprising of an entire tribe in that area.

They were just blocking off the dangerous area to keep others from entering into similar peril there. After being detained until around 2 am in the night, they were finally informed by the police it was safe to leave and continue their trip back to the original town where they had started their day. Security warnings that came to us all after that attack took on new priority and concern once again.

Eternal Security

Sitting with a friend one time who has changed his loyalties to Jesus brought up a fascinating point of conversation. In that part of the world, people said God has ninety-nine names that describe all the essential aspects of His character. For the Christian who sees these names, it is always unbelievable but later not surprising that none of the names mentioned are "love."

We may be familiar with *rahman* (merciful) or *akbar* (greatest), but one I had never noticed was *maakir* (capricious or crafty). As my friend reflected on his past life as a Muslim, he said that this name of God, *Maakir*, had always scared him in the back of his mind.

A famous story told by one of their most significant leaders, Omar ibn il Khateeb, one of the *mubashereen* (ten blessed companions of Muhammad), said that he feared *Maakir Allah*. Omar said he was like a man standing at a door with one leg in heaven and one leg in hell. Even if you did everything God commanded—prayed five times a day, fasted for Ramadan, gave alms and went to Mecca, God may send you to hell almost as a joke if He was in a bad mood or feeling fickle.

My friend knew Omar ibn il Khateeb felt that way about his eternity and even the islamic prophet Muhammad also said he was not sure if he would go to hell or heaven at death (Sura 46:9). If that was so, how could he ever have any security in his own future?

Security issues were certainly a huge facet of our lives as we struggled to follow our calling and also protect our family using the ordinary means God had given us. However, from an eternal perspective, those concerns of security were always ultimately only about physical and emotional issues and never about spiritual concerns.

It absolutely breaks our heart to know the doubt and insecurity of so many friends there when we treasure and take for granted such a sure salvation in Christ daily. We struggled with security issues as a family at times, but we always knew God was watching out for us and would solve the problems in the eternal, if not in the present.

We could only imagine how that would affect your daily life if you knew your eternal life was dependent on a fatalistic understanding of a capricious God. It made all these security matters we dealt with seem pretty small in comparison with the spiritual security issues of our neighbors. If they had no ultimate security in their lives, how could we remain too concerned about our temporal security and make that the priority?

It was a struggle and remains a struggle as we contemplate God's calling on our family to reach the least of these. May God encourage us to pray and work so that we can have opportunities to express our spiritual security policy more often and more boldly with our Arab friends back home and abroad.

PART 3

IN THE DESERT
WITH DENTISTRY

Chapter 15

GO EAST, YOUNG MAN

I'm not sure if I could have endured very long on the field had I not had the opportunity to get out of my little dusty, podunk town and regularly go out on adventures into the outlying and obscure desert places. My wife Grace was a perfect saint, harboring many virtues I lacked to stay in town with her work and with the primary responsibility of our kids' education. But for me, part of my job included community healthcare and I was happy at times to dust off my boots and hit the road and see where the Lord led.

There is of course always uncertainty with any work on the field, but I often felt a certain energy and excitement surrounding a new venture into a distant village full of strangers. It was always intriguing how the Lord would often lead us to the right person through an old relationship at the clinic or even from a wrong turn off the roadway that would lead to a predestined conversation. Seeing how God may answer and meet a need in a novel way and in a unique place was something for which I often found myself hungry.

All parts of the desert had a unique personality. There were differences in geography, but there were also distinct variances in the spirit and character of the people in each region. I assume those distinctions are interconnected because of the requirements that come with the type of living that developed there.

Even now when I think of the East, I think of a barren, black and rocky landscape populated by people living on the edge. There were living on the edge of poverty and on the edge of civilization and new influences coming from a developing country that was quickly modernizing through-out its urban centers.

They were also being edged out by a country who was not recognizing their citizenship and right to be there; simply put, they were disenfranchised with all the baggage that comes with that reality.

Buba Zeraded and the Pasalmees

The first time I made the trip East, it was at the invitation of a refugee camp. We arrived in order to provide much needed dental care among foreigners to the nation who were living in this camp. Some of them had lived in the camp their entire lives and I was surprised many of them were able to speak workable English, having taught themselves the language during their years of confinement.

In the camp, they had large donated tents and many of them even had big screen TV's which was a bit of an anomaly being so remote. They said they received money as refugees monthly and there was nothing really to spend it on, so they had enriched themselves with electronics.

Being non-citizens it was easier to share the good news with them flagrantly, and we quickly found that they had quite an appreciation and understanding of the message we gave. They nodded to each other in familiarity with the Bible stories as we shared about the life of Jesus.

However, the name of Jesus was completely unfamiliar to them, but they realized they believed all those exact things about a person named *Buba Zeraded*. When we inquired about *Buba*, we found that he was born to a virgin and suffered and died on a cross for sins which sounded pretty familiar.

We asked them where they got this information and they told us they had a couple of holy books that spoke about *Buba Zeraded*. The names of the books were Matthew and *Pasalmees*.

We were immediately intrigued and showed them our Bible which contained both of their books, except with the name Jesus used for the main protagonist. The people were ecstatic and couldn't believe we had the same books, but even more of them!

They begged us to give them our Bibles and we were happy to oblige. We had brought a box of 70 with us, realistically hoping to give out two or three to interested people during our outreach. However, the word spread throughout the camp and we were quickly besieged by refugees crying out for God's Word. The box of 70 Bibles was emptied before our first full day of work was done there amidst a clamor of excitement and enthusiasm!

Work that continued throughout later years with local people outside of the refugee camp was never quite as fruitful and easy as that day. In those places, the people were often quite suspicious of us or even resentful. They had suffered a lot in their living conditions and especially because they were politically unrecognized their identity was not valued.

We quickly came to see that if we were going to serve a suffering group of people like this one, it was necessary for us to absorb some of this suffering ourselves. At times it felt like we were going to have to out suffer them to get an opportunity to share in their lives.

Vandals and Heroes

Some of the troubles we saw over the years of ministry were simple nuisances and others were quite harsh. The first time I went to minister to them, we realized as we got ready to leave that the gas tank of our clinic truck had been filled with handfuls of desert sand. This was not only logistically difficult to deal with because of our distance away from a main town, but it was also thousands of dollars to handle the repairs later. A gas cap lock would make this occurrence the last of its kind, although keeping up with the gas cap key was the resultant hassle.

Other times we would witness damage to our personal vehicles or other items. I have to give them credit that they would usually not do anything bad until all the services we could provide had been rendered. Once they realized we were ready to depart we had to be on high alert, lest they vandalize our transportation.

One time a friend's car was completely debrided of its chrome accessories, and another time we came out with our luggage to see the back tires on the car were out of air. Most recently, a window was broken out right before it was time to leave.

We have found bloody legs of goats outside our living areas, we have received spit on our car windows from thankful patients, young men have torn up Bibles and cast the pieces into the wind and kids have even broken into our living area and stolen our bananas! Through it all, God has generally given us patience and the ability to continue our work and absorb the abuse, although I have to admit there have been times of total frustration and screaming when we couldn't keep the emotions at bay.

We tried to handle the criminal activity once by reporting it to the police, but all they did was station an army officer with us. At first, we thought this may be a great option, but after we found he demanded we feed him every meal, house him and drive him around, we realized this blessing wasn't helpful.

While there were discouraging times, on the other hand, we have been blessed by our patients and friends living there. They have invited us into their homes to feed us and make us part of their wedding celebrations or other festivities.

One friend, Isa, who early on professed faith took us out for a fun evening in the desert for a barbecue. We ate a lot of good food and explored an old castle. Later that night we fired his old Russian shotgun that was barely still holding together. He taught us how to chase desert rats using a flashlight, a jacket, and a lot of gas in our vehicle as we chased them for hours into the night.

We had quite a few normal mechanical failures with our vehicles and equipment as we served in villages in the area. The temperatures were often scorching, and the wind and dust were detrimental to most of the working parts of our engines and machines.

I particularly remember a fuel pump supplying the generator died, and it was going to prematurely end a long-planned outreach and require us to drive three hours away to get parts. Suddenly, a man appeared out of nowhere and offered to take a look at it for me. He pulled out a box of tools and removed the fuel pump and installed a new one in its place. We were back in business and almost as soon as we had seen that the equipment was all working again, he had left without receiving any recompense. We called this mysterious mechanic our angel and thanked God for His provision.

We generally loved our time with the people of the area, but maintaining a deep interest in spiritual things for new believers was always hard. Even with our friend Isa, we found that he was very content to enjoy a very surface level of faith. He could articulate the gospel very well and even share with us all of the things he believed that Jesus had taken care of in his life including his sins. The old ways in his life were long gone he would tell us as he distanced himself from the teachings of the majority religion in the area. However, he never really wanted to get much deeper than that.

One time several of us were meeting Isa, and we had been doing a study with him for a few weeks. As we started to get into some interesting parts of the study about Jesus' temptation in the desert, I got a text message. I looked at my phone and the message was from Isa. The man next to me then got a message from Isa and then the next man.

We asked Isa, "why are you texting us during the study? Aren't you interested in seeing what happened to Jesus?"

He replied, "I believe in Jesus with my whole heart. I am 100% a follower of Jesus and I don't need to know anything else." He stood up and within a few minutes had left our meeting.

This surface understanding of the gospel caused me to reflect. I came to see that for many of these distant people, belief had its share of challenges if not connected more deeply to their lives. Because their former beliefs had been shallow and loosely connected to the practical things in their lives, they inherently thought their new loyalties would work in the same way. Examples were not available to them and it was hard to lift the veil for them to see the richness that came from a life in Christ. Therefore, they were so easily satisfied to have the shallow faith they had previously enjoyed.

Where There is No Oral Surgeon

With any work in a remote area, when you are the "educated" person that comes to help, there are always people and needs that arrive beyond the area of normal training. I learned that to be an expert only means that you are trained a little bit more than the other dentist in the region.

One time a woman came complaining of a bleeding sack under her tongue that was attached to her gingiva (gums). She said that the sack had been excised before but it always came back. She had come a long way because she was confident I was an expert and could take care of her problem.

I examined her and saw that she had a pyogenic granuloma. This mass is a type of vascular tumor that was attached to her lower vestibule area in the anterior. I had never even seen one of these before, let alone excised one, and I knew that they were often recurrent. I wasn't really sure how I could do any better than anyone else, but kneeling down on the floor, I prayed beside her and we began the small surgery.

There was quite a bit of blood and kneeling on the floor while she laid on a simple mattress made it very difficult to get the right position or even to see very clearly. Still, I was able to do a pretty good job for the conditions and get her sutured back. I hoped I had removed enough to prevent reoccurrence. When I finally ran into her a year later, she was so happy and I was relieved to hear that it hadn't returned. All I could acknowledge was that God had done something special there through some untrained hands.

At other times I had guest dentists visit me so I would take advantage of the extra man or woman power and drive several hours to a remote village. One time I got to a remote village after a long and difficult drive, and my guest dentist and I slumped down onto the floor of a simple apartment where we would be staying the night. We had split up duties, and he had helped me pack all the supplies.

After sitting there relaxing a few minutes and unwinding he suddenly exclaimed, "Dr. Adam, I just realized that I totally forgot one of the things you asked me to pack!"

I cringed and slowly asked him what he had forgotten. He responded and told me he had forgotten to bring all the packs of gauze I had laid out and written on the list.

I replied, "Whew, I thought you were gonna say you forgot to pack the anesthetic that I asked you to put in the suitcase. We would have been dead in the water without anesthetic, but we can make it without gauze."

There was a long pause. He then slapped his head and said, "Oh Dr. Adam, I just realized that I forgot to bring the anesthetic!"

Another time a talented female dentist, Dr. Eva, came and worked with me. She was doing a lot of great dentistry for us; when a patient came in with a loose third molar, she called me over to take a look at it.

I normally don't like to take out third molars or "wisdom teeth" back home, but when you are the only hope of people in pain, you have to get pretty good in remote areas, sometimes even without the aid of x-rays. I had taken out hundreds of wisdom teeth at this point, but this one was different.

This molar was fully mobile and even rocked up and down in the socket. I asked her what the matter was—it seemed like a slam dunk extraction. She told me to gently pull up on the tooth as if I was going to extract. I did and the tooth slowly moved up but then quickly bounced back when I let off the pressure. It was like it was attached by a rubber band to the jaw.

I said, "It almost feels like the roots are fully encircling the inferior alveolar nerve." She nodded and said that she was thinking the exact same thing. Because extracting the tooth might lead to permanent numbness of the lower right part of her face and jaw, we decided to leave it be.

Running on Empty

When we weren't challenged by the people we were serving, we were sometimes tested by our local help. One trip, when it was time to drive the clinic truck back the long three-hour road home, a dentist friend and I noticed that the gasoline gauge was on about 1/8th of a tank. We knew there was a place to buy gas in the village, so we told the local driver that he needed to take it over there and fill up the tank before we left. We had already given him the gas money on the front end.

He refused to go and get gas saying that we had plenty of fuel left and the winds would be behind us the whole time back anyway. That was impossible, so we suspected he was not wanting to spend the cash on gas so he could do something with the money later.

As he left to get lunch, my friend and I got into the clinic truck and drove it to the gas area. My friend was just going to use his own money to get gas because, after a long week, the last thing we all wanted was to run out of gas on the way home and be stranded.

As we got out of the vehicle and went around to fill up the tank, we realized our plan had been thwarted. In our excitement, we forgot the gas cap had that new lock and the local driver was the only one with the key.

Just about then we got a phone call from the driver who had just noticed that we had "stolen" the vehicle away. He soon arrived at the gas area and chastised us up and down for our deception. We begged him now that the vehicle was there to let us at least pay for a little gas out of our own pockets. We wouldn't make him spend the gas money we had paid him. He told us he was the experienced driver here and he knew for sure that no more gas was needed for this trip home.

We began the long ride home, dejected and with our heads down from shame at the failure of our plan. Thirty minutes into our trip home, the vehicle began to shudder. It began to misfire and huff before it finally came to rest on the edge of the road. We were out of gas.

It's a little funny now to remember that event, but still quite painful as I think of the verbal exchange that ensued in the car following our breakdown on the road. A car came to our aid, and we and the driver with empty jerrycan in hand packed into this auto already stuffed with people in order to go find some gas.

After a tense thirty-minute ride back to the exact gas pump where we had struggled to fill the tank and a thirty-minute return ride back to our vehicle, we were on the road again. We had learned that you had to put a lock on the gas tank to prevent harm from those wanting to harm us. Now, we realized that gas was another way people could steal from us. Sadly, the local drivers were never again given the authority or funds to purchase gas on their own after that.

Chapter 16
FAR FROM DIXIE

Author Clyde Edgerton said about distinctions in the US, "Because I was born in the South, I'm a Southerner. If I had been born in the North, the West or the Central Plains, I would be just a human being."

There was a similar distinction among the people we worked within the southern deserts. They were just a different cohort with the dirt baked deep into their faces and hands; distance removed them a little further from civilization than the rest. They had maintained their ancient customs and way of life with more purity and orthodoxy.

If possible, these people weathered an additional layer of poverty compared to those living in the East and West. This difference was attributable to several factors, including greater distance from resources, less access to education, and more intense weather patterns, to name a few. My time with them was always enjoyable as I loved their simplicity and their paradoxical contentedness with life as they squatted on the dirt floors of their tents and prepared simple meals and welcomed distant guests as they had for millennia without change.

One area that we worked in for over six years was a disputed tribal area that had a history of spiritual and political darkness. People living there were at odds with the country and would usually foment riots and rebellion periodically.

Christians had worked there over the years, but they had routinely fallen victim to many troubles and were forced to leave after short amounts of time. We felt that if we could get through one heavily troubled area, we could go farther and have general safety as we worked in the more remote villages among these tribal people.

The first time we ever went there, it was at the invitation of a women's society who had urged us to come and help them with their oral needs. This invite gave us the boldness to go, and we made our way into the area problem-free after a pleasant drive of four hours. Up ahead, we now saw the outskirts of the troubled town we needed to traverse and felt the palpable heaviness of darkness in the area.

Maybe it was just in our minds from the stories we had heard or from the riots we had seen on the news, but we braced ourselves to journey through with our large vehicle. We knew that the people there had just attacked the local police and burned down a small police post building in the center of town.

About that moment, the whole truck started to kindle up warning lights on the dashboard, and the heavy vehicle thundered to a halt on the side of the road. We were sitting literally outside the town sign.

We tried to restart it, but it was utterly dead and showed no hint of life. None of our team were mechanically inclined with automobile engines, so after talking to maintenance folks back home and flagging down some help off the highway, we decided to get a mechanic to come over from the local town.

Arriving reasonably quickly, a local man greeted us and then inspected everything in and out of the truck, mysteriously not finding any cause of our problem. By that time, there also had arrived another curious local driving a tow truck. He intimately involved himself in the problem with the mechanic, all the time staring at us and taking a great interest in these out of place foreigners and their truck.

The mechanic said the only thing to do was to tow it to a large truck stop in the middle of town where we could try to get some repairs the next day. We had already spent several hours working on the problem at this point, and it was getting late in the day now. The other man who had attached himself to us, happily readied his tow truck as he was excited to get some business.

One pertinent question for us was where we would sleep that night. One friend back home reminded us on the phone that we were in a volatile area. He was concerned that during the night, the locals might strip our vehicle of all of its parts and likely steal all of our dental equipment and tools as well. He recommended we consider sleeping outside on all four sides of the truck to guard it throughout the night with our flashlights for the deterrence of any possible thieves.

I appreciated his considerations about the truck and its expensive equipment and readied my heart to spend a night out on the pavement. But, I reckoned, *If the police have trouble with these people, what are our chances?* That made total sense from a distance, but looking around, I was more concerned for myself and my team members than the truck.

We had a guest apartment available to our group about 45 minutes away, but it would leave our truck and dental supplies completely exposed. We made a group decision at that point to get the truck to the mechanics' shop, but then leave it behind and retreat to the guest apartment for the night and pray for the best.

We piled into the tow truck, and the driver started his large rumbling vehicle that would bring us to the mechanic shop in the city. The mechanic had told us that we only had to make one left turn and then go about two miles into the town, and we would see the shop lit up.

The driver of the tow truck agreed, and he put his rig into gear, and we were finally on our way. It was now fully night, but we could see lights up ahead and to our left demarcating a busy part of town. As the designated left turn approached, I reminded our tow driver to turn left, but he didn't seem to make much change. I told him again and pointed to the left turn with rising urgency in my voice, but to my amazement, we just careened straight past the desired left turn.

It wasn't just that we missed the turn, but I realized the state of the roads was going to make it almost impossible to turn our large vehicle around and go back the correct way.

However, that wasn't a concern for our driver at all. He now informed me he had missed the turn on purpose. He claimed that the mechanic we had dealt with was a very unsavory character who was trying to do us harm because he was connected with the radical group of people in town.

At that point, we didn't have a name for it, but later we would come to know this group as Daesh or ISIS. The tow driver said they would destroy the truck if we brought it to the shop the mechanic recommended, so he was instead going to bring our truck and park it beside his house during the night. He said that he and his friends would all guard it for us during the night and we could stay safely somewhere else.

He could have been telling the truth, but because he had already deceived us once, I wasn't going to go along with his new plan. For all I knew, he actually was the ISIS operative, and he and his "friends" were going to steal and destroy our vehicle during the night. I didn't trust anyone at this point.

We all started to yell at him that we refused to go to his house; he needed to pull over immediately. We saw three or four glaring towers of lights shining down on a building that looked like a well-lit fort, and we demanded that he pull over there and let us go.

He was annoyed and told us we were making a huge mistake but relented when he saw we were not going to go to his house peaceably. He unloaded our vehicle right below one of the banks of lights, and we looked up to see that there were armed guards in the towers of the fort watching us. This garrison was a new police fort that had recently been built out of stone.

He talked to the police officer at the gate, and the officer decided to allow us to park our vehicle there until morning so that we would have some protection. We breathed a sigh of relief and thanked God for providing this unseen protection in the middle of our need.

We packed up as many of our dental tools as we could and then got a ride to the guest apartment for the night. It was a relief to get out of the troubled town for the night; we would come to see black ISIS flags plastered throughout the city squares in future years of ministry in that area.

We departed the next morning for our destination, bypassing our dead truck parked at the police fort and going on another road that would get us there. My friend Job was mechanical, and he had agreed to take a look at it and take responsibility for either getting it fixed or towing it back to the capital city for us.

Pressing on, we arrived in the remote village and set up a straightforward dental clinic in a small building used for public health. Almost as soon as we got started, we got a call from Job with our vehicle. He said it was running and would be with us in an hour.

We couldn't believe it because it had been entirely dead the previous night. He remarked that he had checked the fuses, and when he pulled out one fuse for the electrical system and plugged it back in, the truck had started right up. Was it a coincidence that a fuse had popped out on the outskirts of this spiritually dark town after four hours of uneventful driving, or was there something more at work here?

Regardless, we knew that in God's sovereignty, even over all the dark spirits, none of this had happened contrary to His will. Looking back, we were thankful to have gotten many opportunities to despair of our self-confidence and self-reliance in the first 24 hours of this outreach. Willing or not, we had been pushed to pray and seek His help, and we knew there were no coincidences in this life, but also no forces of darkness that our Lord could not overcome.

Earning the Right

Our vehicle finally growled into town, and we transferred our equipment back over into its more spacious interior and continued to see patients.

The unique thing we were noticing about these patients was that they almost, to a person, avoided talking with us, and clearly, they were not interested in praying with us. It was almost like there had been a village warning or discussion beforehand to be careful of the foreigners. Still, we provided the best dental care we could, and we gave the opportunity for patients to take a Bible if they wanted one, although few actually showed interest.

The next day, the headwoman involved with our invitation to the village came to us blessing us for our help. In addition to her praise, she also brought us stacks of pamphlets and tracts purporting the fantastic qualities and teachings of the Quran and their prophet.

We politely thanked her for giving us these materials, and then she suddenly asked us if she could have some of our literature.

"Sure!", we heartily offered and she hungrily started to take multiple Bibles off the shelf, cradling a tall and growing stack of them in her arms.

I finally said to her, "Well, how many Bibles do you actually need?"

She replied, "I want to take all of them!"

Understanding her motivations now, we then began to unload her arms and told her that she was welcome to have one, but we needed to keep the others in case someone else wanted them. She started to argue with us, wanting us to get rid of them and stop distributing them, but we stood our ground and said we only treated patients if we had literature available. She finally deferred and left angrily with a huff— only one Bible left in her hand.

After a few days of serving these villagers and especially a large number of women from this tribe, the headwoman returned to us while we were treating patients. Digging in our heels a bit as we waited to see what she wanted, we were surprised that she invited us over to dinner at her house.

We accepted and had a marvelous time dining in her home and getting to know her a little bit better. She really appreciated us being in the village now, and her countenance had dramatically changed from the opening day when she tried to take all the Bibles. The suspicious attitude was primarily gone, and she happily welcomed us to the resources of her home. The women of our team were invited to spend the rest of the nights in her house. They had been sleeping in a bedouin tent in the cold, so they happily agreed and got to take showers for the first time since our exodus from home.

In the end, they got to spend a lot of time with her and share about the hope they had within them. This initially angry woman would end up being the facilitator and a critical lynchpin responsible for us returning to the village and region periodically over the next five years.

Sharifa, Revisited

In one of those later visits, we had the happy occurrence of reuniting with the woman, Sharifa, who had been possessed by the three demons that I described in an earlier chapter. In the intervening years, some of our coworkers had regularly visited her and spent time with her teaching about the power of Jesus' name over the demons. She had been very receptive to their message and to their friendship.

She had heard from those women that we were in the area, so she came in for dental treatment. I was a bit nervous based on the last incident, but all went well, and she didn't have any seizures this time as we helped her with a deep cavity.

I had some time with her in the dental chair while we were waiting on her to get numb, and she was asking some thoughtful questions about what I believed.

I sense that many times, when people are challenged with a new idea or truth in their life, they often confront it with the same pattern. First, they will try to assimilate it into their current worldview without changing any of its basic foundations. If that proves impossible, they must then decide to adopt it which will change their worldview or completely reject it. I witnessed this dilemma many times when introducing the radical claims of Christianity to someone who had never heard.

For Muslims, I would often observe them trying to figure out if they can solely add a more important role for Jesus into their current religion and try to have it both ways. Then they could feel like they were friends with both sides as they integrated these differing points of view.

Ultimately, as time moves on and they learn more about the Bible, they start to run into walls with these competing worldviews. They realize that this combination of "Chrislam" can never work because Jesus and the Quran teach precisely opposite things. Then, they finally come to that point where they have to make a decision for themselves about their spiritual journey. They either reject the new ideas they are hearing about Jesus altogether or they adopt them entirely. I was always very happy to have them reach that place.

I felt like Sharifa was on the same path, so adapting a line of questioning I had heard previously in a sermon about John chapter 1, I chatted with this simple woman of the desert in the same way as I had heard the pastor talk that day.

I asked her, "If I told you that I knew another woman well, but later you found out I had never even talked with her, would you agree that I knew her well?"

She responded, "Certainly, you would not know her well. You can't know someone well if you have never talked to them."

I agreed with her but countered that you could, however, know a lot of information about people without talking to them. This knowledge about them can fool you into thinking that you know them. Unless you converse with them, what makes them tick, and the intricacies of their personality will always be hidden from you. Words are essential for relationship.

She agreed.

I asked her if she would like to know God better than she already did today, and she responded definitely in the affirmative. I then asked her, "How can we have words with God to get to know Him better and not just know things about Him?"

She said she didn't know.

I questioned her, "Who was called the Word of God?"

She correctly answered, "Jesus," and I was very thankful for this one similarity that not only is Jesus called the "Word of God" in the New

Testament, but also in the Quran. That name was carried from the Gospels into the Quran where Jesus in Arabic is called the *Kilamat Allah* or Word of God.

The Quran assuredly has a very different understanding of who Jesus is, and I certainly never try to use their book to study Him, but Muslims at least have that title already in their subconscious that Jesus is called the Word of God.

I challenged her to have words with God by praying in the name of Jesus and reading the teachings that He had left behind in the Gospels. Only by interacting with Jesus, God's Word, can you have a deeper relationship with God.

At the end of the treatment, she asked if someone could come to visit her in her tent and bring a Bible. She really wanted to have her own copy but didn't want to receive it in such a public location. We welcomed that opportunity and set up a time for some women to visit her the next day.

When they returned from their visit the following day, they told us that they had enjoyed a beneficial time of Bible study with Sharifa, sharing with her everything she needed to know for salvation. She had been excited to be with them and was eagerly licking up God's Word and wanted a deeper relationship with Jesus.

However, when they were almost done, her husband had returned home unexpectantly and walked into the tent, eyeing them with the Bibles in their hands. He had gotten very upset. Yelling, he had asked the women to leave and take all of the Bibles with them at once.

Sharifa was very sad and distraught at first, but as her husband kicked the guests out, she had suddenly switched her personality and told them sternly they should never return with those Bibles.

My friends were disheartened about this dramatic turn of events, but on the other hand, truly felt that the Spirit had been moving during their visit. They were pretty convinced that Sharifa had changed personalities at the end only as a sham trying to cover up for herself and maybe alleviate a beating or some other punishment she could receive from her furious husband. They couldn't hold that against her.

We reflected on the amazing power that men have in this part of the world to control every aspect of a woman's life. They can control where they go, what they wear, and what they do. In this circumstance, it made us feel like they control even what they believe and their eternal destination. How many women out in the deserts have been blocked from the saving message of the gospel because of unbelieving husbands who want to retain their power and control under the bulwark of Islam?

Still, we gave thanks that God was more powerful than any misguided husband. If He wanted women in remote parts to hear His message, He would make it happen because the gospel is no longer bound by the power of Satan (2 Tim 2:9).

In fact, Sharifa had heard everything she needed to follow Jesus, even if it was to follow Him with only a child-like faith, and we continue to pray for her heart to grow in that faith.

City on a Hill

Another region that we often visited in the South was my home for several months over the course of my ministry there. This place was desolate, frigid, and windy to my Southern sensibilities. The people there were very poverty-stricken, and we could tell it not only in the way they dressed and lived but also in their expectations for dental treatment.

In many poor places, people would be very anxious to have a tooth filled instead of an extraction, if at all possible. Sadly in this village, they were usually content to have as many teeth extracted as feasible, and they would almost prefer that treatment modality over a filling because they were resigned to the idea that everyone loses their teeth in the end. As a result, our percentage of fillings would always drop here, and it seemed like it largely became an extraction clinic.

One little girl I had to privilege to treat and know in this village was Hashmi. Sweet four-year-old Hashmi had been born with a particular syndrome that affects the nerves and sweat glands. Syndromes and particularly deafness are common traits among these desert peoples. This phenomenon is because of centuries of intermarriage among small people group populations.

Other children with the same syndrome as Hashmi tend to die at very young ages because their bodies cannot adapt to heat quickly enough. Besides that, they don't feel pain in many parts of their bodies, so they tend unknowingly to do exceptional damage to themselves. She was only alive primarily because of the work and care of a Christian woman who lived nearby.

It's hard to imagine how thankful we should be for the sensation of pain until you meet someone like her. She had sores in her knees that were the result of crawling on the ground. You or I would stop crawling after we had bloodied up our knees and created sores, but this little girl didn't feel anything and had kept crawling along the rocks until the bone was nearly exposed.

It would take months and months to bring healing to those tiny legs. Pain not only can lead us to God spiritually, but it ends up being the thing that literally keeps us alive physically in a lot of ways.

Hashmi had come to us because she couldn't feel anything in her mouth or lips. As a result, she had bitten off her lower lip with her teeth over several days and spit it out. When I looked at Hashmi with her missing lower lip, I also noticed that she had broken out a lot of her teeth. She had no proprioception or sensitivity in her teeth, so she would often bite on a rock or pebble hard enough until something broke and it was usually her tooth.

The recommended dental treatment for kids with this syndrome is the removal of all teeth because they can do great damage to their mouths, face, and hands if these numbed teeth remain. That was a hard treatment plan for me as a dentist, but I consented to try and help her as best I could, so at least she wouldn't bite off the rest of her lips and damage her hands.

Her caretaker insisted she couldn't feel anything and didn't need anesthetic, but I still used some in the first area because that was hard to believe. She truly didn't seem to be bothered by anything and just sat there for me as I extracted a molar.

I didn't numb her up for the other teeth, and it was a weird sensation just going tooth to tooth as she sat there daydreaming. Thankfully, their teeth usually don't have much root, so they all came out easily. Finishing up, she gave me a bloody smile and seemed not to resent me at all. If only all my other patients felt this way about my oral surgery!

Lord of the Flies

Another young man who didn't have quite as an enjoyable experience sought out my help out in this village as well. He allegedly had some mental disabilities but clearly could point out a large abscess in his mouth by his lower molar.

The villagers said that he had some trouble with wicked *jinn*. It's hard to know if that is what they blame mental disabilities on or if there had truly been some spiritual component to their accusation. All we noticed was as soon as he entered our tiny clinic, the place was full of flies. They swarmed all around him as I tried to take a look at the work that needed to be done. I noted that he had a scar on the same side of his face as the abscessed tooth, but it seemed to be old and had healed. We worked to get rid of the flies, but they were persistent. We decided we would need to find some spray during the next break period to get rid of them.

Regularly, with an abscessed tooth, you would like to get the patient on antibiotics for a few days to lessen the swelling and make it easier to get them numb. I didn't have that luxury since this man had traveled about an hour to get there and could not come back at a later time. So, I decided to do my best for him, and we would see if this "hot tooth" would get numbed.

After a nerve block injection, I began to inject more anesthetic around the tooth. I noticed that the tissue was not expanding as it typically does to hold the anesthetic liquid in that area. With flies buzzing all over my goggles and face, I then took in the big picture and realized that every time I injected some anesthetic, it was instantly squirting like a water gun out of the little scar on his face. I had made quite a mess on the wall and the floor but was also intrigued and amazed by how far it would squirt! It didn't take much sometimes to amaze this dentist.

Presumably, this tooth had been infected so long that the building pressure of the pus had found a path of least resistance to release the tension. Instead of being discharged inside the mouth like normal, this fistulous tract ran all the way to the exterior of his cheek. This tooth had died long ago, and the release for the infectious pus had been external to his oral cavity for a long time at this point.

Finally, getting his tooth numb and extracted, the young man was anxious to go back to his tent in the desert. We tried to slow him down as we gave him some information about what to do over the next few days, and he then hurriedly departed. To our surprise, not a single fly was left in the dental clinic. They had all departed with him!

Tooth Camp

One father, Abed, living in this village had shown quite an interest over a few months in talking to some longtime workers we knew there about spiritual matters. In the course of that relationship, his twelve-year-old daughter, Madi, who he was raising by himself, had enjoyed learning about stories from the Bible and had spent some time learning English with some of the women.

When I examined her mouth for the first time, I couldn't believe how much damage had already been done to her permanent teeth. She had only had her first molars for six years, and already two of them needed extraction, and the other two required large fillings. Aside from these broken-down molars, I quickly charted an additional eighteen fillings that she would need, some of them relatively large and heroic.

I told her father that I could help her with a couple of problems while there in the village, but to fully rehabilitate her mouth and get her into a good habit of oral hygiene, I would need her to become a patient in our clinic back home for a month. It would be a kind of "tooth camp" for the summer.

We all encouraged him in this step because we knew she would be losing most of her teeth in the near future without getting all the cavities fixed. Besides, we told him that we could include her in all of the women's Bible studies, and she could learn from the Bible almost every day while she was with us. We had already discerned that he was concerned about her spiritual health.

He was really excited after hearing about those possibilities and decided to let her come with us. We let her ride back with some of our female staff, and over the next month living in the clinic, I logged a lot of hours fixing her teeth in the dental chair.

We first thoroughly cleaned her teeth and then drilled and filled almost every tooth in her head until there was no more active disease in her mouth.

Over that month, her teeth, her smile, and her breath were undoubtedly improving, and her understanding of the gospel was blossoming as well. I would often see her heading to a Bible study with a wry smile on her mouth when she saw me. When she left to go home, we were encouraged that she had fully participated in the studies and seemed to be happier and more excited about life in general than before. We didn't know her heart, of course, but it seemed like Jesus had become an essential part of her life.

Unfortunately, life back home was not as free as she had gotten used to in the clinic. Her oldest brother, Islam, was very concerned about this newfound faith of his dad and sister, and he felt threatened and embarrassed by the possibility of it getting leaked out to the community. He started to place himself as an obvious barrier to any of our efforts at being part of their lives and continuously tried to insert doubts in their minds.

Trying to contact them at their home now became more complicated, and I particularly remember Islam filtering phone calls and not forwarding messages we would leave for his dad and sister. He would talk harshly to his dad trying to get him to return to his previous faith and pretty much held us with disdain if we ever visited their house.

When one of the foreigners living nearby visited them soon after that, he heard the sound of shattering glass and saw a rock had been thrown through the window of his truck. The son was clearly not providing any kind of protection for our visits, which would be reasonable for hospitality in this culture. On the contrary, he was likely stirring up anger at us from the community with the endgame of getting us out of their lives.

As a year went by and summer came again, we offered Madi a chance to come back for a second "tooth camp" at our clinic. She sadly had a couple of new cavities that showed her habits had not completely changed, but she was anxious to return and get out from under the thumb of her brother and the narrowness of her village.

This visit, however, was not as auspicious as the first. It seems like Madi had begun counting the cost of what it would mean to become a follower of Jesus. She would go to studies and interact with the women, but one woman finally told me that Madi was different this time, and her spirit was heavy and hopeless. She was not ready to make Jesus Lord and feel all the pressure from her home and community about this decision, so she had pushed back at the idea of making a significant change in her life.

We were disappointed by her change in direction, but at the same time, couldn't imagine the pressure she was under inside her home where the older brother held sway over most aspects of her future. In her place, anyone would have the same doubts and struggles; we could only pray that the Holy Spirit would move and give supernatural help to this situation.

One for the Road

Another complication that occurred while working in the South at a different time was the disappearance of our clinic truck. I was not on this particularly infamous trip, but the dental team had finished their work after a genuinely long, but agreeable week.

Exhausted, they began the long track back home. The professional driver they hired to drive the truck had eagerly departed early, which wasn't a problem because the truck went very slow, and they knew they would catch up after only a short time.

The problem was that the farther and longer they drove they still didn't see the clinic truck. At first, they were angry at him for ruining the engine by driving so fast. As time passed and it became theoretically impossible for him to be ahead, they realized he had not driven the truck in the direction of home at all. No one knew why, but it seemed he was hijacking our clinic truck for some nefarious purpose.

A leader at our clinic postulated that whatever had happened, the truck would still end up back at the clinic at some point because the driver would not want to be incarcerated for theft, which was a severe crime in our part of the world. He thought that the mischievous man would likely try to return the truck at night and then deny that anything unseemly had happened.

We put out the equivalent of an all-points bulletin for the truck and warned our clinic security guard to be alert at night in case he came back in the dark. Finally, the police reported back to us that the truck had been seen on the road going in the opposite direction from the clinic.

Later we received notice that someone had seen the truck pulled off the side of the road near customs, and it seemed to be stuck in some sand. They called the driver's family, and they claimed not to know where the driver had gone and said he had not called them at all.

A call came from the police at 3 AM on the third day after the disappearance. The driver had stealthily returned in the middle of the night and was attempting to sneak the truck into the clinic parking lot when he had been arrested. Part of a fender was missing because the truck had been towed at some point and a hard-packed sand bank had ripped the fender off in the process of getting it back on the road. More interesting was when the police entered the clinic truck only to find it stocked full of cigarettes and beer.

We finally understood the purpose of the theft. The driver had used a clearly marked volunteer clinic truck to smuggle a truckload of taxable goods past customs. His plan was then surely to make a lot of money selling all these tax-free items at the regular price.

The consequence of his little adventure was that he lost his job immediately and was placed in jail for a few days awaiting his hearing. At the time of his hearing, he simply said that he drove the truck right back and never stopped anywhere. He denied that he had purchased anything to place in the truck and claimed that his arrest in the middle of the night had never happened. His bald-faced lies in the face of all the facts were incredible, but an unsurprising symptom of trying to avoid shame at all costs.

Rising Tension

We are always meeting people and getting to know them in order to help them with their needs but also to be a vehicle and conduit of the Holy Spirit. Even though we often remind ourselves that He is the one really doing the work and we are just called to be obedient, it's hard not to get discouraged when you see rising oppression against the name of Jesus.

The last time I made a trip to one particular area in the South was heartbreaking because instead of seeing revival, we actually saw a retreat of sorts from spiritual truth. True, we don't know what is really happening behind the scenes in hearts, but the evil one was not going down without a fight in this area.

Some young boys who had generally been very kind to us in the past were clearly hostile when we arrived. As we tried to make conversation with them, they began to howl curses at us for being Christians and were harassing us as we walked from place to place. It increased to the point where the boys were demonstrating sexual motions towards our female colleagues and were cursing Jesus.

We confronted them that even in Islam, you don't believe those things, and we reminded them how it was so shameful to act this way, but they persisted. They could care less about the judgment of God on their actions as they showed no shame in their behavior.

Later, a young boy who was apparently still holding us in favor approached us. We were glad to at least see one kind face out of all of these boys we had cared for over the years. He confided to us that the *imam*, or spiritual leader of the village, had come to the school that day and warned all the kids about the foreigners who were coming to do a dental clinic. The boy said that this occurrence was the reason for their behavior earlier because they had been empowered to do that by their elders and spiritual leaders.

I felt so sick in my heart about the verbal wounds I had received, but mainly about the darkness of this village and the knowledge that it wasn't just coming from troublemaking kids but from the adults at the top. They would greet us with welcomes and smiles when we arrived, all the while devising evil against us in private.

Luke's passage about Jesus' teaching in 6:22-23 was comforting in that moment:

> *Blessed are you when people hate you, when they exclude*
> *you and insult you and reject your name as evil, because*
> *of the Son of Man. Rejoice in that day and leap for joy,*
> *because great is your reward in heaven. For that is how*
> *their ancestors treated the prophets.*

It was hard to feel like leaping, but we also remembered that they rejected us because they were really rejecting Jesus. We were only His messengers, and it was not a message that anyone in spiritual leadership in this village wanted to hear.

Why don't they want to hear about God's love and the free forgiveness of sins? It's hard to know for sure, but the human soul in its fallen state rebels against anything else that would claim authority over it. The heart of man in its pride would prefer to work harder and harder to make God accept him and therefore put God in his debt. This dedication gives the person the illusion of control and the pride of accomplishment but is an impossible task and a total misunderstanding of the character of God. It's a delusion that Satan loves to encourage.

In addition, man-made religion that leads people into slavery and more and more rules tends to bolster the power of the people at the top. No man in charge is going to willfully let people fall away towards the grace of the gospel in Christ. That would weaken his power and take away the fear he holds over people's hearts; the thing that keeps him in business.

Grace and forgiveness may lead women to be held as equals which to him would be ruinous in this male-dominated place of multiple wives. A whole gender mistreated by some as simply another commodity waits to be freed by the gospel.

The truth is that I must often confess and fight against very similar sins in my own heart. A desire to control my destiny, a desire to put God in my debt, a desire to live for self is my daily struggle. It's no wonder that these choke points in Islam are so insidious because these areas of sin are so hard to fight against in my own life. Every day I wake up and try to earn my salvation all over again and only succeed when I reorient my mind to the salvation of grace that comes through the work of Jesus.

How can I expect them to progressively improve the quality and freedom of their society without the power of the Holy Spirit? It's only in that power that they have any chance of change and that we have any chance of hope.

Chapter 17
CENTRAL COMMUNITIES

It was always an encouraging development to make a new contact with a Bedouin and then find out that they dwelt in the vicinity of our town where we could maintain a tighter relationship with them. It was exciting to travel and live in distant villages for short periods, but it also required a lot of energy and planning.

These friends who were close to home did not require us to stay overnight with them to be in their lives. Instead, we could stay home and travel there often whenever we wanted to visit them and therefore have a more prolonged and deeper relationship with them.

The first connection I ever made to a nearby village was through a coworker who had become friends with the sheik of a modest but vibrant community. Driving over on a visit, he introduced us, and we planned out a time for us to come and do dental screenings and treatment in his village.

This project would be a "door opener" event that would address some felt needs and help us get to know the community better. The sheik was thrilled about the upcoming campaign and welcomed us with a big smile.

After we arrived on the appointed day and began to treat people with their dental needs, some realization started to sink in about the context of what we were actually doing. As people walked up to get a place in line, we couldn't help but notice that the sheik was telling the people, "Look, I brought you an American dentist to take care of your teeth! Vote for me in the election."

We hadn't realized that the election was coming up in the next few weeks, and this sheik, who is what we call the mayor of the town, was running for reelection. This reality didn't discourage us because we knew that he needed us as much as we needed him.

It actually motivated us to openly pray with the patients and care for them while having Bibles available to anyone interested. The sheik was certainly using us for his election campaign, but we at least got some benefit from him that allowed us to work in this village, a spiritual quid pro quo of sorts.

We started to notice that some wealthier looking people began to show up at the clinic, which was contrary to our agreement to see primarily the poor. He pleaded with us to see them because they were influential people in the region. We agreed to see one of them for every two poor people, and that seemed to be a good compromise.

The sheik noticed that we were giving out toothbrushes and toothpaste to our patients to which we had taught oral hygiene instructions. He asked if he could be the one managing the boxes of toothbrushes and help us by giving them out. We didn't give in to that request, because we could see his desired outcome pretty well, but that illustrates the tit-for-tat we developed back and forth throughout the day.

Indecent Proposal

We felt like things were going very well in this gambit, and we continued driving to this village for the next three days, serving the felt needs of these Bedouin and apparently the sheik's election campaign. I specifically remember how hopeless some of the people were in this community. That desperation was underlined in the actions of Fati, one of the most memorable female patients I met.

While doing a filling on her, she suddenly reached out her arm in fear and grabbed my leg. The action of a woman touching a man in any way is highly unusual in the culture and took me by surprise.

I robotically lifted her hand off my leg and returned it to her side. She seemed to calm down, so I surmised it had been purely a fear-based reaction to the whine of the dental drill.

However, as I continued working, her hand gently snuck back over to my thigh, and she grabbed me. My female dental assistant immediately rebuked her, and I calmly returned her hand to her side and scolded her, saying she needed to keep her hands to herself if she wanted me to finish the work.

After finishing, in broken English, she told us again and again how much she appreciated our help and how great a dentist I was. We dismissed her, and I thought that was yet another confusing interaction, but I would surely never see her again.

My prediction was shown to be false the next day when she showed up again for treatment. We denied her a second treatment since there were so many people waiting for their first treatment, but she persisted in passing on a letter to me through my assistant.

We opened up the letter and read it together. The letter stated again how great a dentist I was and that she was trying to learn English and would dedicate herself to speaking English fluently over the next few months. She further said that she would like to be my wife, and she would do anything I wanted her to do and would move to America as soon as I would like that to happen.

We concluded that we needed to talk to her directly to nip this in the bud, so my assistant called her over so we could talk to her together. I thanked her for the touching compliment of proposing marriage but informed her that this could never happen, because I was already happily married. We told her she needed to look elsewhere for a husband, and she should not come back anymore.

To our surprise, she responded frankly by saying that my being married was not a big issue for her. She would be happy to be my second wife; she just needed out of this village however possible.

Initially, I hadn't blamed her for her radical actions, because I jokingly reasoned I must be a pretty hard catch to resist. However, I quickly returned to reality as it sunk in that the true situation was much different. She must have a really difficult life in this village.

It was sad to realize she was ready to do almost anything to leave her town, including marrying a total stranger and being just slightly better than a household servant as a second wife. We dismissed her again and reflected on the desperate situation in which so many of these people lived.

Halcyana

Another village we went to nearby was Halcyana, an impoverished district where the Bedouins were working as farmers. We generally didn't see Bedouin working in this fashion as farmers, but here there was a massive government farm fully irrigated and maintained where they could work. Outside the fence, where the people lived in their tents, lay only rock with no grass and little opportunity for industry of any other type besides a few flocks of sheep that were eating who knows what.

As a dental team, we were overwhelmed with the needs of the people to receive basic dental care and quickly filled up our appointments for several days. There were some large private wheat farms nearby, and we began to treat several of their farmhands who were dealing with painful dental issues.

Such a mixed group of shepherds and farmers and Bedouins from several different countries led to a few interesting encounters. One man brought his wife, fully clad in a black *niqab*, to fix a broken tooth that he said needed a filling. I asked her to lift up the *niqab* veil covering her face so I could look at the tooth and make a diagnosis about how we could treat it. The husband quickly countered my request and asked me if I couldn't just do the filling on his wife without removing her veil. I asked him how could I possibly do that, and he informed me I could just go up under the veil with my dental drill and make the filling.

After refusing his suggestions as impossible, the man finally relented and let me see his wife absent the veil over her face. In these moments, I was always wondering what I was actually going to see at the "big reveal," but she had a healthy and pleasing appearance.

The usual cynical joke I always heard from Muslim men is that the husbands that make their wives wear a *burqa* (head to toe covering) or *niqab* (a veil revealing only the eyes) all the time do that for two reasons. Either because she is gorgeous and they don't want other men to covet her or because she is unsightly and they don't want anyone to know.

Another woman patient I looked at needed an extraction. After getting everything ready to get this tooth out, I could tell she was not settled—she had something on her mind. She quietly leaned over and asked me if it was okay to extract a tooth because she was menstruating. I had never heard that question before but calmed her worries about that being a contraindication. She didn't want to require a blood transfusion, and thankfully my dental surgery didn't lead to that outcome.

In a similar vein, a young man asked me another question there that I had never encountered before. After extracting his tooth and giving him some home care instructions on how to take care of the socket, he waited for my assistant to leave and then beckoned me over for a question.

He asked me, "How long do I need to wait until I have sex?" The inquiry took me by surprise, but I was able to rally quick enough to tell him, "Don't have sex for three months. If you do, you'll die." His eyes got big as that thought slowly sunk in, but then I quickly let him off the hook and told him there was no delay needed—I was just kidding and he was very relieved.

The people there were very thankful, and we developed a long relationship with many of them over my entire time in the country. The owners of the private farms were very kind to us and thanked us for taking care of their day laborers because we were helping their farm production in the process.

They informed us that an ancient jar had been found during an excavation that was full of wheat dating back to the Roman Empire. Scientists were able to get seeds from this ancient wheat to germinate, and now they were growing this ancient Roman wheat in their fields. The realization that the history of this area was having an impact on even present-day life was intriguing.

These same men took us on a tour and drove us around on these sand flats at high speeds in their trucks. The men were pretty adept at hitting the wheel in one direction and then the other and getting the vehicles to spin all the way around. It made for a memorable finish to one of our work weeks there.

When the Moon was Cleft Asunder

When I reflect on another village area that was near our home, I can't help but be nostalgic about the sweet and happy experiences I enjoyed in that district. The times I spent there resulted in many good interactions with several men and even some women who became friends as we got to know them and their families over the years.

We worked in that place with a school and also with a cultural center; primarily entering the lives of villagers yet again through our skills in dentistry. We got involved in starting a toothbrushing program for some of the school children as well as providing dental relief for many of the students and female teachers.

Out of all those interactions, one memorable woman, Batul, was an English teacher in the school who sought our help for her teeth. After spending some time with her in the dental clinic over a couple of different days, she had noticed that we had *Injils* available for patients to take home with them.

She talked with my friend Kent who was visiting the dental clinic that day, and she told us she had been taught many negative things about the *Injil* over the years by other Muslims, but she had never read the *Injil* for herself. She said she would like to take one and read it with her husband, Hamdi. This request was unusual indeed, and we could tell she was a more highly educated woman who had a curiosity about the Scriptures. I felt like this was an authentic interaction; like the Holy Spirit was working in that moment, and it was not just a polite action done superficially to thank us for our hard work.

Typically, in a similar situation with a man, I would quickly exchange contacts with him and follow up in the near future. However, with a woman like this one, it was impossible, but I didn't want to lose contact with her if I could help it. I was mystified wondering what I should do.

I excitedly gave her an Injil and asked her if I could give her my wife's phone number. I told her that my wife Grace would love to talk to her and even study the *Injil* with her. She took the information and the *Injil*, thanking me with a big smile, and walked out the door. I wasn't sure if I would ever hear from Batul again, but I told Grace about the circumstances just in case she ever got a phone call.

About one week later, Grace told me Batul had called. She had been reading the *Injil* and wanted to meet with us! Batul remarked that we should come over for a meal because Hamdi had been reading the *Injil* also and wanted to talk to me about it. Grace felt like she was very pleasant and excited on the phone, and we made it a priority to meet with them as soon as possible.

A short time later, we found ourselves back in their village and trying to hunt down their small home, which ended up being in a neighboring village and not the actual town that had the school. They greeted us with open arms and joyful hospitality, and we also got to meet the extended family outside before we made our way into their home. They lived in a home next to several other small homes housing their parents and brothers.

Batul had a wide grin on her face as she asked us to sit in the salon of their simple painted cinder-block house. The floor was covered in a variety of carpets, and it seemed like they had several conveniences in their home, probably due to the fact that Hamdi worked in the army, and Batul had income from the school.

What we call DINKS (double income no kids) in the West is a very unusual circumstance in the Middle Eastern life and is often a result of infertility, although I knew one other educated woman who had told me she wanted to delay having children. In this particular situation, they did have small kids, but the grandparents were watching them as Batul went to work.

We sipped tea with them and enjoyed the usual near-hour of pleasantries with them until we finally got to a discussion of what was dear to our hearts. As we began to discuss the Gospels, Batul had several thoughtful questions for us about what she had read.

Receiving the *Injil*, they had started at the beginning in Matthew, and it was apparent that she was fascinated by some of the radical things Jesus was teaching in the Sermon on the Mount. As we gave her a little context and explanation about some of the harder things to understand, she seemed very accepting of what it said about life and the way Jesus said to live it.

The disappointing thing was that Hamdi kept pointing out things about verses that he didn't like or that were troublesome. Unlike his wife, he had not been reading Matthew to learn what it said, but rather to find problems with it so he could bring up things about which to disagree.

He told us, "I could never follow these teachings. Jesus tells everyone to pull out their eyeballs and cut off their hands. It's completely crazy to believe someone like this."

Before we could counter his misinterpretation, Batul quickly looked at Hamdi with squinted eyes and countered, "You know that is not what He means in that passage! Jesus is telling us how important it is to flee from sin. He's not actually saying everyone should take out their eyeballs!"

The conversation continued like this for some time with Batul asking real and heart-felt questions while Hamdi would distract with ridiculous interpretations of any verse with a hint of hyperbole or symbolism in Jesus' teaching. Hamdi finally said that since he had spent time reading some of the *Injil*, I should spend some time considering how the Quran correctly described that the moon had been sliced in two and put back together.

I had absolutely no idea what he was talking about when he said that—I almost thought he was making a joke. Hamdi wasn't smiling; he was serious. He quoted for me Sura 52:1, which says, "The Hour is nigh, and the moon is cleft asunder." Then he told me that that verse described how the moon had been split into two parts by a miracle of the prophet Muhammad and then put back together.

Just in case I didn't believe that it happened, he showed me a short YouTube video that stated it happened, showing a picture of a line on the moon which therefore proved it. I was thoroughly unimpressed and unconvinced by the verse and YouTube proof. This one verse seems very poetic and not literal at all. It doesn't talk about a miracle of Muhammad, or the idea it was put back together.

Sadly, most of the Quranic proofs I received during my time in the Middle East were YouTube videos that are poorly done and can only convince someone who is already on board. I told him these sentiments as gently as I could, but he insisted the Quran was not poetic at all about this fact but is a very literal book. I brought up the verse in the Sura 18:85 that says the sun sets every night in a spring of muddy water and asked him if that is fact or poetry. Their famous Abu Dawud in his Hadith writing also records the prophet Muhammad saying directly that the sun sets in a spring of warm water.

Logic wasn't his strong suit, and he didn't want to go down that path, so he just offered to show me a few more YouTube videos that he said would be wholly convincing. Instead, I decided to end my unfruitful conversation with him and asked him to show me his animals outside. Leaving the house ended up letting Grace have a chance to share more with Batul in private.

We chatted outside and looked at his homemade birdhouse full of pigeons as well as his goats and sheep. Being an army man, he also showed me the militarized border area adjacent to his house, and we discussed politics. All the while, I knew the women were having a good discussion inside and quietly prayed that the Spirit would open Batul's heart to hear and believe much like Lydia in Philippi. I prayed the same for his husband. I truly wanted to see them both loving God to the fullest.

When we finished and returned inside, Grace had spent well over an hour with Batul in her house. We rose to go and made our final goodbyes to Hamdi and Batul. Hamdi told me that he didn't want to read any more of the *Injil*. He would love to have us come back some time and visit, but he didn't want to discuss the Bible anymore.

Almost as a strange consolation, I remember Hamdi addressed us as we were leaving and said, "You should realize that we are the first people in our family and in this whole village who have ever read the *Injil*. No one here has ever seen an *Injil* here, let alone ever read or studied it, and you have made that happen. You should feel good enough about doing that."

I was pretty sad about the conversation with Hamdi, but excited that God had been able to use Grace is such a great way during this time. It felt strange considering his words that we had enjoyed the privilege of being the first to bring the Gospels to this village. It was exciting to hear that confirmed with his backhanded compliment, but also sad that no one had been there before.

The realization came that as awesome as that was, in the absence of repentance and faith in the Creator, it was disappointing. I desired results beyond that, results that included people and hearts and not just checking a box.

We had Batul and Hamdi over to our house later as well, but the subject of the Gospels was never able to be broached in-depth again. I wasn't the Holy Spirit, and we could only attempt to be as obedient as possible and share as much as we could. We pray that the seeds we had planted in hearts would spring up in time, though we may never see the fruits ourselves.

My Sheep Hear My Voice

A shepherd in that area once told me a truly remarkable thing in the middle of a pretty dull conversation. I was trying to keep the conversation going, which was hard sometimes when you have so little in common with these simple, shepherd folk in the rural areas. So, considering his area of expertise, I asked, "How do you know which ones are your sheep? Do you tag them or brand them with some distinguishing mark?"

At that time, his sheep were mixed collectively with the sheep of several other shepherds. The large group of over 100 animals was grazing on what grass they could find in this lonely desert place.

He responded that none of them marked their sheep in any way. He said that they all knew their sheep by their shape and coloring, so branding was not necessary. Plus, he told me—his sheep all knew him by his voice.

A short time later, he shouted a few words that his sheep had unmistakably heard many times before. His sheep extracted themselves from the midst of this intertwined larger group and came over to him. Another shepherd then fingered a short tune on his little lute, and all his sheep perked up and went in another direction towards him.

John 10:25-28 describes this very phenomenon when Jesus uses this picture of shepherd life to illustrate God's relationship to His elect people.

> *The works that I do in my Father's name bear witness about me, but you do not believe because you are not among my sheep. My sheep hear my voice, and I know them, and they follow me. I give them eternal life, and they will never perish, and no one will snatch them out of my hand.*

We didn't always know who the sheep of the Father were, but we believed God's promises that He had called people from every tribe, nation, and tongue, and those people were just waiting for an opportunity to believe. It was such a blessing to speak into the lives of people out in the desert and pray that the Batuls and Fatis and even Hamdis might be ready to hear the voice of the Father.

We couldn't convince anyone with our words—that work had to come from God Himself. It gave us confidence that wherever we went He was calling his sheep to Himself. We must only remain faithful and obedient to proclaim His message.

Chapter 18
COMMUNITY HEALTH

Although sharing about Jesus was the spiritual fire and lifeblood at the heart of our ministry, I always loved it when we could find opportunities to enter into discipleship with patients, neighbors, or villagers interested in following Jesus. Our first interaction in people's lives meant that the majority of our work included sharing with tribal people about the gospel of Jesus for probably the first time in their lives. However, that never took away our conviction that we were ultimately called to discipleship whenever it was possible.

While the Great Commission uses several participles like "going," "baptizing," and "teaching," we know from the original Greek text that the only imperative listed in the Great Commission of Matthew 28:18-20 is the command to "make disciples."

> And Jesus came and said to them, 'All authority in heaven and on earth has been given to me. Go therefore and make disciples of all nations, baptizing them in the name of the Father and of the Son and of the Holy Spirit, teaching them to observe all that I have commanded you. And behold, I am with you always, to the end of the age.'

This making of disciples was difficult in our context. Not only was it challenging to find a private place or time, but it was infrequent to meet what my good friend Kent often called a FAT person. That is someone who is Faithful, Available, and Teachable. When we encountered such people, we were always excited to dig in and grow together with them as we studied and prayed together. Sometimes we discipled new believers to increase their faith. But quite honestly, in our context, we often discipled non-believers hoping they would come to faith in the process.

Theory and Practice

Theoretically, the basis for our method of carrying out discipleship was not our idea but based on biblical concepts that have been around forever and have been forgotten and subsequently rediscovered over the centuries. This pattern of lost and found is usually the case with good ideas, and I was blessed to be around people who had studied these thoughts and wanted to put them into practice while challenging me to do the same.

In the Three-Self Church model that emerged 150 years ago, new thinkers were trying to energize newly planted churches. They emphasized ideas that arguably are described in the book of Acts: self-propagating, self-governing, and self-supporting church bodies. Following examples that can be witnessed in Paul's church-planting method, these leaders challenged churches not to create something that could only be managed and maintained by the outsider. Preferably, they should build something with the DNA that could last long after the planters had left town. If it was founded in the culture, style, and leadership of the local peoples, it would have a better chance to endure.

In the same way, our goal with discipleship was to create a gathering that self-propagated, self-governed, and self-supported itself and had the DNA to help it last without Western influence.

To do that, we ideally wanted the Bible study to be simple and very reproducible. This goal meant the study couldn't be taught unilaterally from a seminary-educated Westerner but should empower all members of the group to lead and participate in the meeting even from the beginning. If you have ever conducted a Bible study, you know that the one leading the study always learns the most, so we wanted that to happen with new believers or interested people and not just the longtime believers.

We also wanted discipleship to occur with means that could be reproduced in the villages. We didn't use PowerPoint or any other audiovisual helps that they couldn't regularly use themselves. If we did, that would communicate to them that they could never do something like this on their own and create a debilitating barrier.

We usually desired the style of teaching to be easily copied. This objective traditionally happened by reducing the study of Scripture to asking four questions, much in the vein of a discovery Bible study.

After reading a particular passage, the leader may first ask a volunteer in the group, "What did it say?" A person would then put the verses in their own words or in some cases, recite it almost entirely. We found that in an oral society, the memory of people was specially developed. After that, they would ask the group if anything was left out or was all the passage covered, and that would give a chance for others to fill in any missing parts of the passage.

Secondly, the group leader would ask, "What did it mean?" Many people could answer, and all were encouraged as long as it wasn't outright heresy. Longtime believers would try to lay back during this part as much as possible. In the case of problematic interpretation, maybe another Scripture could be gently recommended because "only Scripture interprets Scripture."

Thirdly, the group leader would ask, "How do I apply this to my life?" Sometimes this would be a hard section, but it was always critical to be sure we were not just teaching knowledge. "Teaching them to observe" or obey all that Jesus had taught as the Great Commission commands was an essential goal of this process.

Lastly, the discussion leader would ask, "Who can you share this with today?" We wanted the teaching not just to be learned in a bubble but for new learners to process this with their family and neighbors. Then, if they had a dramatic change in their lives, it would be more natural for them to communicate it to loved ones with which they were already in conversation. Once the study began, we would often ask at the next meeting to find out who they shared it with during the previous week so we could build accountability.

I used this method over and over in our time in the Middle East, but truthfully it became my preferred method for discipling my kids as well. Going through these questions with them opened up doors for spiritual learning and application in their lives. It also helped to develop my style of doing this discipleship with others.

Working for God

My first outside experience at doing this method was to join in a Bible Study on the book of John already in progress with two Christians and two other Muslim background believers. I knew the theory as I described above, but it was eye-opening for me to see that this study time was being led by a man who was very new to the faith. He did terrific leading the discussion on chapter six and asking the group the first two questions about what we had read and what it meant. When we got to the application, he surprised me because, at that moment, a light came on for him as we tried to apply the passage to his and our lives. He read John 6:28-29, which says, "Then they said to him, "What must we do, to be doing the works of God?" Jesus answered them, "This is the work of God, that you believe in him whom he has sent."

He was clearly surprised by this verse. He told us he had always thought the works God demanded were to pray the shahada and other prayers five times daily, fast at the proper times, give alms, and visit Mecca. He had done those things but had failed so many times under the weight of their burden. But here, Jesus was not saying we had to do these works at all. With a big smile of evident relief on his face, he exclaimed that the only work God wanted him to do was believe in Jesus, who God sent to do the works for him!

I saw through later study times in the Gospel of John that the Scriptures themselves would prompt this same man to ask great questions as he grew in faith. We read about baptism, and he wanted to know if he could be baptized. We learned about the Lord's supper and came to find out he had stockpiled some bread and wine in his room for the occasion because he had been reading ahead. It was amazing to see God's Word bearing fruit among these people.

Creating Collisions through CHE

As I mentioned, the main difficulty in carrying out our plans regarding discipleship was often a lack of participants. To find more people that we could meet and interact with, we had to be creative with using our time. One of my leaders, Henry, had challenged us that the goal was to create as many natural collisions as you can between yourselves and outsiders. This terminology stuck in my mind. The more collisions that you created, the better the chance you would have at meeting a person who was ready to learn more.

One of the most promising ways that we went about trying to create these collisions for initial sharing and discipleship was the idea of CHE or community health evangelism. This program of working in rural communities has the goal of promoting holistic health among the people by empowering them to take charge of the solutions. While doing emergency dental care among the villages was great for relief work, CHE allowed us to move from relief to development. With development, we had more long-term interactions with people as we tried to help them make lasting changes to their communities.

CHE was a good fit for us because it incorporates a lot of the same strategies we used in the Bible studies. We wanted all of the leadership and vision to come from the people themselves and tried hard not to point out any negative matters ourselves. We had the villagers self-determine on which health issues they wanted to work and just offered our expertise as a temporary jump-start for a program of health that they could continue to carry out long after we were gone.

CHE training for the villagers developed initially in Africa where there are often believers you can use and send out as community health workers to multiply your efforts. You could train them with holistic health messages that combine physical and spiritual health, and then they would go out and teach these same lessons to several households by themselves. Although it possibly is frowned upon by the developers of the program, we ultimately had to adapt and modify some of these principles to better relate to our context where villages would not have even a single believer in the vicinity. We could expect our ministry mainly to be towards the small group of healthcare workers we were training. Because they were not believers, we didn't necessarily expect them to carry out the spiritual teachings to other households, although we hoped they would.

For instance, we had several dental trainings that incorporated good ideas about improving their oral health with spiritual insights that would make them think as well. A favorite story that always came up during dental times is the teaching of Jesus about the defilement that comes from inside. He said, "Listen and understand. What goes into someone's mouth does not defile them, but what comes out of their mouth, that is what defiles them" (Matthew 15:11).

When a dental patient walks in smoking in one hand and eating candy with the other, it's usually pretty obvious what is causing the decay you are going to see inside. It's almost like taking a dare to say, "Open up." Much more eye-opening for patients is to hear that if bad things are coming out of their mouths (speech, anger, hate)—those actions indicate a much more dangerous diagnosis; they reveal a heart that's sick. The basic teachings of Jesus continue to be profound for people who previously have never had a chance to hear them. Like a good doctor, His teachings and life expose the diseases in our lives and our patients' lives. We were happy to teach them that He provided the cure at His own expense.

Trial and Error

Our history of using CHE in the villages was a rocky road that we often didn't get right, but overall it delivered enough results that we kept using it. With each mistake, we continued to hone our understanding and practice until it was getting a little better each time.

One of the first times that we made a cold-call approach to a village to use CHE, we quickly were directed to the mayor of this small village. Abu Fayez was a kind man, and he dressed the part wearing Western business style dress in the middle of this very rural village. He welcomed us into his home and invited several key people to meet with us. It was a cigarette-fest inside the salon of his house as an administrator from the town came as well as the religion teacher from the local high school.

We explained ourselves and our goal of assisting and empowering their people to make positive changes in their village. We complimented them on all of the good things we had already seen in their village from schools to clean water and asked if there were any matters there that they wished were a little different. We did not show our hand and tell them our areas of expertise because we wanted to let them freely decide how we could help them.

These key men brainstormed a little bit and listened to a parable story we shared with them about another hypothetical village that had taken ownership of a problem. With just a small assist from outsiders, this village had tackled a vital safety problem and fixed it sustainably, so they never again needed outside help with it.

The men were excited, and so we asked to meet with them again the next week. We also implored them to invite some key representative women from the village so we could hear precisely from both men and women where they wanted help. We promised to share with them another parable story the next week and begin to figure out some areas of need.

We thought it went well overall and were encouraged to return the next week and continue the conversation with a handful of leading men and women from the village. We planned to tell another story that gave a lesson on how villagers can help themselves far better than outsiders can help and then have a vote on what the priority needs list was for this village. The only disconcerting thing was that as we got in the car to leave after this first auspicious meeting, one of the men asked if we could bring presents with us next time, maybe new bicycles for the kids.

We had just spent two hours talking about it, but we reminded them that our work did not include presents or bicycles or other handouts, but involved empowering them. They waved as we left, and we discussed among ourselves how this gave us a bad feeling in the pits of our stomachs. Usually, this means that some well-meaning organization had already been there and given out handouts. Once that has happened in a village, the people only equate foreigners with donations in the future, and it's tough to change their expectations.

Arriving the next week at the mayor's home, a young man frantically waved at us to follow him. He said the meeting today would be in their new Youth Center. We hadn't seen anything new in this village but ended up following him for a mile or so down a small hill to the back of the settlement. As we turned a corner around the hill, a massive brand-new building came into view, which prominently said "Youth Center" across the front.

It was a beautiful building, especially for that region and we walked in and looked around at many spacious and empty rooms. The young man told us that USAID had recently paid for them to build this immense building for their village, and although it was ready, they had no staff or furnishings to make it useful. We certainly didn't see any youth.

He told us that everyone was already there and waiting on us as he quickly led us into a hall that was set up with chairs. Our eyes bulged as we walked into the gym, shocked that at least 50 women were eagerly staring at us with Abu Fayez and the other two men we met previously in the front row smiling. We noticed that there were four chairs assembled in the front of this hall facing this considerable assembly.

Abu Fayez welcomed us and waved his hand at the crowd to show us how he had succeeded in getting women to come this time. We realized we must have shamed him a little by mentioning the lack of women last time, so now he had honored us by bringing almost every woman in the village to this meeting. We had brought materials and prepared to sit on the floor and talk personally with five or six people, but now we were prized speakers for a colossal event.

After stumbling through a few exercises that were properly designed for a small group, we began to ask the people to dream about how they would want things in their lives to improve. We weren't going to give them any suggestions, because we wanted the ownership to come from them. After a lot of awkward silences, Abu Fayez happily interjected that he wished they had better dental care in their village. Another one of the men said they could use some instruction on asthma since many of them had problems with the blowing sand causing breathing problems.

We then again inquired of the women in the room what was relevant to them. They all as a group started to chime in that they wanted help with their teeth and asthma. We realized that culturally, they almost had to agree with these leading men since we had put the women and the men in the same room. We never did it that way again.

The other curious thing about these freely determined healthcare selections was that these men (and women) had chosen dentistry and asthma needs. It was curious because three of us happened to be trained in the dental field, and another nurse in the group was trained especially in asthma care. We had never mentioned or hinted about our skill sets or occupations, but it seemed like these men had done their homework and figured out who we were.

Now that we were committed, we carried out a dental hygiene program over the next few months and did a short series on asthma. Unlike other programs we would do later with CHE, these people just never quite took ownership of doing anything on their own. Almost every time we came, people would expectantly ask us if we brought them any cash or presents. When we responded in the negative, some people would then start to wander off.

Overall, we found their attention lacking, but we did learn a lot from our mistakes in the process. Regardless of the attendance, we still got to share many spiritual things with the mayor, his family, and other people who came to all the meetings. We began some new relationships this way, and I think they all improved their dental health or at least dental knowledge as a result.

However, following this village, we always tried to scout out villages that previously had not received handouts. Once people receive gifts, their mentality is of dependency, which was the very thing we were trying to avoid. We also never had the women in the same meeting as the men. We conducted these two meetings separately having women on our team meet with the village women. Only after all the votes had been cast, we would bring the men and women together to look at the results and discuss what challenges they wanted to tackle as a community.

In a later village, we made a new mistake of opening up the vote to anything they wanted to address, which is the true CHE style in Africa. We were horrified to see that they voted for us first to stop the drug problem in their village, and second they wanted us to help them start a union so they could go on strike against the government and get their wages increased. These were not things we were particularly skilled at, nor did we as foreigners want to start something adversarial to the government who was letting us live there. After that, we always limited the vote to healthcare items—issues that we could legally help them with inside our country.

Zaytoona

Our most successful CHE village was a tiny outpost of Bedouins that we found while looking for a past patient who had come to faith. In this windswept little village of Zaytoona, some intermarried families were living in the same proximity amid a rubble-strewn field. These families had only simple tents, a patchwork of colorful plastic tarps and canvas.

They certainly did not live like more well-off Bedouin in their unmistakable *Bayt Shaar* tents made of tightly woven black goat hair. No, these people had only a few sheep and goats for their livelihood, and they spent all of their extra time doing day labor work in nearby fruit orchards.

There was no mayor here or sheik but merely a patriarch of the family. We met him, and he gathered around him his many sons, all of whom had married and represented one of the many tents in this rocky land. After talking to them for some time, we made plans to return over the next few weeks to begin a CHE program in their tiny village.

Weeks later, after we had explained many health principles and even enacted them in a drama to the family's delight, we were ready for a vote. We split them up according to our hard-learned lesson from the past. When it finally came time to vote, the women voted for help with acquiring baby formula and fixing their teeth, and the men wanted help with building homes out of rock and filtering their water.

Other than building them all permanent homes, these were reasonable requests. Those of us connected to dental began by addressing the dental needs of the families and initiating a hygiene instruction program that we hoped they could replicate with others as they had the opportunity.

It is supposed to take 21 days of doing something new to make a habit, so we developed a four-week training course on brushing your teeth. Of course, like all topics with CHE, you don't need any previous expertise, but it was fun to work on a topic we understood. We introduced tooth brushing the first week and passed out everything they needed to get started, including a calendar sheet where they could put sticky stars down for every time they brushed. The kids were very excited to get a star on their sheet for brushing! We also introduced a spiritual lesson from the Bible as we typically enjoyed doing at these times.

The next week we returned not without a little trepidation because we knew we would see if they had really been interested or not. We were excited to see that the kids and adults had indeed been actively brushing their teeth every day. Some of the kids quickly displayed their charts to us, showing us how many times they had brushed through the symbolism of the stars. We curiously noticed that amazingly, some of the kids had already brushed all of next week as well, which made us doubt the accuracy of some of the star records.

We continued our teaching by covering flossing, diet, and smoking by the end of the month. It seemed this large family had indeed been making new habits that were good to see for their oral health. We also knew that they had learned simple concepts about the ideas of sin, forgiveness, and God's love in the process that could have eternal worth.

The only disconcerting meeting we had came later after we arrived for one of our typical holistic health visits. We had called ahead so they knew we were coming, but the atmosphere was much different. It felt like we caught them in the middle of something, but they didn't mention anything as they welcomed us and had us sit down and drink tea with them.

The women kept going in and out of the meeting, and we detected there was quite an elevated amount of anxiety within the group, so we finally inquired if there was something the matter. They then told us that they urgently needed a ride to get to the *Umrah*.

"The *Umrah*?" we inquired. That was the name of one pilgrimage that Muslims take to Mecca in Saudi Arabia. When Muslims go to Mecca for *Eid al Adha* and celebrate the *eid* there, it is called the *Hajj*, and this is one of five pillars of Islam that is required of all Muslims who can make the trip. The *Umrah* is a different pilgrimage.

For *Hajj*, Muslims spend five or six days in Mecca, and they must circumambulate the Kaaba seven times in a counter-clockwise direction. Moreover, they must walk between two different "hills" called Safa and Marwah many times. Thankfully for them, these hills are now connected by people-movers inside air-conditioned corridors as Saudi Arabia is hot. Next, they go and stand on Mt. Ararat for a day, supplicating God before gathering pebbles on the plane of Muzdalifa. Finally, they throw these stones symbolically at Satan, who is represented by three pillars, and shave their heads. Once they have accomplished all of these tasks, they are officially known as "*hajjis*" in the community, and Islam teaches that all of your sins committed beforehand are wiped away.

The obvious remaining problem is that you continue committing sins for the rest of your life. So, most people repeat the *Hajj* many times or just wait until later in life to get more bang for their buck, because it is a costly trip. The whole goal is at the end of your life to have more good works tipping the scales against the bad things you have done that weren't washed away by *Hajj*.

During different parts of the year, if you make this same trip, it is called *Umrah* or the "lesser pilgrimage." You only do a truncated set of actions for *Umrah*, and it does not replace the *Hajj*. Some Muslims say that four *Umrah*s equal doing one *Hajj* or one *Umrah* done during Ramadan gets you the same benefits as *Hajj*.

Sitting in this tent in the middle of nowhere, we didn't understand how a pilgrimage could have any relevance to what was going on with us there. I asked the group, "When are you trying to go to the *Umrah*?," and to my surprise, they heartily all answered, "Now!" They said that a bus crossing the border would leave in one hour, and they weren't sure how seven of them were going to make it there on time. The woman then asked us if we could take them.

To be honest, we didn't want to take them to the bus station. First of all, we were right in the middle of our health lesson, and secondly, as

Christians, we felt weird about supporting them in going on a Muslim pilgrimage.

Despite all of our misgivings, we looked at each other, and knowing this was the best way we could meet their present needs, we made the decision to abort our health lesson and give them assistance to the bus station. Thankfully we had brought two cars since there were five of us, so we added their seven to our load and made a very uncomfortable trip to the bus station pressed in together against the doors and the roof of the cars.

Every speed bump along the road (and there were many) brought pain and groans, but we finally pulled into the bus station with five minutes to spare and dropped off our eager passengers. They thanked us profoundly and then sprinted as much as they could in their long robes towards the bus that would begin their very long journey to Mecca.

We had strange feelings and doubts about what the future might hold for our meetings, but to our surprise, a few weeks later, they let us know that they had returned from *Umrah* and now wanted to continue our meetings. It later became difficult to keep meeting with the men because the harvest had started, and they were very busy trying to make ends meet for their families. However, the women were eager to keep meeting again, and the women of our group continued meeting with them.

They first discussed issues of cleanliness, hygiene, and diarrhea, which are important topics for life in a tent. As time went on they began to talk about all kinds of other issues related to women's health like breastfeeding. Each of these studies was mixed in with Bible stories from the Old and New Testament.

Breastfeeding was one of the key issues that these simple women had voted on requesting help. It seems like none of the new mothers were able to breastfeed their babies. This was causing a lot of expense to their families because they were forced to purchase formula from the nearest town.

As the ladies on the team got to know these Bedouin women, they also got to understand their lifestyles. While at first, the breastfeeding problem seemed to be connected to the newborns not latching on, they soon noticed in spending time with them that the women drank very little water during the day. When they encouraged these new mothers to drink more water during the day, the Bedouin women refused. It seems that they could only use the restroom when it was dark outside. These women didn't drink much water so they could hold it better until the evening time.

Once this issue was discovered, the team went about teaching them the importance of using the restroom during the day and setting up simple but private privies near the tents. Once the women were liberated from evening-only bathroom breaks, they began to drink more water throughout the day.

When that next baby was born within this family, the women's team quickly visited the new mother. The baby latched well, and the new mom was the first one for years able to produce plenty of milk for her baby. She didn't need to buy expensive formula anymore, and the women were really encouraged that they had helped with a real problem.

Around this time, the women's community health team received a delightful surprise. These Bedouin women they had been helping made a new request from them. They told them they appreciated them doing these health and spiritual lessons with them, but asked if they could stop doing more health lessons and only spend all the time focusing on studying the Bible with them.

This request, of course, was precisely what they were hoping for, and this group ended up being one of our best results in doing community health work while I was there. We reveled in being able to follow the example of the Master, mixing Word and deed, even if it was in a small and weak way.

As the founding woman in our ministry reminded me one time, the book of Luke thirteen times describes Jesus interacting and working with a single person. We love to see significant people movements happen with a tribe or village, but the reality is that we spent a lot of time with small groups or even individuals in our work. This type of discipleship is not strategic from a numbers point of view, but it is Christian in that it follows the example of Christ who invested so much in so few disciples who went on to change the world.

It is encouraging to see through Christ's example that all individuals are valuable to the Lord, and no time is wasted on that work. From the poor shepherd living deep in the rocky desert to the hard-working Bedouin woman struggling to raise her young ones in the dirt of her tent, we loved having the privilege of going to the rural places of the barren desert to give the Bedouin people a reason to smile.

PART 4

THE TIMES THEY ARE A-CHANGIN'

Chapter 19
WRITINGS ON THE WALL

Returning back from a short home assignment in the summer, I found myself feeling a new sensation as I went through my daily routine at work. I couldn't put my finger on it specifically, but over July and August, I realized that what I was starting to feel on a daily basis was boredom.

Initially, I fought this feeling and felt guilty about even having it. Were not people back home supporting me and praying for me to be out here and do this work, and wasn't this something God had called me to do? I mentioned it to Grace, but she didn't report being bored in her work. In reality, I probably got to do more things that were somewhat more exciting and curious, with travel to distant villages and visits to remote areas.

One day, in particular, I came home after a great day at the dental clinic where I had explicitly shared with two patients, and one had asked for a Gospel to continue reading. It had been an exciting time of talking and conversing about what Jesus had done for us, and I had loved it in the moment. But as I left the clinic to return home, I had this overwhelming feeling of boredom return to my consciousness.

Gradually I had to admit to myself that it was real, and it wasn't going away. It was there when I woke up in the morning, and it was there whenever I wasn't actively busy. I confessed it in an email to my friend Job, who was out of the country, because he often helped me work through things like this a bit, and we often tried to keep each other accountable. I asked him how a Christian can share the gospel with people and find himself bored at the same time.

I told him about the exciting day of sharing that took place and how I felt genuinely bad that I could have such a negative emotion of boredom on that very same day. We worked through a lot of options; exploring family issues, personal issues, and turning to Scripture to see what we could find. It was hard to find anyone bored in Scripture, especially in the book of Acts, but it was also hard to pin what sin or sins were exactly behind it.

I watched several sermons about the topic of boredom in the life of a Christian, and nothing crystallized for me, but I just knew it wasn't good and pointed to a lack of faith.

Spiritual Gifts and Spirit Renewal

A few months later at our annual conference, I went for a walk with our member care person. I had faithfully been carrying out my duties seeing normal successes and failures over the previous months like always, but I had still been dogged with these low feelings for a while and decided I needed to see what a professional counselor would think of such thoughts.

"Was it open sin against God or something she saw from time to time in people in ministry?" I asked her.

She quickly told me that while it's true that some people will start to get a "seven-year itch" after years in ministry, more often, she saw people have feelings of boredom when they were not exercising their natural spiritual gifts over a long period.

She did a quick assessment and asked me what my spiritual giftings were, and I told her usually what those tests showed was that "teaching/ discipleship" and "faith" are at the top. She asked me where "evangelism" was, and I told her while I thought it super important and did it more than anything, it was always closer to the bottom of my spiritual gifting list.

She told me that based on that, even if I was evangelizing and having success at times, in the absence of teaching or discipling people deeply, I would probably be experiencing boredom by now. I was mainly spending time doing things outside of my spiritual gifting.

I didn't discount the sin aspects of my feelings, but her comments hit home for me as I thought of the best years and seasons I had known in the Middle East had always included a close relationship to a man or men with whom I was studying Scripture. However, at that point, those men were all gone.

The problem for me was that our ministry and many ministries towards unreached peoples are evangelistic and seed sowing. We were often praying with people, sharing a Bible story, and offering Scripture. While everyone wanted to "make disciples" and disciple them long-term, it was much harder to do this because of our role with the clinic where people would not be staying forever.

Our advantage of treating sick patients who were taken out of their social networks and pressures went towards helping them spiritually. Conversely, long-term discipleship in their homes after they left was more difficult.

This introspection helped me make some new plans for the coming ministry year because I knew I could not just keep going on with these feelings of boredom, even if the work was going well. I spent a day for prayer and vision to think about what could change and how I could move in that direction. I realized how thankful I was to be discipling my kids every morning as my most crucial crew of disciples, but I wanted to see if God had some other ways for me to nudge in that direction and what new men he might put in my path to disciple.

In God's planning a couple of new things happened during that next summer. We stayed in the Middle East that summer to carry on the work, but as always, half of our staff left to do their routine home assignments. This summer evacuation always leaves us short-staffed, so you usually have to wear a lot of new hats during those months and learn new roles and jobs which can be exciting but also daunting. We were all busy with work and ministry trying to fill all the gaps that summer. We looked forward to some relief as one of our key ministry leaders, Titus, was returning who led many of the men's studies. Tragically, we got a call from him the night he arrived that he was at the airport in the Middle East, but that he had been barred from reentering the country. He had to get a ticket and fly back to the US. As we counseled with an attorney, we realized that he had been blacklisted and would not be coming back no matter what.

It was quite a blow to us because we all loved him and his family and they filled so many niches we couldn't begin to think about how to replace them. Out of necessity, we all stepped up and split up his roles with the Bible studies, and for the first time in the clinic, I was tagged as a teacher. It wasn't something I had ever aspired to because I felt that

I was really blessed in my role and already got to have a lot of patient interactions and to share opportunities that others did not.

I had always felt like the patient meetings should be reserved for those in departments that didn't directly get to do ministry during the day, so they would have an avenue to do direct teaching. But, with the lack of personnel, it was clear they needed all hands on deck, and finally, my Arabic was probably after all of these years ready to take on a direct teaching role. I was already somewhat comfortable with small group discussions or one-on-one, but this was more of a larger group setting with teaching from up front.

Yusef

In addition to my new teaching role, some new patients arrived, and one of them was named Yusef. He had come because of COPD (Chronic Obstructive Pulmonary Disease), which is essentially an incurable condition where the cardiovascular system is in maximum overload trying to perfuse the body with enough oxygen. People usually have up times and down times, but it always is fatal in the end. We can only prescribe treatments that may ease the patient and make them feel better to get through a low period. He insisted that he didn't want to be admitted, but our doctor told him it was impossible to see any improvement without a three to four week stay as an in-patient, so he finally agreed.

A short time later, he boldly told us that now he knew why God had sent him to our clinic; he had learned about Jesus and had decided to follow him! The fun thing for me was that I had found he desperately needed dentures and so we had decided to prolong his in-patient stay so we could continue to address his COPD and have enough time to make him some teeth while he was getting some discipling in as well. As I got to know this man, it was beautiful to see his simple but unwavering faith in a place where it was so hard to carry out a public faith in Jesus, the Messiah. I think he could get away with it more than most people because he was so bold about his new faith that no one was going to question his integrity on it without knowing they had a big fight on their hands. Besides, he was an older man which always garners more respect, and at least from the authority side of things, he was a refugee, so he was under much less scrutiny from the government.

He used to help me prepare lessons in Arabic that I would use in teaching some of the patient meetings that we did with the men. Full of opinion, he would not hesitate to tell me that I couldn't speak Arabic well or that my examples were complete rubbish. During the first patient meeting that I led while he was there, he suddenly interrupted and asked the room if anyone could understand me because he couldn't understand a word I was saying. Thankfully, all of the other men quickly responded that they understood everything I was saying and told me it was because of his foreign dialect. That probably wasn't entirely the truth, but it was a factor because I often struggled with the differences. He often couldn't understand my Arabic dialect, even when I was speaking as clearly as possible face to face. As time went on, I got to where I could understand him better, and he got accustomed to our dialect and my own unique "dixie" Arabic.

He became a dear friend, and after he was discharged, I continued our relationship by visiting him in his home and always bringing my latest Bible lesson in Arabic so that he could critique and basically tear apart my syntax each time. Still, it led to a lot of great conversations about faith and life over the next months. One time, my friend and dental assistant Max and I arrived only to find him curled up on the floor with blue lips and gasping for air. It was a bad day for the COPD, so we helped him to get a mask over his face for a nebulizer treatment. He perked up after about 30 minutes and insisted we go ahead and study the Bible together even though he had seemed almost dead a short time before.

The first time I had come, he invited his daughter-in-law and wife into the conversation, but later, I had noticed that he met me very privately. Also, at times, he would ask me if I could bring meds from the clinic and do other things for him. I didn't want it to just turn into a dependency relationship where he was inviting me to get stuff, but I also honestly wanted to help him because he was poor, and I could see that he didn't have much. I was trying to walk that line between real help and creating a "rice" Christian who only meets with you because of the stuff you can bring them.

Jesus dealt with people like this in John 6:25-26 after he had fed the five thousand.

When they found him on the other side of the sea, they said to him, "Rabbi, when did you come here?" Jesus answered them, "Truly, truly, I say to you, you are seeking me, not because you saw signs, but because you ate your fill of the loaves."

Often when we help people with external things, they can't help but see us only as a connection for getting even more things, which is just human nature.

I was growing a bit concerned about whether his faith was even legit at all. We usually say that it's best to wait two years, and then you will find out if someone is really a believer or not. He had been a believer about 18 months when I decided to probe a bit further. I was sitting in his home, and the call to prayer rang out over the city. We had just finished studying a passage on Romans 4 that did a pretty good job of distinguishing between Abraham who believed by faith and others who try to earn their salvation by works. I asked Yusef how he saw himself. Was he trying to earn his salvation, or was he 100% trusting in Jesus for his righteousness?

I also asked him if he still went to mosque sometimes to pray, because that had been something he had always done in Islam his whole life. He stared at my face and tilted his head to the side a bit, and I noticed he was a bit perturbed.

He said, "Dr. Adam, why do you ask me this?—You know there is no other way to be saved except by faith in Jesus."

He went on to tell me how the life of doing good things trying to get points with God was rubbish, and we had clearly taught him that at our clinic. So now why would I ask him such simple things?

As for the mosque, he said, "Dr. Adam, how could I ever go to the mosque again? I am a Christian. I am not a Muslim anymore. You should know there is no grey area with God. You either follow him 100% or none at all— I will follow Jesus 100%."

I was so excited and relieved to hear his confession of faith, which was a convincing refutation of my doubts and also a seeming rebuke from this elder man not to doubt my own faith. There is no way I had given him these responses at all, and in fact, he had surprised me with the depth of his feelings on these matters. Thank you Holy Spirit!

Muathim

A younger man that had been with us previously for treatment returned once more around this time to the clinic after his health took a downturn. Muathim had fair skin, being a young man in his mid-twenties and he was also fairly thin; he wore a toboggan hat eternally on his head and usually sported some unkempt facial hair as well. The first time he had come to the clinic, he had listened well to what we shared but had been a little bit hot-tempered, leading to some rough interactions among the male patients. His background had been living in slum housing or even sometimes on the streets in the capital, where he had been involved with drug dealing and other lower than desirable pursuits. Somewhere in the process, he had come down with a severe infection and needed some long term treatment, which led him to us the first time around.

The difference this time around compared to the first time he came was that he started to have a new countenance about him. He was usually smiling and friendly, and he had gotten involved with an additional Bible study with Titus before he had left the country. It seemed like the wheels were really starting to spin as he began to understand Scripture more and more and declared himself to be a Christian.

After Titus had left, not to return, I took the opportunity to start meeting with him. He was lonely and appreciated the one-on-one time, and I enjoyed the chance to dialogue with him and get his perspective on passages from the Bible. As I was still leading Bible studies at this time, Muathim was accommodating for me as I would try them out on him, and he would correct my Arabic or even tell me that certain things didn't make sense to him with his particular background. Then, I would recraft my message until it hit home in what he thought was a meaningful way.

I had to balance spending time with him and Yusef in order to not cause any jealousy, but together they gave me ideas on how to make certain Scripture passages more applicable to older and younger Arabs.

As a new believer, I found Muathim had a fantastic ability to read Scripture and quickly make sense out of it in a way that he shouldn't be able to yet. He would often connect the dots rapidly on something he had never seen before and then exhort me to apply it to my life, even as he was going to do the same thing. I sometimes wondered who was teaching whom during this time, because he had a lot to say as he encountered some of these passages for the very first time in his young life.

One time, in particular, I encouraged him for drawing something out of a passage that I had never seen before in 30 plus years of following Christ and studying Scripture.

He turned to me and said, "You know what, earlier this year, I could have never done that. I used to sit here and try to read the Bible, but it just seemed so dry to me, and I could never understand what it was talking about. Then one day, I opened it up, and it was so clear and exciting to read. Now it makes total sense of everything in my life, and I just love reading it."

I was stunned to hear him say that and said, "Do you want to know how that happened?" I wanted to tell him.

He said, "Oh, I already know how that happened—the Holy Spirit— He opened my heart to understand it, and now I do."

His unearned insights like this were always so surprising and heartening to me. His sanctification and discipleship continued through a lot of key men pouring into his life at the clinic. He still struggled with his temper sometimes, and sadly he and another believing patient at the clinic at that time became enemies. This conflict actually gave us all plenty to talk with him practically about how following Jesus changes our actions regarding forgiveness and jealousy and love.

He struggled to leave the clinic to find a job and get into a good life pattern. He always was tempted to go back to what ironically were the "comforts" of street life but were just the habits he had learned over many years.

Like Pavlov's dogs, we all always have a taste for those sins that we came out of, and it's so easy to salivate and think we'll find peace going back into those very things which really want to enslave us again. It was hard to break those cycles, but with the Lord's help, he began to make a new life for himself in the capital. He remained a faithful and connected friend even after he left.

Uthman

One other dear friend that I had lived a lot of life with over the years was Uthman. He was a sweet, gentle man who had a fairly dark complexion having migrated a great distance. He said that in his home region there were ethnically many descendants of Africans who were thought to have been brought to the area years ago by the Romans as slaves. When I first met him in the dental clinic, he had recently become a Christian and literally had the scars and stories to prove it. His story was sadly quite typical for someone who has become a believer and then either announced it or been discovered.

In his case, after coming to faith, he had initially kept his faith to himself, nightly reading and studying the Bible and other Christian literature in his room by flashlight. But one night, as he was studying with everyone in the house asleep, his brother knocked and then quickly cracked open the door to say something to him. He quickly shoved the Bible under the sheet and responded to his brother, but he wondered if his brother had seen anything or not.

The next day as he arrived home from work, he saw his mom, dad, brother, and wife all out in front of the house. They were gathered around a large fire, and as he walked up, he looked at the fire and saw that it was his Bible and many other Christian writings that he had hidden in his room. He told me that for him, those books were his very life and before they could restrain him, he grabbed what was left of his Bible and the other books straight out of the fire. That explained the genesis of the scarring that was visible on his hands and lower forearm.

He said that after he had been treated for his burn wounds, his family had put so much pressure on him to recant and reject Jesus. He refused over and over, and they finally kicked him out of the house when he wouldn't return to Islam. Then his wife's family told him that she was going to divorce him in court and would list as the reason for divorce apostasy from Islam.

This threat was severe because it would not only lead to the divorce, but this would then put him into the Sharia courts where he would be tried for apostasy and would likely never leave prison. He agreed to meet with them, and they put his wife across the room from him and told him that all he had to do to get his wife back and to never go to prison was to reject Jesus. In a show of resolute faith, he told them that he loved his wife very much and never wanted to leave her, but he could never turn his back on Jesus. He loved Him more.

As Uthman put it, "It is like Jesus has plucked me out of Satan's army and put me into His heaven. How can I ever go back?"

The result was that he had no one to go to and nowhere to go. As a result, he had returned to the clinic, where he knew there were faithful Christians who could help him. He was readmitted temporarily to reassess his past illness, but also to give him a chance to rest and recoup for the fight for his life in court that was ahead.

We prayed earnestly for several months for God to show Himself and intervene in the terrible situation. The word had spread, and Uthman had already lost his job back home because he had now been black-marked by the secret police. The chances of him ever getting a good job again may have been compromised by his family. It seems he may always remain a marked man. We hoped this would not be his fate but it was for now.

Moreover, many times, the people who had been outed as apostates had never had the chance to even go to jail. It was common for a family member to murder them before that because of the shame it brought onto the family. Once she brought the charges to court, his very life would hang in the balance.

In the intervening months, I had the privilege of going through some discipleship training with Uthman. Much like Muathim, he almost wanted to share more things about the Scripture with me than I could share with him. As we continued through the material, he was always going through highs and lows as he tried to bear the stress of his upcoming court date. He often had nightmares and dreamed of terrible dark things that would happen to him.

Around this time, there also started to be some hints that he had started drinking. Sometimes he just wasn't himself, and finally, one day while I was working on a patient in the dental clinic, he stumbled in to talk to me, visibly swaying side to side, intoxicated. As he tried to finish an incoherent sentence, he finally fell down onto one knee on the floor, only catching himself by grabbing his hand onto the top of my patient's head in the dental chair. I yelled at him and shooed him out of the dental clinic, even as he insisted he could help assist me with my patient. I knew I had to confront him, but how?

In the US, we might plan an intervention with a group of people or something like that, but in the Middle East, being accused of having an alcohol problem was one of the most shameful things ever. I talked to a few other staff people that warned me never to bring up the alcoholism; just talk around it but never mention his drunkenness directly. I wasn't sure what to do, but I noticed that our next discipleship lesson was about sin and temptation and it actually used alcoholism as the example to discuss in the lesson. I took this as a sign and prayed that I would have an opportunity to talk about it then.

As we met that time and got to the example of the alcoholic, I asked Uthman if he had ever struggled with something like that. He quickly said no. I told him that as my brother in Christ, he could never do any sin that would make me stop loving him. My relationship with him was secure. He told me that was great, and he appreciated knowing that. I asked him if he wanted to talk about when he had walked into my dental clinic drunk that week.

He said, "Oh, Dr. Adam, you thought I was drunk? No, I wasn't drunk, I had a rash, and I was putting alcohol on it and accidentally spilled the entire bottle of rubbing alcohol all over me. That's why I smelled like alcohol. I wasn't drunk at all."

I paused, taking what he said in and then gently responded, "Uthman, remember I told you that I love you no matter what. Now be honest with me. I'm not stupid. I'm your friend. I know you have been through so much these last months. I'm going to ask you again. Were you drinking?"

After a few seconds, he looked down at the floor and silently nodded his head and began crying. I told him it was okay, and he just needed to give that issue to the Lord, and he would help him escape the temptation like the Scripture we had just read taught. We talked some more and prayed for each other, and by the end, we were both crying and then laughing.

We finished the meeting with some manly hugs and then parted ways. I left that night feeling high as a kite and so exuberated about what had transpired! The Lord had really moved among us, and there had been a real catharsis about this whole issue in his life. I had been so worried that he would be too ashamed to admit it, but his heart had been soft after all, and we had made some significant steps together with the Lord's help.

The next morning when I returned to the clinic, I looked forward to seeing how Uthman was doing. Before I could find him, a male nurse stopped me and asked me when I last had seen Uthman the previous evening. He also asked if anything strange had happened.

I told him I had seen Uthman before I left around 6 pm, and as I left, he was heading back to his room in a good mood. I didn't want to tell him any details about what we had discussed. He informed me that Uthman was missing this morning, but another patient had reported seeing him climb over the clinic fence last night sometime after 6 pm and run straight out into the desert. I began to have doubts about if he had felt the same way as me the previous night.

We ended up not seeing Uthman again for three months. He never would answer his phone anymore, and he just seemed to have dropped off of the map. I was afraid to call his family because they didn't need to know anything else about what was going on with him, and I didn't want them to know that he had left the clinic. Finally, one day, I just noticed that he was back.

We exchanged greetings, and he made some excuses about why he had been gone so long. I didn't dig too deeply, and I didn't bring up his drinking again that directly ever again. I had concluded that though our conversation had been real, the shame of it must have really hit him after we parted.

I must assume he just couldn't face seeing me or the other doctors the next day after he had been exposed as having an alcohol problem. If it had been evident to me that he was drinking, he must have realized it was obvious to everyone else in the clinic as well, and the embarrassment must have been too high.

Finally, the time arrived for the court meeting, and Uthman left to face his fate. After a few days, he soon returned unchanged in character and seemed jubilant as we asked him what happened. He said that in the end, his wife had loved him so much that she couldn't go ahead with the divorce which would have outed him and destroyed him as an apostate.

He had met again with the family and drawn up a compromise. He would remain married to her, but he could never have a Bible or any Christian literature in the house and must not talk about it to her. He agreed to the terms and decided to live with her as with an unbelieving spouse, praying for her every day to know the Lord.

She was always hospitable to me when I would go to their house to visit them, but Uthman had to be careful with what he said in front of her. However, I felt like I was free to say whatever I wanted to say because I had made no agreement.

When I brought my whole family over for a visit one time, along with an Egyptian friend, it was the first time in my life that I had met someone who was that vocally angry at Jesus. She said she not only didn't believe in Jesus's teaching, but she hated Jesus and thought he was from Satan. She was really in a lot of pain you could tell.

We reminded her that even Muslims don't think Jesus is from Satan, he is a holy one from God, but she told us that Jesus had totally ruined her life, and she could never forgive Him for what he had done to her through her husband. We disagreed with her point of view, but I could see how things must have looked. I hoped Uthman could live his life in such a way that she would see the difference in the coming years and change her mind.

Abu Abdul Kareem

By the middle of May, the temperatures in the desert are picking up, and all of the beautiful lush greenery that has arrived in April is quickly fried into a brittle brown. This period also is a time that we routinely refrain from going out on dental outreaches. For one thing, it is challenging to hydrate and help all of the people waiting outside for hours in the brutal sun. They tend to come into the clinic dehydrated or with high blood pressure after roasting outdoors for several hours.

Another issue was that Ramadan fell in the summertime that year, so during that month, no patients would even bother coming out because they were afraid of swallowing something and breaking the fast. Regardless, as we went out on one of the last outreaches for our Spring season, I had been studying the Gospels in particular and taking note of how Jesus dealt with these crowds who were always clamoring for his "services" whether they were miracles, justice or teaching.

We certainly could not match the kind of gifts that Jesus offered to the people. Still, in a minimal way, we always experienced some of the difficulties He must have struggled with as we used our small skills and gifts amid overwhelming need and demand. Ultimately, whatever we did was just a drop in the bucket compared to the dental needs in every community in which we arrived. The amazing thing to me was how Jesus always handled this overwhelming demand. He mixed healing and teaching but never in the same proportions. You can't make a formula out of it—He doesn't want us to do that. He always showed compassion, and Scripture seemed to emphasize how Jesus showed compassion even in the absence of gratitude from the people or even proper decorum from them.

On my first outreach into a village years ago, some young boys had yelled at me and demanded treatment ahead of the other people who had been waiting. When I refused, they announced to the entire crowd outside the dental clinic that I had promised them in the morning that I would see them first, but now I had shown that I was a liar by not seeing them. They were trying to shame me. If I had been an Easterner, that might have worked splendidly, but being a Westerner, it didn't shake me at all, because I knew the truth, so I wasn't ashamed.

When I didn't flinch or show any emotion, one of them suddenly grabbed our appointment book and ripped it into a hundred pieces and flung the pieces all over the ground. Gone was our full record of who had come that day and in what order we needed to see them and what they all needed. Shame hadn't gotten to me, but now this treachery had worked pretty well, and I was seething hot.

Seeing a policeman nearby down the street, I ran over to him and told them that those young boys were harassing me. Coming back, I figured the policeman would soon finally get rid of these meddlesome boys as I told them I would never treat them now, no matter if they waited until next week.

To my surprise, the policemen came over with a fellow officer, and they started cursing the boys and beating them with their police batons. The boys screamed and fled, holding wounded limbs as the police literally chased them away, running for their lives.

Dr. Ron, who was standing with me at the time, said, "Good work Adam, I think that's exactly how Jesus would have handled it."

Ouch. With those words, it felt like someone had plunged a dagger in my heart.

Dealing with crowds is easy to read about in the Gospels, and you can imagine yourself being the same sweet way as Jesus would be with the demanding people. When you are in the middle of it, it's a tough thing to do.

You'd think that after all of these years with crowd control, I had matured a little bit at least with how to deal with them as a Christian. However, if I have a room full of people and one was yelling at me or cursing me, it was still my protocol at that time to typically put them last or not even want to see them.

I mean, I didn't want to enable bad behavior and encourage it by still seeing them, right? If people want me to help them, they should at least be respectful or decent first. I am a doctor trying to help them for free with my time, so why should I put up with abuse? But reading the Gospels at that time, I was convicted that Jesus kept doing exactly that.

In Luke 17, Jesus famously healed ten men who were lepers. They yelled at him, demanding mercy, and He responded by sending them to the priests. They were then miraculously healed on the way. Only one ever returned to Jesus to thank Him, and that was a Samaritan, an enemy of His people.

Jesus never required thanks or gratitude before he performed a healing or a miracle. His healings, in the rare case, received praise as a result, but they were never performed with that as a prerequisite.

I had to remember that the poor and needy people He saw and we saw were truly suffering, and they always were going to share that suffering with whomever they came in contact. Jesus was ready to take it all on Himself and out-suffer them so that He could finally give them what they needed, and that was on my heart as I entered this village.

Having that attitude helped my heart, and that week I wasn't too affected by the occasional complaining person who demanded to move up the line. Even when I had helped people with long and exhausting treatments only to see them quickly leaving the dental clinic without even saying thank you, it was fine. I knew I was working for a different cause and purpose. But then, Abu Abdul Kareem walked in.

Abu Abdul Kareem was notorious with our clinic. Many of us had spent years being involved with his life only to see him reject help from us at every turn and continue in personally destructive behavior. We knew him well because he had married a local nurse in our village. After he got a promising job with the Army he requested she not work so they could start a family and they left town.

Once you have a job like that, you are set for life, but in his case, he soon got thrown out of the Army because of drugs.

We helped him get back on his feet, but he had soon gotten into trouble again because he borrowed money that he could not pay back. Before we knew it, he was in prison, leaving his wife and three kids to fend for themselves. We helped them with some of their needs for food and clothing, and after about a year, he was released. Sadly he returned home where he seemed just to lay in bed and become a worthless eater.

His wife told us that he never worked or did anything for the family. I had been in their tent with my family and received gracious hospitality from his wife and mother-in-law, who was a believer. He had never budged to welcome me or lift a finger and host me as his role being the male of the tent demanded. I pretty much chalked him up to being a black sheep because he didn't care for his family's needs and he was spiraling down deeper into this destructive lifestyle.

So, when he came into the clinic in the middle of a busy day, my good mood and better attitude started to fade. I figured, *Great, here is another problem to deal with. I wonder what he wants?*

We told him that the schedule was already full for the day, but he could come back tomorrow early in the morning like everyone else if he wanted to get his teeth checked.

He said, "No thank you, I appreciate you seeing my wife and daughter today, and I just wanted to come in here and see the Jesus film if you still have it here like last year."

Does this man really think we're going fall for this? I thought. *It's so obvious what he's doing.*

Putting the film on, I told my assistant, "He'll start watching the Jesus film, alright, to get on our good side and then he is surely going to ask for treatment or toothbrushes or some handout. Just wait."

The next time I came through about 15 minutes later, he was sitting there with his daughter in his lap. Not seeing me, he was pointing at the screen and telling his daughter what was happening as Jesus resisted the temptations in the desert. I walked up and discussed the scene with them both some more and was surprised that he seemed interested. But going back to my patient, I thought, *This is going to be really rich. He's putting on such a show this time.*

A little bit later, as I finished my patient, he was finishing watching the Jesus film. He started to walk up to me, and I braced myself as I was ready for "the big ask" that was coming.

However, he surprised me by asking if I had a copy of the Jesus film on DVD that I could give to him. As I handed him one of our copies, I couldn't imagine what he was now going to ask me. I mean, I figured before that he was going to ask me to sneak him into the line or something, but now by asking me for his own copy of the Jesus film, he must want something enormous.

Instead, he simply turned around and started walking out the door. I was dumbfounded. I stopped him and said, "Abu Abdul Kareem….don't you want to ask me for some dental treatment…or something?"

He said, "No, I just wanted to have my own Jesus film because it's a good movie."

What in the world was happening? I wondered.

I quickly grabbed a New Testament off the shelf and asked him, "Have you ever read the *Injil*?" He took it from me and looked it over and said, "No, but maybe sometime you could come to my tent, and we could read it together."

So much for learning my lesson. The man I had completely written off in my mind for the Kingdom of God was one of the biggest responses we saw that week. I was able to follow up with him and study the Bible a couple of times in his tent in the following weeks.

In my hard, sinful heart, I hadn't even given him a chance. He was the Samaritan, the tax collector, the drug dealer, the prostitute. The ones Jesus always hung out with that I thought was so cool when I read about it in the Gospels, but in my own life, I don't consider doing it practically because I write those people off as lost causes.

God was always showing me in these situations the hardness of my own heart and my utter lack of compassion. Thankfully, he does not treat me the way I have treated so many "undesirables" in my own life. Maybe I didn't see fruit in every patient I spoke to, but it was often clear that God was bringing forth the fruit of repentance and conviction in my own heart and loving me before I ever did anything to merit it.

While taking on some of these new responsibilities at the clinic for teaching Bible studies and now having a few new or returning men that I could spend time with talking about spiritual matters, I soon had come to find my boredom had disappeared.

Life was exciting again and hectic as I always was spending time doing dental work or leading a Bible lesson or preparing my Arabic to convey the ideas needed to lead the next one.

In addition, we were enjoying a productive discussion at home every morning as Grace and I would sit with our three kids and take that special time to be sure that they were being discipled as well. They were, in fact, our greatest charge and responsibility at that time, and we knew those years were so formative for them.

We loved our time with them as parents, but we also were concerned during those months. The education and social development of kids are always issues when you live in a remote area.

Of Corban and Sacrifice

One of those undercurrents that we felt arriving on the mission field was an attitude of intentional self-sacrifice. That's expected, because it's exactly what we want to have at the forefront of a ministry worker's mind. I mean, we want these people who we are supporting with our hard-earned money to work hard and be ready to serve others before themselves as we send them out to the world.

It's biblical too, because Jesus taught and led by example that life for the Christ-follower should be full of self-sacrifice. And don't we all know that as we go out we are supposed to sacrifice a little bit more? The average person needs not carry their cross in the same way. Well, I guess that illustrates a piece of the problem in itself.

We have these expectations for foreign workers that we don't often apply to ourselves back home, where we are called to be salt and light among our neighbors and friends. In the US, if I worked a 40 hour week in the office, that was a full week's work that I could be proud of, and Grace was busy at home taking care of our three children. Maybe we could do some ministry on the side with foreigners or attend a Bible study once a week and make it to church as well.

Serving away from our home, it was assumed that I would be putting in at least 40 hours and that Grace would be putting in her 40 hours a week as well with the women. But, if we couldn't do that before as a family in our home culture, so how does that work overseas?

We often had to remind ourselves that if we were back home, we would never be attempting to do this without expecting things to break apart. Maybe it was just us and no one else feels that way, but there was always that pressure or expectation from ourselves and from others to work harder and do more because we had a spiritual job title.

God had called us to sacrifice, and certainly, we would take Him up on it. It's a role we in the church have prescribed for church workers, and we were just as culpable in prescribing it and applying it to ourselves and others as our supporting churches and friends were, if at all.

What it often leads to is a competition of sorts to suffer the most. In the US, we are all very competitive in another way. We compare our houses and cars and all aspects of life trying to keep up with the Joneses. But that's because we're a prideful and sinful culture often trying to measure everything to see who has it better. But here's a dirty little secret—foreign workers are sinners too.

Our particular prideful sin was to measure and see who had it the worst. During a brutal summer of 110 degree weather a friend once told me, "You're paying $25 per month on water? I've never paid more than $8. You guys must be wasting a lot of water showering all the time or someone is just stealing it from you at night."

The five of us were taking showers two to three times per week and doing minimal laundry. Someone else told me they only let their family shower once per week on Sundays to conserve water. Another colleague bragged to me that they had worn the same outfit for ten days to cut down on laundry water.

In America, you might boast about taking a needed weekend vacation to a beachfront resort with your family. On the field, any kind of expenditure that wasn't attributed to a special price or fire sale was often embarrassing to admit.

Sacrifice might not be a big deal when you're debating shower time, but it all really came to a head when things started to get tough on our family in other ways. As we were considering where the Lord was leading us for the coming year, we often bumped up against this idea of sacrifice quite a bit.

Along our journey, we periodically monitored each of the children's mental, physical, and emotional well-being. Grace was particularly good at having an intentional dialogue with each child every six months to evaluate how they were doing in these areas and worked to tweak anything necessary along the way. This regimen felt healthy for our family and the children hopefully knew they were not forgotten behind the ministry. Truly, they were an important consideration as we annually evaluated if we could stay for another year.

We had a few new concerns as we evaluated this particular year ahead that were relevant to the idea of sacrifice. We wondered how we were going to meet the educational and social needs of our kids without high-school teachers and full-time classmates. If Grace and I took on the burden of teaching a full high school curriculum to two of our kids, when would we actually do any ministry? We would be teaching all day, and they still wouldn't have friends to help them with their growing social needs. Moreover, our kids had vocalized for the first time ever that they were ready to leave, which was concerning.

Previous ex-pat families from the area had needed to leave with older children because of psychological hardships. Our kids were still relatively happy, and they didn't even know what they had been missing in terms of social possibilities. They had been blessed with friends who filled their hearts with happiness, but almost all their classmates had left now.

Additionally, at what point is it no longer reasonable to raise three kids in a town with increased security problems and drop them off at a school location that one group had now classified as a "soft target" for a terrorist attack? Are these acceptable sacrifices we should make to continue God's work or should we look for other solutions?

I might discuss these dilemmas we were having as a family with different colleagues and get totally different and well-meaning answers. One type of friend would recommend to us that it sounded like it may be time to depart while we could still leave without any major crisis going on in our family. Another of our leaders commented that there was no shame in taking the basket over the wall, much like wise Paul did when escaping from Damascus in Acts 9:25. Paul saw it was time to go and took the opportunity with no shame.

But often I would notice the same people with that type of argument would not feel any pressure at all themselves to leave. Were we just being too jumpy, or were we like that proverbial frog being boiled to death slowly in the pot? Having the temperature slowly raised and slowly raised until we just died without taking the hint to jump out.

On the other hand, a different type of friend may remind us of why we were there. Didn't the Lord call you to come to the Middle East and accept some risk? When the going gets tough, don't you just dig into your calling and trust God more? If you are where God called you, aren't you in the safest place? If your kids get messed up or have psychological, social, or academic deficiencies, don't you think that God will take care of those problems if He called you to come here?

I couldn't disagree with any of those assertions necessarily. Still, it did bring up that there was that annoying spectrum to be evaluated between the sovereignty of God and the responsibility of man. We might be unfaithful to leave, but might God just as quickly disapprove of us staying when the signs of impending danger were getting pretty clear?

One morning I was reading Mark 7 when these ideas all came together for me in a new way. It was the little innocuous passage, almost a side note in a longer passage where Jesus condemns the traditions of men. In verses 11-13, Jesus describes the situation of a man who had a responsibility to care for his parents.

"But you say it is all right for people to say to their parents, 'Sorry, I can't help you. For I have vowed to give to God (*corban*) what I would have given to you.' In this way, you let them disregard their needy parents. And so you cancel the Word of God in order to hand down your own tradition. And this is only one example among many others."

Whatever he could have done for them to assuage them in their need, this man in the passage gives it up in the name of "sacrifice" to God. The Greek word used directly in many translations of this passage is "*corban*" which is the exact same word we use in Arabic to denote making a sacrifice.

For the Jews, this was the common word to describe any type of Levitical sacrifice or offering that they would make to Yahweh. As a result of this man declaring he was giving up everything as a "*corban*" or sacrifice to the Lord (we don't know whether he means time, money, or work), he now feels no obligation to carry out his duty towards his family members.

God will take care of them. Jesus says that a man like this stands condemned because he has put the traditions and wisdom of men over the natural responsibilities he has for his family—particularly his parents in this case according to the fifth commandment.

I was extremely convicted as I read this passage with new eyes towards my situation. I actually asked several pastors if I could even interpret these verses in this way while knowing I had felt that it had hit me right between the eyes. The easiest thing for me was to stay in my same situation. I was enjoying work again. All the boredom was gone. I couldn't imagine going back to the craziness of life in the US, which we had left behind.

We also had been settled in our newer apartment for two years now, and moving was always a considerable stressor. It seemed like we had just gone through all of that recently. But for me, I felt like this was a turning point that I kept coming back to every time I would assess our future plans.

I didn't feel like I could play the sacrifice for God (get out of jail free) card anymore without feeling guilt and concern for my family's needs. After many months of discussion and prayer with Grace and others about all these matters, the writings were on the wall. It was time to go home.

Chapter 20
ALL GOOD THINGS

Our last few weeks were bittersweet, as we reserved proper amounts of time for making final visits to our friends and colleagues. It was nice to spend such intentional time with each one of them but sad to say goodbye for now.

It is said that as you leave a ministry field, many people may take the opportunity to ask more intimate questions or risk more vulnerability because they know you are leaving. We kept this idea in mind and shared as much as we could in each situation, but with each goodbye and each hug farewell, it felt like we had just not spent enough time in each of those people's lives. It was hard to believe it was over; all the time suddenly dried up and gone.

Where did the time go? How were we here for years and only got in a limited number of visits with this family or this person? It's incredible when you think about it how much time it takes just to live in a foreign country and culture. When I thought of how much time I spent on different things that took me away from interactions with people, it was amazing. Countless hours were needed to acquire water for my family or to maintain the apartment appliances or to deal with the car or go to government offices for my visa renewal. How many more hours were spent writing newsletters for supporters back home and calling them to check-in? All good things, but also diversions from the main goal I had arrived in the Middle East to accomplish.

Ecclesiastes Wisdom

*I hated all my toil in which I toil under the sun, seeing that
I must leave it to the man who will come after me, and who
knows whether he will be wise or a fool? Yet he will be
master of all for which I toiled and used my wisdom under
the sun. This also is vanity. So I turned about and gave
my heart up to despair over all the toil of my labors under
the sun, because sometimes a person who has toiled with
wisdom and knowledge and skill must leave everything to
be enjoyed by someone who did not toil for it. This also
is vanity and a great evil. What has a man from all the
toil and striving of heart with which he toils beneath the
sun? For all his days are full of sorrow, and his work is
a vexation. Even in the night his heart does not rest. This
also is vanity. —Ecclesiastes 2:22-23*

Thinking about the work we accomplished there in light of
Ecclesiastes can be a little depressing. Thankfully, it usually hasn't felt
like that, but the rub is the same. How about all of the dental work I have
provided for my patients over the years? The reality is that much of the
dental work I've done in my life is already six feet under the earth, and
the rest will be there soon. That one denture patient had already told me
that all my hard work on his first denture was blown up. If that's true of
his dentures now, how can I even hope in the rest?

The truth is that while I've put much effort into the physical work, I
haven't placed my hopes there. Instead, Grace and I have striven from the
beginning to provide a legacy here in terms of eternal relationships. But,
as we look out at the last season of years and try to find some meaning and
consequence from the connections that we've made, the same nagging
issues persist. Those people who are so special to us—who will look after
them or teach them or visit them after we leave? Who can ever consider
them and be concerned for them the way we have been? Will it all lead to
nothing?

*There is nothing better for a person than that he should eat
and drink and find enjoyment in his toil. This also, I saw,
is from the hand of God, for apart from him who can eat*

or who can have enjoyment? For to the one who pleases Him God has given wisdom and knowledge and joy, but to the sinner he has given the business of gathering and collecting, only to give to one who pleases God. This also is vanity and a striving after wind. —Ecclesiastes 2: 24-25

We remember the truth is that we have ultimately been working for the Lord here, and every good thing has come from His hand. On the whole, we have thankfully found great enjoyment in the toil here and offer it up to Him. Despite our concerns for its legacy, Scripture seems to say that even the desire for legacy is a vanity in itself. The only thing that has meaning is working unto the Lord, and He will do whatever He wishes with our efforts.

Legacy aside, we are still thankful that God so quickly provided for us people who can step into our roles at the clinic, so at least there is not a void. This is what we were praying for as another sign that we could leave our ministry and return home for this season.

In fact, our replacements came so easily and quickly, considering the location and the job skills required, that it almost felt like God was purposely humbling us. I was kind of thinking, *Come on God, couldn't you have made this at least a little difficult for the clinic to have filled our positions?*

Even if we thought we were indispensable members of our team, we certainly couldn't enjoy considering ourselves irreplaceable very long, because God filled those needs within a very short time. Though humbling, this was the right answer to our prayers and the key provision that gave us the freedom to leave and pass the baton to those who certainly will come after us as wise people to continue the work.

This answer included a new, highly trained dentist who took over the dental ministry role to take it to the next level I could never reach. His wife joins him as well as another woman who has come into the mix, and both have giftings with art and a desire to visit and work with the female patients.

Rocks for Sale!

Many of our efforts honestly have seemed ridiculous at times. For all of the strategizing we have done to share the good news with our friends, we've often found ourselves getting to that interesting point only to feel like we're offering something that they must think is crazy according to their world view. At best, to be reconciled with their creator through Jesus who loves them may lead them to many severe troubles, but at worst, death.

Because of this reality, sharing amazing truth with some people has often reminded me of the little boy I met in a tourist stop for an ancient ruined city. "Rocks for Sale, Rocks for Sale!" this little boy yelled out to me as I walked down the trail into the heart of the city. I looked at his blanket laid out, stacked with all kinds of different rocks, and it seemed so ridiculous that anyone would ever even try to sell rocks when the whole countryside was full of them.

Because of how pitiful he was or maybe because of how ridiculous his product was, I went over and bought some. He gave me a special deal—three rocks for one dollar!

I've often empathized with this little boy, because there are such barriers in place culturally, educationally, and spiritually that we feel we're just like that little boy selling our rocks in a rocky desert.

Our Lord in John 15:18 did call himself a *scandalon*—a "rock of stumbling and offense." That must be exactly how our neighbors and friends sometimes have looked at the gospel that we presented them.

We often prayed and will continue to pray for the Spirit to work in our neighbors and for the Spirit to work among us for them. Without that, there can never be any shift in the hearts of men and women. The teachings of Christ are just craziness from the world's point of view. We're thankful that in this desert, He did still send people to us. Many poor and sick and weak of the world have found Him not as an offensive roadblock, but as the refreshing shadow of a great Rock in a dry and weary land about which Isaiah 32:2 prophesied.

Oldest Church in the World

After years in the Middle East, we finally got around to visiting the oldest church in the world. At least they claimed it was the oldest church, but later we found out there were about fifteen oldest churches in the world. We certainly believe ours is the most authentic though.

It happened to be not far from our house in the ancient ruins of a former Christian town. Like almost all of the churches in our area, it is largely just rubble, with the border of the building still remaining and various mosaics peeking out at points through the drifting sand which covers them.

An altar in the back of the lower level is the oldest part, going back to the first century. As a cave, the situation and environment remain largely unchanged, although it is covered with much evidence of wear and black soot with years of use and multiple cooking fires.

When you go to the Middle East, it often is with the desire to go to the most unreached people groups as we had longed to do. I have driven many times for an hour, three hours, or five hours into the vast reaches of the utter desert to bring the good news to people who have never heard it, let alone even seen a Christian before.

The truth is that while we often pride ourselves on going where the gospel has never reached, the reality is that as remotely as we go, especially in the Arab world, we commonly end up sharing and doing outreaches in areas surrounded by ruins of ancient churches. Many of these places are, in reality, old Christian towns where you sadly can no longer find a single believer.

I specifically remember being in one of the most remote areas I had visited, and a Bedouin man wanted to take me to see some ruins next to an oasis. I asked him what those ruins were and found out they were a Monastery. Christians had lived there and studied there for hundreds of years some 1500 years ago, and now it was just a quiet place where sheep and camels could come for an uninterrupted drink.

What shall we conclude? That the gospel is all in vain? It's a dark thought to imagine the church in America is only one generation away from looking like these ruined churches in the Middle East. On the other hand, we also remember that the church here is only one generation away from reviving millions of Arabs for the gospel.

Though we tend to see our two cultures as starkly different in this black and white modern world, in another way, we are really just the same; two groups of broken sinners who require a great rescue. This is something my friend Faoud helped me see clearly years ago.

In the US, there is a difference, not because we are better, but because we have many benefits derived from recent generations of Christian believers and an underpinning of Judeo-Christian teachings and ethics in our society. Opportunities abound with churches on every corner and the message of the gospel readily available on TV, radio, or in print. We have enjoyed the spoils coming from having the teachings of the good shepherd organically intertwined with our lives in visible ways.

In the Middle East, that availability of exposure is not there as the people are born into a sheepfold that is rigorously guarded by a different shepherd, a hired hand, who is not looking out for his sheep.

As John talks about these differences in his Gospel, we see the differences between the two groups are not inherently in the people. We all are lost sheep, but some people have the benefit of a good shepherd ready to lay down His life for the sheep, and others are guided by one who has come to kill, steal and destroy. It has been our hope to lead those from the neglected sheepfold to the good shepherd who continues to call to us.

> *I am the good shepherd; I know my sheep and my sheep know me— just as the Father knows me and I know the Father—and I lay down my life for the sheep. I have other sheep that are not of this sheep pen. I must bring them also. They too will listen to my voice, and there shall be one flock and one shepherd. —John 10:14-16*

While it's slow work in the Middle East, it's encouraging to see changed hearts in the messy lives of people as we have pressed forward in the model of the One who came down to us. We have hope and assurance that on the last day, like pictured in Revelation 4 & 5, we will look around us to the right and left only to see many Bedouin and other Muslim background believers among the throngs of people in white robes praising the Lamb and finding ultimate healing and redemption in the new heavens and earth of His kingdom.

I think this may surprise many people in the West who call Arabs heretics or enemies of the people of God, but our Lord is a God of many surprises, our own salvation being one of the best. By His grace, He has cast out the bad shepherd and called us in our own weakness to be His ambassadors to a people He loves who are in darkness and longing to see a great light and be guided by a good shepherd. May He continue to bring Arabs, Bedouins, and all peoples into His heavenly fields.

www.ingramcontent.com/pod-product-compliance
Lightning Source LLC
Chambersburg PA
CBHW051716020426

42333CB00014B/1005